MW00805737

Critical Studies of Education

Volume 12

We live in an era where forms of education designed to win the consent of students, teachers, and the public to the inevitability of a neo-liberal, market-driven process of globalization are being developed around the world. In these hegemonic modes of pedagogy questions about issues of race, class, gender, sexuality, colonialism, religion, and other social dynamics are simply not asked. Indeed, questions about the social spaces where pedagogy takes place—in schools, media, corporate think tanks, etc.—are not raised. When these concerns are connected with queries such as the following, we begin to move into a serious study of pedagogy: What knowledge is of the most worth? Whose knowledge should be taught? What role does power play in the educational process? How are new media re-shaping as well as perpetuating what happens in education? How is knowledge produced in a corporatized politics of knowledge? What socio-political role do schools play in the twenty-first century? What is an educated person? What is intelligence? How important are socio-cultural contextual factors in shaping what goes on in education? Can schools be more than a tool of the new American (and its Western allies') twenty-first century empire? How do we educate well-informed, creative teachers? What roles should schools play in a democratic society? What roles should media play in a democratic society? Is education in a democratic society different than in a totalitarian society? What is a democratic society? How is globalization affecting education? How does our view of mind shape the way we think of education? How does affect and emotion shape the educational process? What are the forces that shape educational purpose in different societies? These, of course, are just a few examples of the questions that need to be asked in relation to our exploration of educational purpose. This series of books can help establish a renewed interest in such questions and their centrality in the larger study of education and the preparation of teachers and other educational professionals.

More information about this series at http://www.springer.com/series/13431

Linda Ware

Editor

Critical Readings in Interdisciplinary Disability Studies

(Dis)Assemblages

 Springer

Editor
Linda Ware
Independent Scholar
Corrales, NM, USA

Critical Studies of Education
ISBN 978-3-030-35307-0   ISBN 978-3-030-35309-4   (eBook)
https://doi.org/10.1007/978-3-030-35309-4

This Springer imprint is published by the registered company Springer Nature Switzerland AG
The registered company address is: Gewerbestrasse 11, 6330 Cham, Switzerland

Acknowledgments

In appreciation of all the voices that contributed to this work--by example--we show that, indeed new conversations on disability across disciplines are possible.

In loving memory of my little brother, John.

And always, for my son Justin, who continues to resist.

Contents

About the Editor

Linda Ware *[Dis]Assemblages: Critical Readings in Interdisciplinary Disability Studies—An International Reader* draws attention to recent, critical developments in the academic field of interdisciplinary disability studies and extends this scholarship to merge theoretical and pragmatic perspectives. The notation of "critical" in the title is not intended to suggest that disability studies ever was anything less than a "critical" treatment of disability. Rather, its use is intended to underscore the necessity of sharpening a critical lens when reflecting on disability today. The contributors to this volume include a robust mix of scholars in the academic field of disability studies. Some are among the early leaders who established disability studies in literary studies; education; sociology; women's studies; communication; media, technology, and design; and museum studies. Others are budding scholars who may have yet to commit to disability studies exclusively; however, all are bound by a clear recognition and respect for the complexity that disability-related topics incite when taken up in conversations within the academy and beyond.

Personal/Professional Background

The opportunity to edit *(Dis)assemblages* serves on many levels as a project at the intersection of my personal and professional interests in disability studies. This book stitches together multiple "peripheral" experiences from the selection of the chapters that make up this Reader. To begin, I live in the world as the mother of an adult disabled son whose lived experience significantly informs my professional framework. At each phase of my son's interaction with medical and education interventions, social contexts, and bureaucratic systems, ours was a partnership that more often than not was in conflict with the status quo. However, my parenting experience and my son's lived experience are distinct sides of the same coin. My professional path is peripheral, in many ways, to my son's disability as his experience is not mine to appropriate as my own. Ours has been a reciprocal learning experience and one that I cannot easily and distinctly split into the personal and the professional claims.

Professional Background

Of equal influence is the fact that I have invested decades in public education, first as a classroom resource room teacher—early nomenclature for special education classrooms that served students with the highest incidence of disability. At that juncture, I served as a district-level coordinator of inclusive curriculum that I developed for district implementation. These experiences influenced my doctoral research in K-12 classrooms committed to "inclusive education" and ultimately into a professional career in teacher education at several universities in the USA.

In much the same way that my son's life informed my perspective on disability, professional tensions at each of the junctures I noted above also transformed my worldview, i.e., turmoil and tensions followed, when as a special education teacher I refused reductionism and worked instead to create meaningful curriculum for my middle school students informed by contemporary cultural content (Ware, Brill series 2020). Such an approach was far from the norm for students generally viewed as damaged and in need of repair—yet it was the same approach I used to teach my son. I operated on the periphery of the bloated bureaucracy that is special education until I could no more. The most problematic structural barriers that I confronted would, years later inform my doctoral research (Ware 1994). This qualitative research study richly informed my professional critique of special education as a flawed and outdated institution. But it traced back to experience as a parent and then as a teacher, and well before my doctoral studies.

Professionally, I operated on the periphery of special education, although I forged a career in teacher education where my research and publications align with the evolution of critical special education/inclusive education/disability studies (see Chaps. 15 and 16). In this role, I held firm to the belief that teachers can imagine disability as an experience that cuts across the lifespan and cross-cuts race, class, economic strata, and identities. I advanced a version of teacher preparation informed by discursive and performative practices to be understood as enacted in and beyond schools, not only inter-institutionally but also intersubjectively and intergenerationally. The tensions and repercussions that followed from voicing such a critical challenge to status quo attitudes, beliefs, and assumptions about disability were never fully reconciled in the programs in which I worked. The established paradigmatic intolerance for alternative perspectives on disability within special education remains. Further, the consensus among general education colleagues—even those who positioned their scholarship through a critical lens—found disability studies interesting but unworthy of meaningful integration as their work, they often reminded, did not specifically "consider" disability. This book represents a clear departure from the above, as a collection of voices considering disability across multiple perspectives. It aims to generate conversation on disability and move readers to consider disability beyond the constructs inherited from medical, psychological, and social science perspectives.

Melding Inspirations

The evolution of the inspiration for this collection also traces back to the summer of 2000 and a National Endowment for the Humanities Institute on Disability Studies, held at San Francisco State University (hereafter, the Institute). This four-week professional experience was codirected by the noted disability studies scholars Paul Longmore (History) and Rosemarie Garland-Thomson (English), and with the support of the NEH, convened the first summer institute on disability studies. The then-nascent field of disability studies was fuelled by scholarship in the humanities and growing activism by scholars who pressed the Modern Language Association (MLA) to explore disability as "a subject of critical inquiry and a category of critical analysis" (Snyder– et al. 2002, p. 3).

At the time, just a handful of academic books considered cultural interpretations of disability and/or rendered the lives and worth of disabled people through other than a reductionist, rehabilitative lens. In its early days, disability studies was cast as an "emergent" field of scholarly inquiry that mounted a new conversation in the academy. Disability studies was propelled into a vibrant, legitimized academic field by many of the Institute presenters, who included Douglas Baynton, Brenda Bruggeman, G. Thomas Couser, Lennard J. Davis, David A. Gerber, Sander Gilman, David T. Mitchell, Sharon L. Snyder, Katherine Ott, Tobin Siebers, and Anita Silvers. As the conveners of the Institute, Longmore and Garland-Thomson contributed, along with the participants, in what amounted to a provocative cascade of voices in reaction to the material within and across our developing professional and personal interests in disability studies. Most days, our conversations spilled over into the evening hours when the participants—many of whom now represent the second wave of disability studies scholars—pondered and planned ways to bring this content to life in their scholarship, research, and teaching. Among the seminar participants were Licia Carlson, Sumi Colligan, Jim Ferris, Ann P. Fox, Kim Q. Hall, Diane Herndal, Martha Stoddard Holmes, Cathy Kudlick, Cindy Le Compte, Robert McRuer, Carrie Sandal, Susan Schweick, Tim Thomson, myself and others.

The Educator Outlier

As the only education faculty member in attendance, I initially wondered how my approach to disability as a critical special educator would mesh with the perspectives of my fellow participants. My peers were unversed in the distinction between special education and *critical* special education and the educational histories I cited were laden with educational jargon embedded in educational contexts. I espoused an unyielding critique of education's overreliance on medicalized and rehabilitative discourse on disability and was pointedly critical of special education in particular. Paradoxically, I was a former special education teacher who completed a doctoral program in special education and at the time was teaching in the second of what would become a string of academic appointments in special education teacher preparation.

All Voices Welcome

Both Paul Longmore and Rosemarie Garland Thompson welcomed the critique of special education as an "insider" as outlined in my application to the Institute. They were excited to consider how humanities-based disability studies could engage with general and special educators. Paul Longmore in particular was optimistic that we might somehow advance disability studies in teacher education along the lines of curriculum as "intervention." In his letter to confirm my acceptance to the Institute, Longmore reiterated the importance of including educators in conversations on disability as a cultural construct. To this day, I believe that the support he provided was pivotal to the efforts of my peers and myself to advance the subfield of disability studies in education.

Another earlier influence on my thinking about disability that predated the Institute was my coursework with the noted sociologist, Daryl Evans (University of Kansas). Evans originally coined the term "normate" and was a founder of the Society for Disability Studies (SDS), an organization of disabled individuals and those who supported their interests both in and beyond the academy. At the end of my doctoral program, I happened into "Stigma & Disability," a course Evans taught that was not a doctoral requirement. I had to secure institutional permission to substitute "Stigma & Disability" for the required course, "Medical Aspects of Disability." Evans, a sociologist, was recognized across campus for his courses that integrated film, music, performance, art, and various nontraditional pedagogies. Students from various programs of study enrolled in this course to consider a critique on disability that was largely unknown to them in advance of his course. Evans outlined the then-emergent critique of disability among sociologists in the UK advanced by Michael Oliver and others dating back to the early 1980s, as well as scholars in the USA who, like Evans, founded the Society for Disability Studies (SDS). This critique cross-cut my doctoral studies that concentrated on critical special education as developed by the education theorist Thomas M. Skrtic, who advocated an "alternative" paradigm to reform special education and general education in an era when disability studies was not yet on the map. Like Evans, Skrtic drew on critical analyses by British sociologists, particularly Sally Tomlinson and Len Barton, who located their critique in education and social inequity with an emphasis on disability. Neither Evans nor Skrtic connected the dots within their analyses, nor did they explicitly draw from the nascent humanities scholarship on disability (for a more complete discussion, see Ware 2001, 2017). Although they were acquainted in social circles, because they were siloed in their academic homes they never made a professional alliance related to disability studies content prior to the untimely death of Evans.

Threading Disconnections

I recalled these early experiences during the Institute as interdisciplinarity was emphasized in a way that was wholly missing from my doctoral studies. Collegial exchange among the Institute participants and the interpretations that followed from our discussion of the readings cut across our disciplinary homes to influence the loose strands that were ultimately braided into our teaching. It was during those conversations that I began to consider how, as a teacher educator, I might advance the development of disability-related content into the K-12 curriculum, "imagining" what schooling might become if educators "dared" to do disability studies (Ware 2001). I reasoned that educators would benefit from exposure to more critical ways to understand disability through a humanities lens, given that such content was typically excluded from teacher preparation coursework. Teacher training, mired as it was and remains, is overburdened by the impulse to train discrete skills, conformance to scripted instruction, and the delivery of prepackaged curriculum content. My proposals called for a cultural critique that would clearly disrupt the status quo. The goal became to provide teachers with the opportunity to engage as learners with disability studies content and to support them in the development of curriculum.

In very short order, I was awarded two NEH grants to advance disability studies in education. The first project was designed to promote collaboration and conversation among humanities-based disability studies scholars (many of those listed above and others) and public high school teachers in general and special education in Rochester, NY (2000–2001). The second project built on this success, and with my colleagues David T. Mitchell and Sharon L. Snyder (then University of Illinois professors), we received funding for the first NEH disability studies summer institute exclusively for K-12 educators (Chicago 2003). Taken together, these experiences led to the call for "curricular cripistemologies"—those "teachable moments organized around crip/queer content that interrupt normative cultural practices" (Mitchell et al. 2014, p. 302).

Critical Disability Studies and the Launch of Disability Studies in Education

This early history of the institutional support from the NEH was instrumental in the launch of my work in disability studies in education (DSE). All three NEH projects described above continued to inform my commitment to encourage conversation and collaboration across traditional academic disciplines and among educators and

humanities-based disability studies scholars. The value of these mutually informa-
tive and generative conversations cannot be fully appreciated in the absence of continuing to develop similar initiatives. This book is intended to continue this effort,
organized to spur a conversation prompted by a range of interdisciplinary interests
in disability that need not be viewed as *exclusive* to educators, or to art majors, or to
history majors, or English, or any other circumscribed academic field of study.

(Dis)Assemblages conveys the reach of disability studies as it has evolved from
the mid-1990s to the present. The contributors offer fresh thinking that recognizes
the value of igniting an interdisciplinary conversation on disability that need not be
tethered to a singular disciplinary home. Sixteen chapters appear in three sections:
(1) Disability Theory and Critique; (2) Disability Representations Juxtaposed; and
(3) Disability Pedagogical Interventions. In many ways, categorizing the chapters
beneath a section header defies the aim of the intended conversations across the
chapters and the contributors. I am hopeful that each will summon a conversation on
disability with readers and their peers, students, fellow instructors, and administrators—anyone who has yet to understand the reach of interdisciplinary disability
studies. Because the Reader will consider global themes and topics related to disability, it is my hope that this integrative approach will herald more powerful ways
to imagine disability.

References

Longmore, P., & Garland Thomson, R. (2000). National Endowment for the Humanities Summer
    Institute on Disability. San Francisco State University, San Francsico, CA.
Mitchell, D. T., Snyder, S. L., & Ware (2003). Integrating disability studies into secondary cur-
    ricula. National Endowment for the Humanities (NEH) Institute. Final report to the NEH,
    Washington, D. C.
Mitchell, D. T., Snyder, S. L., & Ware, L (2014). "[Every] child left behind": Curricular criptem-
    plogies and crip/queer art of failure. Journal of Literary & Cultural Disability Studies, 8.3,
    295–313.
Snyder, S. L., Brueggmann, B., & Garland-Thomson R. (2002). Disability Studies Enabling the
    Humanities. The Modern Language Association of America New York, NY.
Ware, L. (1994). Innovative instructional practices: A naturalistic study of the structural and cul-
    tural conditions of change. Doctoral dissertation, awarded by the University of Kansas.
Ware, L. (2001). A collaborative inquiry on understanding disability in secondary and pos-second-
    ary settings. National Endowment for the Humanities, Project #ED-21977-00 at the University
    of Rochester, Rochester, NY.
Ware, L. (2017). Section Editor, "The disability yet to come. In: Lennard J. Davis (Ed.) Beginning
    with Disability, A Primer, (pp 275–305). New York & London Routlede.

Part I
Disability Theory and Critique

Chapter 1: *Disability Studies and Interdisciplinarity: Interregnum or Productive Interruption?*—Julie Allan, University of Manchester. Allan considers the positioning of disability studies, by its own exponents and others, as a discipline in its own right and in relation to other disciplines. It draws on Taylor's (2006) historical analysis of the development of disability studies and disability studies in education, which demonstrates how the early critiques of labelling, stigmatization, and the medicalization of deviance have formed the basis of what we know as disability studies today. The chapter offers some comparisons of the developments and tensions within disability studies in the USA and the UK, some of which have arisen from the diverse perspectives and theoretical orientations that comprise it (Taylor 2006). It explores questions of voice and power that have arisen through efforts to articulate and position disability studies as a distinctive field and in relation to other disciplines.

Chapter 2: *Alternative Agencies: Materialist Navigations Below the Radar of Disability Studies*—David T. Mitchell, The George Washington University and Sharon L. Snyder, Independent Scholar. These authors trouble the impact of the default equation that "disability = oppression." This foundational formulation in disability studies is embedded in our collective conscience as integral to understanding the social model of disability. The challenge for readers will be to recognize the need to move past the reification of the social model as a starting point for understanding the ever-evolving such that a rigorous conceptualization of "peripheral embodiment" and its implications for those "experiencing lives of 'low level agency.'" Early in the chapter, Mitchell and Snyder, informed by the work of (Abbas 2011; Weheliye 2014), pose a series of questions that critique of "Liberalism's overdetermination of the concept of agency. This critique is carefully situated against the experience of their daughter who required multiple surgeries over two years to reconstruct her esophagus, but became blind in the process.

Chapter 3: *The Cost of Counting Disability: Theorizing the Possibility of a Noneconomic Remainder*—Tanya Titchkosky, University of Toronto. This chapter examines a common discursive rendering of disability that makes it exclusively a countable matter of economic expense. The focus: common mass media practice of naming an impairment condition and detailing the cost of the condition for an individual, family, organization, or even for a nation. The chapter examines articulations of embodiment counted as an objective expense in order to explicate the actual way the currency of fact is used to count disability as disappeared money, a void, waste, and non-humanness. I show how disability studies can orient an analysis of disability = cost discourse that opens imagination and might disturb the over-naturalized sense of an economic rendering of human life. Addressing these ordinary discursive accounts of disability as costly is also a way to nurture alternative ways of making disability matter, or at least attempting to invigorate a social imagination for the possibility of a non-economic remainder.

Chapter 4: *Theorising Disability and Humanity*—Dan Goodley, University of Sheffield. The chapter outlines seven reasons why we should ask what it means to be human. Drawing on research projects and intellectual moments of engagement, Goodley considers the ways in which disability disavows normative constructions of the human. His use of the term *disavowal* appears in its original psychoanalytic sense of the word: to simultaneously and ambivalently desire *and* reject something (in this case, the human). Goodley clarifies and expands upon this disavowal—with explicit reference to the politics of people with intellectual disabilities—and makes a case for the ways in which the human is (1) a category through which social recognition can be gained and (2) a classification requiring expansion, extension, and disruption. Indeed, an under-girding contention of this chapter is that people with intellectual disabilities are already engaged in what we might term a post-human politics from which all kinds of human can learn.

Chapter 5: *The Metaphor of Civic Threat: Intellectual Disability and Education for Citizenship*—Ashley Taylor, Colgate University. To complement and extend Goodley (Chap. 4), Ashley Taylor introduces what Kliewer, Biklen, and Peterson refer to as the "metaphor" of intellectual disability, the sense in which "we do not literally see mental retardation; we infer its existence" (2015, p. 22). Taylor explains that this metaphor emerges within the context of citizenship education in particular and troubling ways. *We do not see intellectual disability; we infer its existence through manifestations of non-citizenship.* Her discussion shows that intellectual ability—and disability—is actively constructed by and through gendered and racialized attachments to the notion of the ideal citizen. Individuals who are perceived to manifest undesirable differences in cognition, behaviour, communication, or performance appear to threaten notions of civic well-being, of nationhood, and of social reciprocity. In this sense, intellectual disability becomes a metaphor for civic threat. Consequently, educational theorizing around democratic citizenship education advances the metaphor of intellectual disability through a process of negation: the citizen is that which the person with intellectual disability is not *or* intellectual disability is that which is not citizenship.

Chapter 6: *Complex and Critical: A Methodological Application of the Tripartite Model of Disability*—David Bolt, Liverpool Hope University. Bolt considers the "tripartite model" of disability that bridges social sciences and humanities—specifically education, sociology, and psychology—to show that positive identity and disability can coexist sans the presence or promise of cure. The tripartite model is informed by the social model of disability and the affirmative model of disability, but in this chapter Bolt offers it as "instrumental in the methodology of textual analysis" to probe the complexity of disability lived experience. He considers ableism in example, and borrowing from the insights of Carol Thomas, Fiona Campbell, and Gregor Wolbring reminds readers, "ableism is an age-old concept that runs deep in society". Bolt applies his analysis to *Happiness is Blind* (Sava 1987) a British work of fiction that serves as an apt example of the social and cultural influences that produce and reproduce ableism. Bolt digs more deeply to explain the trajectory of normative positivisms that invariably lead to non-normative negativisms and complex embodiment in this work. He concludes with an appeal to literary critics to consider the tripartite model as a means to explore the varied registers of the "complexity of experiential knowledge".

Chapter 1
Disability Studies and Interdisciplinarity: Interregnum or Productive Interruption?

Julie Allan

1.1 Introduction

This paper considers the positioning of disability studies, by its own exponents and others, as a discipline in its own right and in relation to other disciplines. It draws on Taylor's (2006) historical analysis of the development of disability studies and disability studies in education, which demonstrates how the early critiques of labelling, stigmatisation and the medicalization of deviance have formed the basis of what we know as disability studies today. Taylor's ethnographic analysis of a family's encounters with disability, an exemplar of disability studies, is also examined.

The chapter offers some comparisons of the developments and tensions within disability studies in the USA and the UK, some of which have arisen from the diverse perspectives and theoretical orientations that comprise it (Taylor 2006). It explores questions of voice and power that have arisen through efforts to articulate and position disability studies as a distinctive field and in relation to other disciplines. It also considers the boundary work undertaken on behalf of disability studies and the consequences of some of its more policing-oriented manifestations. The extent to which disability studies has functioned as an inter-regnum, marking a gap between disciplines; a more productive form of interruption, which forces an interrogation of particular disciplines; or merely another kind of disciplining, is examined. The chapter concludes with a discussion of the prospects and possibilities for disability studies to become the "default paradigm" (Ware and Valle 2009, p. 113) and the implications of this for the scholars who choose to engage with and within it.

J. Allan (✉)
University of Birmingham, Birmingham, UK
e-mail: j.allan.1@bham.ac.uk

© Springer Nature Switzerland AG 2020
L. Ware (ed.), *Critical Readings in Interdisciplinary Disability Studies*, Critical
Studies of Education 12, https://doi.org/10.1007/978-3-030-35309-4_1

1.2 Not Another Tale of Development: Disability Studies Today

Steve Taylor (2011) points out that it is easier to determine what disability studies is *not;* for example, specifically not special education and not rehabilitation. Linton (1998a) also found the *not* distinction useful, marking a border between the socio-political study of disability and the more traditional interventionist studies and calling the latter "Not disability studies". Nevertheless, Taylor identifies the crucial element distinguishing disability studies from other modes of inquiry, namely the recognition of disability as a social phenomenon, and helpfully shows how we arrived at what we call disability studies today. He offers a sociological lineage of deviance studies from the 1960s (Becker 1963; Goffman 1961, 1963; Scheff 1966; Scott 1969; Mercer 1965) that challenged the "nonsense questions" (Mercer 1965, p. 1) about the incidence and prevalence of disability and asserts that:

> mental retardation is a social construction or a concept which exists in the minds of the "judges" rather than in the minds of the "judged"... A mentally retarded person is one who has been labeled as such according to rather arbitrarily created and applied criteria (Bogdan and Taylor 1976, p. 47).

Disability studies was formally given a status through the establishment of the Society for Disability Studies (SDS) in 1982 (Connor et al. 2008). Taylor notes the proliferation of disability studies programmes within the USA and offers a justification for this by pointing out that disability is part of the human condition and will touch almost everyone at some point in their lives. He also argues, however, that disability studies has the capacity to analyse every cultural and social aspect of life, from conceptions of normalcy to stereotyping and exclusion. Disability studies in education came to focus on the school's role in constructing disability, identifying the phenomenon of the "six-hour retarded child", whereby a child was only retarded within the context of school and on the basis of an IQ score (Taylor 2006), and questioned the legitimacy of segregation. Connor et al. (2008, p. 444) note the significance of the formation, in 2000, of the Disability Studies in Education Special Interest Group (SIG) within the American Educational Research Association for giving a voice to those educational researchers discouraged by the "insularity of special education's traditionalism". Disability studies in education have consistently delivered "fearless critiques of special education" (Connor 2013, p. 1229) that are defensible on account of their rigour and purposeful with their regard—always—for the disenfranchised and disadvantaged other. They have succeeded in "rewriting...discourses of disability" (Ferri 2008, p. 420) and have managed to "talk back to forces in education that undermine inclusive values" (Connor et al. 2008, p. 455). However, these successes have been accompanied by an awareness of the power of the orthodoxy to prevail.

Taylor notes that Dunn's (1968) article *Special Education for the Mildly Retarded: Is Much of It Justifiable?* marked the start of what was for the special educationists (Kavale and Forness 2000) a series of attacks on segregation. The subsequent confrontations between special educationists and the so-called inclusionists have involved accusations by each side that the other is being "ideological" (Brantlinger 1997), with even challenges of "heresy" issued against Danforth and Morris (2006, p. 135). These somewhat unsophisticated attacks, in which the opponents merely trade insults and talk past one another (Gallagher 1998), have led to a continuing enmity between advocates of inclusion and special education that seems incapable of resolution. Whilst in the USA these ideologically "inspired" confrontations have continued to shape the place and function of disability studies, the field of disability studies in the UK has been characterised by internal tensions, with some significant confrontations between the key proponents. Connor et al. (2008) mark the emergence of disability studies within the UK from the publication by the disability activist group, the Union of the Physically Impaired Against Segregation, of the *Fundamental Principles of Disability* (UPIA 1975). Some of the early disputes within the U.K. disability studies field centred on questions of authority and who had the right to speak about disability; others raised challenges about the place of the body in debates about disability and about the orthodoxy of the social model of disability (Shakespeare 2006). In a head-to-head between Mike Oliver and Tom Shakespeare, the utility of the social model of disability, introduced by Oliver and Finkelstein in the 1990s, was brought into question with Shakespeare (2006, p. 9) arguing that disability studies within in the U.K. had reached an impasse and that what has caused it to become "stagnated" (p. 1), the social model, should be abandoned:

> Alone amongst radical movements, the UK disability rights tradition has, like a fundamentalist religion, retained its allegiance to a narrow reading of its founding assumptions (Shakespeare 2006, p. 34).

Oliver responded by denouncing this view and the book in which it featured as "a mish mash of contradictory perspectives" (Oliver 2007, p. 230).

Steve Taylor (2000) provides us with the gold standard of disability studies in his exemplary ethnography of a family's encounters with disability. Taylor recounts the family's success in eluding stigmatising and pathologising constructions of them, through their own immediate and extended networks and through their avoidance of the more austere institutions and facilities "that engulf people in a separate subculture" (Taylor 2000, p. 87). Taylor describes how the more he came to know the family, the more he realised that the questions precipitated by the stigma-oriented studies of the 1960s were not meaningful. He understood that their world was not constructed in opposition to, nor reproductive of, prevailing notions of stigma, but was a collaborative world that they both belonged to and constructed.

The family studied by Taylor, the Dukes, was described officially with labels of disability, mental retardation, or mental illness, with the head of the family, Bill, depicted by his state special school as a product of cultural-familial mental retardation (Taylor 2000, p. 70). Taylor, however, revealed how the master status that operated for the Dukes was familial, daughter, sister and so on, not that imposed by institutions through labels, and family kinship helped to shape social identities and formed strong social bonds. These strong social identities enabled the family members to engage with the institutional labels used on them without being defined or damaged by them: "the Duke family experience shows that small worlds can exist that do not simply reproduce the broader social contexts in which they are embedded" (Taylor 2000, p. 84). Taylor showed the stark contrast between the familial identities and those constructed by the official identities and identified four ways in which the family was able to avoid "the stigma and stained identities"(p. 58) of disability. First, the unit of the family served to interpret and organise everyday meanings, away from institutional constructions; second, the family network was extended and broad, with concomitant resources to draw upon; third, the family was entirely separate from those institutions, agencies, and organisations and from their attendant subculture; and fourth, the family members had acquired extensive competence, not discernible through standardised tests in literacy or numeracy, but nevertheless allowing them to function effectively in the world. This plausible counter-narrative to those that "dehumanize" (Bogdan and Taylor 1989, p. 146) and lead to an "underdevelopment of … consciousness" (Zola 2003, p. 243) underlines the potency and potential of disability studies.

At the same time as there has been a growth in disability studies that seek to undermine the pathologising and segregating of individuals, there has been what Hacking (2010, p. 633) refers to as a "boom industry" in autism narrative, with autism the "pathology of our decade" (ibid). He expresses greatest concern about the proliferation of fictional accounts, suggesting that these have contributed to forming a language with which to talk about autism. This "language-creation" (Hacking 2010, p. 637) plays an important role in helping "neurotypicals" (ibid)—which is how some autism advocacy groups have described ordinary, non-disabled people—understand more about the lives and experiences of autistic people. However, it also, as Hacking points out, feeds a fear and a fascination with the odd and leaves a sense of knowing autistic people in some universal way.

The emergence globally of a more critical form of disability studies is noted by Dan Goodley (2014a), who has of course been part of such a movement. This surfaced in response to a frustration with the materialist conceptions of disability studies, stemming from Marxist sociological interpretations, and their limited analytical capacity. Critical disability studies has also reinscribed the body in analyses of disability and utilised embodiment and the impaired body to force an examination of hetero-normativity. A centring of the disabled person has been effected coincidentally with the construction of the non-disabled person, "in order to look at the world from the inside out" (Linton 1998b, p. 14). Goodley (2014a, b) acknowledges concerns that, in becoming critical, disability studies may have become too much of an academic discipline and lost its political imperatives and its anchoring. He does suggest, however, that the logical next step for disabled people and their allies might be to unpack the complexity of disability.

1.3 Disciplining Disability Studies

Hacking (2008), who declares himself a "complacent disciplinarian" offers a cautionary note about the engagement with one's discipline, based on his experience of individuals who have been "disciplined by disciplines"; that is, bullied by superiors into maintaining traditional structures of inquiry. His most direct experience of this comes from his own discipline of analytic philosophy where junior scholars are afraid, and are denied qualifications and jobs if they do not conform to the narrow conception of philosophy held by many of its gatekeepers.

The disciplining of disability studies, in the USA, the UK, and elsewhere, has come from multiple directions: internally, from within its own field; and from within academia and from other disciplines, through enjoinders to undertake interdisciplinary work. Whilst seeking to avoid the error of reification, I will consider how each of these disciplining forces work upon disability studies and its offspring, disability studies in education and critical disability studies, and reflect on their effects.

1.3.1 External Censure

Disability studies still struggles for acceptance as a serious discipline inside the academy. This struggle goes beyond any effects of the "dis-ing" of disability studies by the special educationists, but includes their efforts at disavowal. Lenny Davis (2013) recounts, albeit gleefully, the putdowns of his work by the medical establishment that draw attention to his literature, rather than scientific, qualifications. Kauffman (2015) rails against the celebratory or over-positive language used within disability studies, emphasising that some impairments are undesirable, and suggests that in particular Emotional and Behavioural Difficulties (EBD) is "actually something that is not so good to have" (p. 170). He goes further to suggest that some kinds of culture may be negative and indirectly criticises the disability studies practitioners for apparently regarding "any cultural difference as sacrosanct" (p. 173) and for actively preventing prevention, by only allowing intervention for "advanced cases or disasters" (ibid). Whilst an attack of this kind may provoke mere irritation at its repetition and lack of foundation, it is nevertheless important to acknowledge the continued need for reproach from the special school yard.

A more significant critique, particularly of critical disability studies, has come from Vehmas and Watson (2014), writers about disability who nevertheless choose to distance themselves at least from the more recent developments within disability studies. They argue that critical disability studies raises ethical issues and insinuates normative judgements without providing supporting ethical arguments and regard this failure to do so as morally irresponsible. They also argue that the concentration on how disabled people are categorised and labelled is inconsequential and demand both a "proper metric of justice"(p. 643) and a recognition of the negative nature of some impairments.

1.3.2 Insider Lament

Disability studies in education, whilst clearly still a discipline in development, has something of an exalted status and is protected vigorously and subject to its own self-discipline. The protectors of disability studies—guardians, rather than police—assume an authority on behalf of the discipline and those who have experienced its effects are not exactly "flogged by [its] institutional structures" (Hacking 2008), but may be kept outside and denied membership. Disability studies in education appears to exist and function as a semi-private club, with activities centred mainly around conference events. At these events, the successes of the discipline and its members are celebrated, rather than any achievements in tackling inequalities. As someone who has been inside and part of this process, this is not an easy criticism to offer, but it seems nevertheless to be an important one.

Connor et al. (2008) articulate some of the tensions produced within disability studies in education—by its own members. They describe how in the early days, much time and effort was spent in articulating what it was *not,* outlining its presence in relation to what was perceived as absent. The creation of this negative space was important in protecting the members from what was seen as a major threat—from researchers practising traditional special education but who were looking to rebadge their work under the more apparently respectable title of disability studies in education. There was, therefore, a genuinely good reason for guarding the gates; there was also an urgent need to define the essence and mission of disability studies in education. This created some challenges, but also brought a recognition that plurality was a significant, and possibly necessary, feature of both disability studies and disability studies in education. Steve Taylor (2006, p. xiii) underlines this:

> Neither Disability Studies nor Disability Studies in Education represents a unitary perspective. Scholarship in these areas includes social constructionist or interpretivist, materialist, postmodernist, poststructuralist, legal and even structural–functionalist perspectives and draws on disciplines as diverse as sociology, literature, critical theory, economics, law, history, art, philosophy, and others.

This plurality does, of course, invite scorn from the special educationists; it also creates an assumption that those carefully guarded gates will be opened, from the inside.

1.3.3 Inter-Regnum

The final mode of disciplining the discipline of disability studies has been through the insertion of an "inter-regnum" (Hartley 2009, p. 127) and an expectation that disability studies will work with and between other disciplines. The language of public services is becoming similarly infused with the prefixes "inter", "multi", and "co", which are forced upon professionals along with the enjoinder that they should work together. And, of course, increasingly there is an obligation to undertake analyses of oppressions that are intersectional, without any clear indication of how these might be achieved. Hartley (2009) points out that the "inter-regnum" (p. 127) within the public services disturbs accepted understandings about school and expectations of professionals and blurs the distinction between consumer and provider. Inclusion, in this new configuration, is thus a shared responsibility, among professionals and involving parents, and one where the lines of accountability are (even) less clear. Similarly, we might suspect that the inter-regnum in relation to other disciplines or to other arenas of oppression could effect a similar blurring or could merely allow a dominance of the more powerful voices.

Hacking (2008) records his suspicion of the inter-regnum visited upon disciplines and seeks to "put in a word for collaborating disciplines that do not need to be, in any important sense of the word *interdisciplinary*". He reflects on whether the anthropologist Mary Douglas should be considered an interdisciplinarian because of her forays into art history, biblical studies, urban sociology, and several other domains, or whether instead she simply "applies her keen and totally unconventional mind and skills where she is interested" (Hacking 2008). He suggests that one way to be interdisciplinary is to be "curious about everything" but appears to be discouraging any interdisciplinary aspirations, advocating collaboration over interdisciplinary work, and characterising the former by an openness, curiosity, and mutual respect:

> In my opinion what matters is that honest and diligent thinkers and activists respect each other's learned skills and innate talents. Who else to go to but someone who knows more than you do, or can do something better than you can? Not because you are inexpert in your domain, but because you need help from another one. I never seek help from an "interdisciplinary" person, but only from a "disciplined" one. Never? Well, hardly ever. (Hacking 2008)

Hacking strongly recommends a combination of curiosity and discipline, the latter inspired for him by Leibnitz, and avoiding the creation of disciples. In the final section of this chapter, I offer some reflections on the prospects and possibilities for disability studies as an inevitable and obvious form of scholarship.

1.4   Disability Studies by Default

Linda Ware (2001) issued the challenge, "dare we do disability studies?" (p. 107), demanding that disability be "thought and thought otherwise" (p. 112) and, in so doing, underlined the requirements for boldness, tenacity, and even humour. Ware and Valle (2009) also argued that disability studies should become the "default paradigm" (p. 113), a necessity particularly within teacher education, to "dislodge the silence buried deep within the uninspired curriculum that restricts teacher and student imagination" (Ware 2001, p. 120). Bogdan and Taylor (1989) see the recognition of the humanness of severely disabled people, achieved through disability studies, as an act of humanity in itself and argue that it is not a matter of individuals' physical or mental condition but a "matter of definition" (p. 146).

Goodley (2014a, b, p. xvi) suggests that the crucial function of disability studies is the help it offers to the "normal" to move out of their "normative shadows" and calls for an politics of abnormality to be embedded within disability studies.

In considering how we might go on with disability studies, some attention to the space in which it takes place, the people involved, and the work undertaken seems timely and these are addressed below.

1.4.1   The Space

The space in which we might do disability studies is necessarily one that needs to be created and made to work for us, rather than involving the capturing of pre-existing and inevitably tainted spaces. Goodley (2014a), following Lash (2001), suggests that such a space should be "lifted out" (p. 641) and should allow simultaneously for thinking, acting, engaging, and resisting, whilst Latour (2004) characterises it as a space of "mediating, assembling, [and] gathering" (p. 248). The space could also be made for demonstration in a way that takes up the "demos", meaning the people, and materialises them through a process of "*demos*-stration", "manifesting the presence of those who do not count" (Critchley 2007, p. 130). Arendt (1958) advocates seeking out spaces for public action, suggesting that these may be anywhere and invoking the *polis* as meaning the "space of appearance" (p. 198) and a space for political action:

> The *polis*, properly speaking, is not the city-state in its physical location; it is the organization of the people as it arises out of acting and speaking together, and its true space lies between people living together for this purpose, no matter where they happen to be (p. 198).

Arendt extends an invitation to the academic to undertake such political work, but recognises that academe has never succeeded in achieving Plato's vision of being a "counter-society" (2006, p. 256). Nevertheless, the civic responsibilities of academics for "pricking the consciousness of the public" (Zola 2003, p. 10) are clear.

1.4.2   The People

In spite of Simi Linton's (1998a) enjoinder to non-academics to challenge the "minimal presence of disabled scholars in their institutions" (p. 538), there is still an under-representation of disabled scholars in higher education. Institutions' equality policies encompass disability but privilege the more visible and measurable gender and ethnicity characteristics. Disclosure of disability within the university as a place of work remains a big deal, especially where this might involve mental health issues. There is much to do in order to foreground the expertise of disabled people in research about disability (and everything else) and in academic institutions generally.

Disability studies is an obvious domain for scholars who want to do work that can make a significant difference and the prospect of joining such an accomplished group will appeal to many. But there are potential risks for early-career scholars entering this particularly charged part of the academy. Many of the dissenters occupy powerful positions within institutions and can exert influence on dissertation committees and appointment and promotions panels. It is vital that established academics use their seniority to advocate for and support more junior staff and to counter negativity from outside the field. Steve Taylor was exemplary in this respect, described as "quiet yet transformative" (Fujiura 2015, p. 1) by one of the many scholars he mentored, and Syracuse, under the leadership of Doug Biklen, has provided a particularly nurturing environment for disability studies scholars. Barton and Clough (1995) urged academics to consider their power and privilege more generally:

> What responsibilities arise from the privileges I have as a result of my social position? How can I use my knowledge and skills to challenge, for example, the forms of oppression disabled people experience? Does my writing and speaking reproduce a system of domination or challenge that system? (Barton and Clough 1995, p. 144).

Linda Ware has been a consistent voice in calling for new alliances with academics in the humanities (Ware 2001) and these disciplines remain our best bet for any kind of meaningful engagement within the academy. But Hacking (2008) encourages a further reach into perhaps unexpected disciplines, guided by curiosity rather than propriety. As has been alluded to earlier in this chapter, Hacking considers it potentially too limiting to call such engagement across diverse spheres interdisciplinary work. He prefers to name it as collaboration, involving not breaking down of boundaries but respect. This is a characteristic of the work being advocated and discussed below.

1.4.3   The Work

The work of disability studies undoubtedly involves critique, whether it calls itself critical disability studies, disability studies in education, or something else yet to be thought of. The academic practising disability studies is, therefore, a critic:

> The critic is not the one who debunks, but the one who assembles. The critic is not the one who lifts the rugs from under the feet of the naïve believers, but the one who offers the participants arenas in which to gather. The critic is not the one who alternates haphazardly between antifetishism and positivism like the drunk iconoclast drawn by Goya, but the one for whom, if something is constructed, then it means it is fragile and thus in great need of care and caution. (Latour 2004, p. 246).

The purpose of critique is to understand the political ends intended by specific practices and to make these explicit, serving, as Said (1995) suggests, "as public memory to recall what is forgotten or ignored" (p. 503). It is not, Foucault (1988) contends, "a matter of saying that things are not right as they are" (p. 154), but rather "of pointing out on what kinds of assumptions, what kinds of familiar, unchallenged and unconsidered modes of thought the practices that we accept rest" (p. 155). The focus of critique is principally the under-represented, the disenfranchised and misrecognised other, with the naming and privileging of their voices and identities, making a discourse of that which has formerly been a noise (Rancière 2008,) and producing rupture:

> For me a political subject is a subject who employs the competence of the so-called incompetents or the part of those who have no part, and not an additional group to be recognised as part of society. "Visible minorities" means exceeding the system of represented groups, of constituted identities.... It's a rupture that opens out into the recognition of the competence of anyone, not the addition of a unit (p. 3).

The critic wades into the "conflict between truth and politics" (Arendt 2006, p. 227) and attempts to "find out, stand guard over, and interpret factual truth" (ibid, pp. 256–257). However, the critical work invoked here amounts to far more than truth-telling, and is positive and constructive, pointing to new ways of conceptualising and critiquing disability and new forms of political action arising from this critique.

Because critique involves engaging in exercises in political thought, practice and training is required (Arendt 2006). Critique, thus, is a form of training that does not prescribe what we should think but helps us to learn *how* to think and offers a fighting experience gained from standing one's ground between "the clashing waves of past and future" (Arendt 2006, p. 13). This is exemplified in Kafka's parable:

> He has two antagonists: the first presses him from behind, from the origin. The second blocks the road ahead. He gives battle to both. To be sure, the first supports him in his fight with the second, for he wants to push him forward, and in the same way the second supports him in his fight with the first, since he drives him back. But it is only theoretically so. For it is not only the two antagonists who are there, but he himself as well, and who really knows his intentions? His dream, though, is that some time in an unguarded moment ... he will jump out of the fighting line and be promoted, on account of his experience of fighting, to the position of umpire over his antagonists in their fight with each other. (Cited in Arendt 2006, p. 7)

A methodology for critique, which enables the identification of erasures, closures, and silences, has been developed by Edward Said (1993, 1999) through an elaboration of the concepts of contrapuntality and fugue, taken directly from Western classical music. This methodology allows for the representation of identity and voice and for the "the telling of alternative stories by those that are currently marginalized and exiled" (Chowdry 2007, p. 103). It seeks to speak of both oppression and resistance to it, achieved by "extending our reading of the texts to include what was once forcibly excluded" (Said 1993, p. 67), but recovering these voices and dissonances. Contrapuntals allow various themes to play off one another without privilege being accorded to anyone. The wholeness of the piece of music comes from that interplay of the themes, which can be as many as 14, as in Bach's *Art of Fugue*, but with each of them distinct. As Symes (2006) notes, "History is a giant fugue of interweaving themes and voices, of subject and reply. A contrapuntal reading of culture entails the entire constellation of its *voices*" (p. 324). Chowdry (2007) points out that contrapuntal analysis is more a simple appeal for a plurality of voices, but is a call for "*worlding* the texts, institutions and practices, for historicizing them, for inter-rogating their sociality and materiality, for paying attention to the hierarchies and the power-knowledge nexus embedded in them. It is also a plea for the recovery of what Said (2000, p. 444) calls 'non-coercive and non-dominating knowledge' " (p. 105). A contrapuntal analysis, characterised by "counterpoint, intertwining and integration" (Chowdry 2007, p. 107), destabilises conventional readings and "reveals the hidden interests, the embedded power relations and the political align-ments" (ibid).

A contrapuntal analysis of disability would involve a reading of disability as culture and of attending to its practices of description, communication, and repre-sentation through which certain narratives succeed in blocking others and whereby particular "philological tricks" (Said, cited in Chowdry 2007, p. 110) allow disabil-ity culture to be rendered distinct from the rest of the world and inferior. Crucially, contrapuntal analysis would also seek out those voices of disability culture "which flow across cultures, that defy space and time, that start local, become global" (Symes 2006, p. 314). Furthermore, contrapuntal analysis has a particularly exciting potential for intersectional analysis and the interrogation of disability in its counter-point with race, class, gender, and other forms of oppression. It takes us beyond analyses of oppression, however, by taking us away from the positioning of antago-nisms, of "absurd opposition" (Said, quoted in Salusinszky 1987, p. 147), and of disadvantage always being presented as caused by another's advantage. It offers instead a "mollifying (though note not solving)" (Symes 2006, p. 320) by allowing different elements to sit in relation to one another in a kind of "fugal resolution" (ibid, p. 321).

1.5   Disability Studies to Come

Nussbaum (2006) reminds us that we still lack a theory that deals adequately with the needs of citizens with impairments and disabilities, as most of these are based on political principles of mutual advantage. We lack so much more in the field of disability studies but also have so much to gain and to give. On the matter of giving, Steve Taylor again provides a measure or a moral compass (Linton 2009), with the mixture of curiosity and outrage, coupled with the most assiduous scholarship, that drove the production of his seminal text, *Acts of Conscience: World War II, Mental Institutions and Religious Conscientious Objectors.* Taylor's (2009) desire to under-stand "how society can dehumanize, marginalize, and systematically discriminate against people with real or presumed, intellectual, mental or physical disabilities" (p. 382) is one that ought to compel us all.

References

Arendt, H. (1958). *The human condition*. Chicago: University of Chicago Press.

Arendt, H. (2006). *Between past and future: Eight exercises in political thought*. New York: Penguin Books.

Barton, L., & Clough, P. (1995). Conclusion: Many urgent voices. In P. Clough & L. Barton (Eds.), *Making difficulties: Research and the construction of SEN*. London: Paul Chapman.

Becker, H. (1963). *Outsiders: Studies in the sociology of deviance*. New York: Free Press.

Bogdan, R., & Taylor, S. J. (1976). The judged, not the judges: An insider's view of mental retardation. *American Psychologist, 31*(1), 47–52.

Bogdan, S., & Taylor, S. J. (1989). Relationships with severely disabled people: The social construction of humanness. *Social Problems, 36*(1), 135–148.

Brantlinger, E. (1997). Using ideology: Cases of nonrecognition of the politics of research and practice in special education. *Review of Educational Research, 67*(4), 425–459.

Chowdry, G. (2007). Edward Said and contrapuntal reading: Implications for critical interventions in international relations. *Millennium: Journal of International Studies, 36*(1), 101–116.

Connor, D. (2013). Risk-taker, role model, muse, and "charlatan": Stories of Ellen—an atypical giant. *International Journal of Inclusive Education, 17*(12), 1229–1240.

Connor, D. J., Gabel, S., Gallagher, D., & Morton, M. (2008). Disability studies and inclusive education: Implications for theory, research, and practice. *International Journal of Inclusive Education, 12*(5–6), 441–457.

Critchley, J. (2007). *Infinitely demanding: Ethics of commitment, politics of resistance*. London. New York: Verso.

Danforth, S., & Morris, P. (2006). Orthodoxy, heresy, and the inclusion of American students considered to have emotional/behavioral disorders. *International Journal of Inclusive Education, 10*(2–3), 135–148.

Davis, L. (2013). *The end of normal: Identity in a biocultural era*. Ann Arbor: The University of Michigan Press.

Dunn, L. M. (1968). Special education for the mildly retarded: Is much of it justifiable? *Exceptional Children, 35*(1), 5–22.

Ferri, B. (2008). Doing a (dis)service: Reimagining special education from a disability studies perspective. In W. Ayers, T. Quinn, & D. Stovall (Eds.), *The handbook of social justice in education*. New York: Lawrence Erlbaum.

Foucault, M. (1988). *Politics, philosophy, culture: Interviews and other writings 1972–1977*. London: Routledge.

Fujiura, G. (2015). Steven J. Taylor: In memoriam. *Intellectual and Development Disabilities, 53*(1), 1.

Gallagher, D. (1998). The scientific knowledge base of special education: Do we know what we think we know? *Exceptional Children, 64*(4), 294–309.

Goffman, E. (1961). *Asylums: Notes on the management of a spoiled identity*. Boston: Prentice-Hall.

Goffman, E. (1963). *Stigma: Notes on the management of spoiled identity*. Englewood Cliffs, NJ: Prentice-Hall.

Goodley, D. (2014a). Dis/entangling critical disability studies. *Disability & Society, 28*(5), 631–644.

Goodley, D. (2014b). *Dis/ability studies: Theorising disablism and ableism*. London: Routledge.

Hacking, I. (2008). The complacent disciplinarian. *Interdisciplines*. https://apps.lis.illinois.edu/wiki/download/attachments/2656520/Hacking.complacent.pdf.

Hacking, I. (2010). Autism fiction: A mirror of an internet decade. *University of Toronto Quarterly, 79*(2), 632–655.

Hartley, D. (2009). Education policy and the "inter"–regnum. In J. Forbes & C. Watson (Eds.), *Service integration in schools*. Rotterdam: Sense.

Kauffman, J. M. (2015). The "B" in EBD is not just for bullying. *Journal of Research in Special Education, 15*(3), 157–165.

Kavale, K. A., & Forness, S. R. (2000). History, rhetoric, and reality: Analysis of the inclusion debate. *Remedial and Special Education, 21*(5), 279–296.

Lash, S. (2001). Technological forms of life. *Theory, Culture and Society, 18*(1), 105–120.

Latour, B. (2004). Why has critique run out of steam? From matters of fact to matters of concern. *Critical Inquiry, 30*, 225–248.

Linton, S. (1998a). Disability studies/not disability studies. *Disability & Society, 13*(4), 525–540.

Linton, S. (1998b). *Claiming disability: Knowledge and identity.* New York: New York University Press.

Linton, S. (2009). *Press release: Acts of conscience: World War II, mental institutions and religious conscientious objectors.* http://www.syracuseuniversitypress.syr.edu/spring-2009/acts-conscience.html.

Mercer, J. R. (1965). Social system perspective and clinical perspective: Frames of reference for understanding career patterns of persons labeled as mentally retarded. *Social Problems, 13*(1), 18–34.

Nussbaum, M. (2006). *Disability, nationality, species membership.* The Tanner human values lectures. Cambridge, MA; London: The Belknap Press of Harvard University Press.

Oliver, M. (2007). Contribution to review symposium (untitled). *Disability and Society, 22*(2), 230–234.

Rancière, J. (2008). Jacques Rancière and indisciplinarity: An interview. *Art and Research, 2*(1), 1–10.

Said, E. (1993). *Culture and imperialism.* New York: Alfred Knopf.

Said, E. (1995). On defiance and taking positions. *American Council of Learned Societies. Occasional Paper No. 31.* Retrieved from http://archives.acls.org/op/op31said.htm#said.

Said, E. (1999). *Out of place: A memoir.* New York: Alfred Knopf.

Said, E. (2000). An interview with Edward Said. In M. Bayami & A. Rubin (Eds.), *The Edward Said Reader* (pp. 419–444). New York: Vintage Books.

Salusinszky, I. (1987). *Critiques in society.* New York: Methuen.

Scheff, T. J. (1966). *Being mentally ill: A sociological theory.* Chicago: Aldine Publishing Co.

Scott, R. A. (1969). *The making of blind men: A study of adult socialization.* New York: Russell Sage Foundation.

Shakespeare, T. (2006). *Disability rights and wrongs.* London: Routledge.

Symes, C. (2006). The paradox of the canon: Edward W. Said and musical transgression. *Discourse: Studies in the Cultural Politics of Education, 27*(3), 309–324.

Taylor, S. J. (2000). "You're not a retard, you're just wise": Disability, social identity, and family networks. *Journal of Contemporary Ethnography, 29*(1), 58–92.

Taylor, S. J. (2006). Before it had a name: Exploring the historical roots of disability studies in education. In S. Danforth & S. Gabel (Eds.), *Vital questions facing disability studies in education.* New York: Peter Lang.

Taylor, S. J. (2009). *Acts of conscience: World War II, mental institutions and religious conscientious objectors.* Syracuse: Syracuse University Press.

Taylor, S. J. (2011). Disability studies in higher education. *New Directions for Higher Education, 2011*(154), 93–98. http://onlinelibrary.wiley.com/doi/10.1002/he.438/abstract.

Union of the Physically Impaired Against Segregation. (1975). *Fundamental principles of disability.* Leeds University Disability Studies Archive. http://www.leeds.ac.uk/disabilitystudies/archiveuk/UPIAS/fundamental%20principles.pdf.

Vehmas, S., & Watson, N. (2014). Moral wrongs, disadvantages and disability: A critique of critical disability studies. *Disability & Society, 29*(4), 638–650.

Ware, L. (2001). Writing, identity and the other: Dare we do disability studies? *Journal of Teacher Education, 52*(2), 107–123.

Ware, L., & Valle, J. (2009). Disability studies as the default paradigm? In S. R. Steinberg (Ed.), *19 urban questions: Teaching in the City* (pp. 113–130). New York: Peter Lang.

Zola, I. K. (2003). *Missing pieces: A chronicle of living with a disability.* Philadelphia: Temple University Press.

Chapter 2
Alternative Agencies: Materialist Navigations Below the Radar of Disability Studies

David T. Mitchell and Sharon L. Snyder

2.1 The Problem of Disability = Oppression

One of the primary problems facing disability studies is the equation of disability = oppression. This foundational formulation suggests that disabled people experience discrimination on a daily basis, or at least as an incredibly common experience; thus, encounters with social barriers are defining experiences in social model research and there has been some significant explication of the equation as part of the history of the field.

UPIAS first formulated this concept in the early 1970s by splitting the experience of differential embodiment into the well-known impairment/disability divide. As a quick reminder of what this critical partitioning involved, we will just say that impairment became the private stuff of the biological that is not the concern of an activist movement in that it belongs in the private sphere. *Disability* sits on the other side of the equation, and involves the discriminatory encounter between social barriers and bodily, sensory, and cognitive differences. It is, in UPIAS's words, a process "imposed on top of our impairments" (UPAIS 1976).

For scholars such as Tom Shakespeare the problem with this formulation is manifold: (1) It means without discrimination one cannot be "disabled"; thus, it forms an exclusionary logic among people who experience impairment but do not recognize their lives as encounters with discrimination; (2) it makes for a significant amount of *orthodoxy-flashing* where one can tell "allies from enemies" based on their use of oppression as the basis of their research/activist claims about disability; (3) UPIAS was compromised almost entirely of white men with physical disabilities (particularly cerebral palsy) whose lives were abandoned to residential institutions. Their experience of impairment was relatively "stable" and did not involve a substantive amount of pain management or chronic collapse into further depths of

D. T. Mitchell (✉) · S. L. Snyder
George Washington University, Washington, DC, USA
e-mail: dtmitchel@email.gwu.edu

© Springer Nature Switzerland AG 2020
L. Ware (ed.), *Critical Readings in Interdisciplinary Disability Studies*, Critical Studies of Education 12, https://doi.org/10.1007/978-3-030-35309-4_2

impairment that might keep them from their political activism; and (4) the embodied nature of the theory of disability as issuing from folks with physical disabilities by definition excluded people with cognitive and non-apparent disabilities. This is an extensive list of limitations from which disability studies may never recover (Shakespeare 2013).

Perhaps surprisingly, we tend not to agree with Shakespeare on any of these accounts. For instance, does the oppression = disability formulation have to mean that one encounters oppression in every aspect of one's daily life? What if discrimination is a relative constant in people with disabilities' lives but not explanatory of every social encounter? Should we have to take oppression as having to be all-consuming in order to call impairment disability?

Second, the "orthodoxy" to which Shakespeare refers may result in some intolerance within human communities (how surprising!?), but his primary complaint is that such a litmus test is overly simplistic. However, like many disability studies scholars, in making this claim Shakespeare fails to recognize theory as an embodied, living, growing thing in and of itself. If it did not show the particular concerns and tendencies of its moment of formulation, it would not be possible to recognize theory as the embodied act it entails. We should welcome the surfacings of the particularities of theory's historical contexts as they are the stuff of embodiment. This is one way we could recognize the subjectivities of cerebral palsy and its collision with masculinities, for instance, without deciding that such an experience has little to tell us other than about the exercise of a hierarchy of power within disability groupings. It does not tell us about everything, but it certainly tells us about some aspects of disability experience that have become critical to disability experience.

Further, if you are creating a way of analyzing a systemic rather than individual failing (and this is at the root of disability studies work) a powerful yet fairly easy-to-apprehend theory might be exactly what one is looking for as an answer to complaint #4: How do you evolve a theory that can be communicated to an activist community that includes people with physical, cognitive, sensory, and/or psychiatric disabilities? One could just as convincingly argue that simple language is the *modus operandi* of the social model of disability from the beginning. Thus, its inherent address of those with developmental and psychiatric diagnoses is in-built from the outset.

So while Shakespeare (2013) offers us some potential ways to understand the limits of the social model (he asks the provocative question of its "outdated-ness as an ideology"), his critiques are not incredibly persuasive for us, and various iterations of the piece offer more of a zealous complaint by someone who feels maligned by disability studies rather than as a convincing piece of scholarship. Of course, Tom has every right to feel maligned by social model orthodoxy in the U.K., but those feelings do not make a solid enough foundation for posing a professional critique as a form of personal reparation.

2.2   Low-Level Agency

We do believe, however, that the disability = oppression equation is the site of a necessary critique that the field needs to develop. One of the courses we are currently teaching at GW is a graduate seminar on Crip/Queer Theory (with a healthy dose of critical race theory), and our readings begin with two important new works that allow us to better understand the problems at the base of the social model of disability: Asma Abbas's *Liberalism and Human Suffering* (Abbas 2011) and Alexander Weheliye's *Habeas Viscus: Racializing Assemblages, Biopolitics, and Black Feminist Theories of Embodiment* (Weheliye 2014). Both offer up an analysis of what we call "peripheral embodiment" in our new book: *The Biopolitics of Disability: Neoliberalism, Ablenationalism, and Peripheral Embodiment.* "Peripheral embodiment" involves the analysis of those who could be characterized as experiencing lives of "low-level agency." There are many gifts that Abbas's and Weheliye's works offer to disability studies, but a key one for us is their serious turning to efforts at thinking about peripheral embodiment at the level of subjective, historical experience (they both refer to their work as part of the tradition of historical materialism at base). What this means is that even in the most leftist, progressive works of political theory there exists an overemphasis on the agency of "politically sturdy citizens" who, although experiencing significant levels of marginality, continue to exert a full degree of claims-based effort in a pursuit of attaining equal rights (Abbas 2011).

In part, this argument is based on a critique of Liberalism's over-determination of the concept of "agency." What, they ask, do we do with people who do not, or are incapable of, performing in the role of the robust, sturdy, minority, rights-seeking citizen? Is there not, even in disability activist and academic circles, a preferential treatment we give to those lives that exhibit the correct level of resistance as a matter of course? Are we not all culpable of excessively privileging (to one degree or another) those who openly and actively challenge a discriminatory political system? What of those who do not perform their opposition openly or even with a knowledge of themselves as oppressed? How might we get to the significant question of identifying how disability and other minority citizens effectively navigate their embodied lives without only finding ways to expose a discriminatory, oppressive politics? Is there anything out there to be learned from those whose lives involve suffering but do not appear to qualify at the basic level of regard we give to our idealization of the "sturdy political citizen"?

For instance, one example we would offer up involves no particular relation to questions of political exclusion at all. Abbas uses a line from the poet Stephen Dunn that sums up her interest in this analysis of "low-level agency": "the privilege of ordinary heartbreak" (Abbas 2010). What we take this phrase to mean is that suffering is the stuff of embodied existence. To experience embodiment is, by nature, to experience one's vulnerability and that vulnerability may be the result of human-on-human cruelty, but that is only one dimension of the complex subjectivities we should be pursuing.

For instance, Abbas convincingly argues that liberalism's personhood is founded on a concept of embodiment as property; to seek one's "rights" in relation to embodiment must be expressed in terms of damage, loss, or defacement of property (including one's body). So one may have lost loved ones in Hurricane Katrina, for instance, but, in order to effectively seek reparations within liberalism's property-based claims system, one has to pursue the systemic recognition of harm in terms of the loss of one's house as a result of the levees breaking, or as the totaling of one's car by a felled tree, or the closing of a business and the ensuing loss of profit which results, or the collapse of an entire economic way of life related to fishing in the now-contaminated Gulf of Mexico, etc. These all represent serious harms to livelihood; they also involve translating harm into infringements of property rights— there is no place in liberalism to define and pursue justice on the basis of things without a property component. Such a situation involves the necessity of turning harms into things we possess and seeking reparations on their behalf. It is, at base, a substitution of limited property rights for a vast range of experiential knowledge upon which we have given up. We might think of hunger or starvation as Abbas's example of visceral experiences that cannot be compensated within Liberalism's property-based logics (Abbas 2011).

Here is another way to think about "low-level agency." How would we capture the significant experience of someone such as our daughter, Emma, who recently spent nearly 2 years in a hospital undergoing a series of staged thoracic surgeries? Certainly there was a substantive degree of suffering in that experience. However, it cannot be effectively explained as "human-on-human cruelty" (i.e., oppression), as the physicians who were performing a life-saving surgical reconstruction of her esophagus certainly inflicted no harm in order to produce a violent effect. Yet she experienced incredible pain during the 2-year period of surgical reconstruction and multiple harms did result.

For instance, because the surgeons were focused on the restoration of her esophagus, they neglected to tend to the rest of her body. Thus, Emma experienced significant muscle atrophy from lying in bed while in a medically induced coma for a great number of months. Second, she came out of that surgical expanse of time with an incredibly effective repaired esophagus but went blind in the process. What is the reparation in this circumstance? Can we get at it with a social model concept of oppression = disability equation? We are arguing that we cannot, and, consequently, there is a massive loss of significant material that we might be contemplating as a result.

This is not, we think, a matter for reparations or courts or lost property claims. It is also not a result of "oppression" in the strict political sense of the way in which Shakespeare uses the word. There is really no way to express the profound gratitude for the medical expertise we received at Boston Children's Hospital during this time, and yet it did have all of these unexpected and unintended impairing consequences. Abbas (2011) and Weheliye (2014) would both argue that what is lost here is not the consequences of power inequity leading to victimization in need of reparation. That is merely the resurfacing of Liberalism's perpetual property emphasis on claims to damages. Rather they both argue that our vocabulary of suffering is incredibly limited because we do not seek out the experience of those who undergo the labor of "low-level agency" (Abbas 2011, p. 3).

2.3   Embodied Suffering

As Abbas (2011) puts it, we ask nothing of those who experience suffering because the point is to usher them into recognizable categories of harm (malpractice, a flooded house, defacing a public work of art) in order to move on to the next case. By taking up some matters of property damage Liberalism effectively silences the ways in which the experience of suffering might bring us new knowledge. There is a decided overemphasis on perpetrators' motives, interests, and practices without a significant effort to access how those who experienced the effects of harmful actions underwent the experience of harm and the creativity of navigating such circumstances. Boston Children's Hospital conspicuously celebrates its doctors and nurses and dedicated staff for helping those with disabilities all the time (and, we would argue, rightfully so), but there is no testimony from patients about what their experience at the hospital entailed. The labor of being a patient goes silently underground and will not resurface unless we coax it into the world as significant.

Consequently, we have so few ways of understanding what undergoing 2 years of surgery, a medically induced coma, and medical interruptions of privacy to check one's vitals and change the sheets on the hospital's timetable unfolds in the psyches of those who experience extended hospitalization. They do not "undo" a person psychically, but they radically alter the way one experiences the world. "Low-level agency" is often about the ways in which experiences of docility in order to allow support to experience its own expanding agency. This is the meaning of living with suffering, and the paucity of language/narratives we have for describing what it brings into the world is due to the fact that Liberalism does not seek to know about the experiential side of these embodied situations.

Why is not this exactly a key terrain of disability studies? If we continually pursue a concept of oppression and injustice as a matter of systemic exposé, how will we show what disability embodiment brings to us beyond our existing knowledge of the perpetrators or carers or supporters—all who circle disabled persons but are not synonymous with the experience of those they treat? As the feminist theorist Lynn Huffer (2010) argues, what is queer studies worth if we cannot say what queer embodiment offers "within a constructive ethical frame that can actually be used as a map for living" (p. 48)? This line of research undertaking might provide meaningful alternatives to liberalism's finite formulas of "inclusion." In Emma's case, we have learned what it is like to be inside of a medically induced coma. It is apparently terrifying in that she experienced a level of inertia that haunted a waking-sleeping anesthetic purgatory in which she existed. We would not have known what this meant if she was not 15 years old and attentive enough to keep track of the experience as she experienced it.

There is almost nothing in disability studies that could have given us an understanding of how one can appear to be a docile subject who spends 2 years as an incredibly cooperative patient and yet refuses to give up her ability to think through her experience as a life-saving and life-endangering process at the same time. What can differential embodiment offer us that can exist so far "outside" of liberalism's conversations about reparations and yet involve so much suffering at the same time?

2.4   Next Thing-Ness

This is how we translate what Weheliye (2014) refers to as the nearly untranslatable experience of peripheral embodiment that proves so worthy of our Crip/Queer studies' pursuits while also not adding to the violence of our times. This is the kind of suffering to which Abbas (2011) refers when she discusses a desire to know about "suffering" that is not born of "human-on-human cruelty" (p. 24) and yet engenders the pursuit of embodiment as the elucidation of human vulnerability. These are not efforts to underplay the significance of resistance or violence or the myriad examples of human-on-human cruelty that saturate our ways of knowing today. They are, however, ways of understanding a different order of contribution disability studies scholarship might make to imagining other worlds of possibility.

Weheliye (2014) calls this the labor of identifying "different genres of the human" (p. 5). That is the project of *next thing-ness* to which we refer in our title. This is a way of approaching the question of the "miniscule movements" (Weheliye 2014, p. 115) of embodiment as an alternative objective of some note for the field, and yet one we have really not even embarked upon to date.

References

Abbas, A. (2010). TedxBerkeley: Doing the unprecedented. Retrieved from https://www.youtube.com/watch?v=rzErTFh67LQ

Abbas, A. (2011). *Liberalism and human suffering: materialist reflections on politics, ethics, and aesthetics*. New York: Palgrave Macmillan.

Huffer, L. (2010). *Mad for Foucault: Re-thinking the foundations of queer theory* (Vol. 27, p. 324). New York: Columbia University Press.

Shakespeare, T. (2013). The social model of disability. In L. Davis (Ed.), *Disability studies reader* (4th ed., pp. 214–221). New York: Routledge.

UPIAS. (1976). *Fundamental principles of disability*. London: Union of the Physically Impaired Against Segregation.

Weheliye, A. (2014). *Habeas viscus: Racializing assemblages, biopolitics, and black feminist theories of embodiment*. Durham, NC: Duke University Press.

Chapter 3
The Cost of Counting Disability: Theorizing the Possibility of a Non-economic Remainder

Tanya Titchkosky

I am a new citizen of the country of your vision.

—Ralph Ellison, *Invisible Man*

3.1 Introduction

Critical disability studies begin from the perspective that whatever else disability may be, it is certainly constituted between people, between the perceiver and the perceived. Beginning from this interpretivist position has real consequences for research. Instead of regarding disability as a pre-constituted, objectively given lack that begs for aid, assistance, or help, we can regard disability as an inter-subjectively constituted situation that invites the researcher to consider how people orient to disability and make this meaningful. This chapter engages one such meaning-making situation, namely the ordinary and ubiquitous ways that disability is expressed as an expense.

Instead of regarding disability as an expensive thing and going on to measure just how expensive it is, or what to do to minimize expenses or make those expenses appear more reasonable, this chapter aims to show the actual ways that mass media "expense talk" is constitutive of a particular meaning for disability. I am interested not only in theorizing how people perceive disability as an expense, but do so by making disability into an expense of a peculiar kind—an expense void, disappeared money, money seemingly spent without profit. Many things in life can be interpreted as expensive, but how some expenses include a sense of disappeared money while attaching this sense to actual people—disabled people—is a curious phenomenon worthy of critical disability studies analysis.

T. Titchkosky (✉)
University of Toronto, Toronto, ON, Canada
e-mail: tanya.titchkosky@utoronto.ca

© Springer Nature Switzerland AG 2020
L. Ware (ed.), *Critical Readings in Interdisciplinary Disability Studies*, Critical Studies of Education 12, https://doi.org/10.1007/978-3-030-35309-4_3

Such an analysis both reveals and grapples with the human imagination that produces this particular representation of disability. By *human imagination* I mean the forms of interpretation, embedded in culture, necessary to render action sensible and that produce a notion of the human necessary for such action (Mills 1959). In this attempt to face the social and political interpretations behind accounts of disability as an expense, my analysis is also oriented to nurturing a need to count (on) disability differently, that is, in more life-affirming ways (Ginsburg and Rapp 2015; Goodley 2007). My overall aim, then, is to explicate the conception of the human involved in the ubiquitous accounting practices that enumerate disorder, impairment, or disability (terms often used interchangeably in mass media[1]) as an expense while simultaneously configuring these expenses as disappeared money.

This common practice is a rather magical form of reading, a way of making expenses appear and simultaneously vanish—where does the money go? To nurture the possibility of change, Paulo Freire (2017) said that a "magical view of the written word" (pp. 9–10) that comes with the quantification of human life must be "superseded" by the need to understand reading and writing as political and not natural. Uncovering the meaning made through the practices that render disability as "in fact" expensive entails showing how the common practice of reading facts regarding disability as an expense is grounded in an unacknowledged cultural assumption that disability *is* wasted human life and, like all waste, disability becomes disposable (Bauman 2004). I will reveal the specific rules for reading disability as an expense that, then, vanishes or is voided as a way to show how such accounting procedures are a vehicle for the transmission of, in Sylvia Wynter's terms, a key cultural fallacy. This fallacy assembles the idea that economic existence is and should be based on a "*representation*-of-the-human-as-a-natural organism as if it were the human-in-itself" (Wynter 1994, p. 49). After explicating these discursive renderings of disability as "naturally" an expense void, I will also suggest how critical disability studies scholarship can open imagination in ways that might disturb this over-naturalized sense of an economic rendering of human life.

3.2   Background

Unpacking the ordinary discursive renderings of disability as an expense is one way to reveal the guiding economic "definition of the situation" that allows for both the ease and the sensibility of conceiving of some humans as costly (Schutz 1970, 72; Thomas 1971). While it is true that within capitalism all human life can be measured monetarily, and while some people argue that such a rendering is necessary in

---

[1] Disability studies has conceptualized the term "disability" in a variety of ways. From within a social model perspective, disability does not refer to conditions, disorders, or impairments, but rather to the inadequate societal responses that serve to disable people who may have conditions, disorders, or impairments (Oliver 1996). My paper attends to dominant language usage of disability found in Western media, where there is often no distinction made between disability and an impairment condition, nor are their clear distinctions made among disability and disease, illness, disorder, injury, etc.

order to access resources, the question of cultural meaning remains. Whether necessary or not, the repetitive expressions that render disability as a costly expense can be examined so as to reveal some of the contours of the imagined human that makes disability into a taken-for-granted and unquestioned economic expense (Garfinkel 1967). These contours include what has been called the "Financialized Imagination" (Haiven and Berland 2013, p. 7), where debt is configured so as to render humans "pure nothing in object form" (Flisfeder 2013, p. 47). The interpretive moves that flow from logics of capitalism and organize the object of disability as a kind of debt not only constitute the disabled subject as a cost that must be counted; but also, once counted, makes it appear as pure nothingness, renders disability as a kind of expense void. Revealing the imagined human that is actualized through this economic discourse allows us to grapple with contemporary common accounting procedures that constitute this form of disability representation.

Since at least the time of the Atlantic trade in enslaved people, there has been a taken-for-granted sense that human life "can" be accounted for in monetary ways (McKittrick 2013; Wynter 1994; Roberts, 2011). "By the beginning of the nineteenth century, insuring slaves was a well-enshrined practice..." and following abolition, says Michael Ralph, "the life insurance industry began to use the concept of 'impairment' to uphold a differential hierarchy in the value of human life" (2015, p. 108). Today, individuals, employers, and corporations buy insurance against the advent of disability, where each impairment condition is given a monetary value that the insured party may receive upon the advent of impairment. Further examples of the ubiquity of the economic accounting procedures that surround human life are witnessed in the World Health Organization's (n.d.) measures of the global burden of disease through its Disability Adjusted Life Years (DALY; Titchkosky and Aubrecht 2015). Such measures reflect the sense that every impairment condition can be given a number representing a loss of productivity which is then mapped as the expense of disability for countries around the globe. This ongoing economic discursive practice that names an impairment condition and details the cost of it for an individual, family, organization, system, or even for a nation may be reasonable insofar as capitalism is reasonable in its assertion that everything has a price; nonetheless, they are also interpretive scenes up for analysis.[2] And this reasonableness is also a little strange.

Here are a few examples of some of the ordinary Western ways of referring to disability as an expense that hint at a strangeness that is of interest to me:

> Neurological conditions such as stroke and Alzheimer's disease cost Canada[3] nearly $9 billion a year, say neurologists, who warn that the health-care system may not be able to handle the increased burden of an aging population. (CBC [Canadian Broadcasting Corporation] 2007, Neurological Conditions Cost)

---

[2] Investigating the corporate profit-drive behind the genesis of these facts is not, however, my focus. Nor am I conducting an analysis of the veracity of these facts. I focus instead on these facts after they appear in public life and generate particular meanings for disability.

[3] To put these numbers in context, the population of Canada is estimated to be 37.5 million (its most populated province, Ontario, has 14.6 million); the UK's population is estimated to be 66 million; the US's population is estimated at 330 million (http://www.census.gov/popclock/).

Or

> The aim… is to increase awareness of the prevalence and cost of psychiatric and neurological disorders (brain disorders) in the UK…There were approximately 45 million cases of brain disorders in the UK, with a cost of €134 billion per annum. (Fineberg et al. 2013, p. 761)

Or

> The Global Burden of Disease study, the ongoing international collaborative project between WHO, the World Bank and the Harvard School of Public Health, has produced evidence that pinpoints neurological disorders as one of the greatest threats to public health. (WHO 2006, p. 11)

What does it mean to count a phenomenon of human life as a condition that costs $9 billion dollars, €134 billion, or the greatest threatening expense facing public health while, at the same time, to depict all this money as seemingly disappeared, or perhaps transmogrified, into the threatening figure of burden? (See also Fig. 3.1.) Does this money disappear?

In order to explore the strange ordinariness of depicting disability as a condition that comes with a cost while also depicting this cost as a burden—that is, non-productive and threatening—I will turn to previously published "facts" regarding the cost of disability that are already in circulation in the Western mass media and that appear to be ordinary facts requiring no specialized knowledge for their sense. These facts serve to represent a "sense-able sayable" (Titchkosky 2011, p. 73); that is, they represent the common cultural act of counting the cost of humans *as an ordinary* practice. The taken-for-granted sense that disability is expensive, is not natural but is constituted by people, and the perception that this is sensible has something to teach us about the culture that makes, make use of, and relies on such facts. There are a plethora of texts that circulate within the mass media, generated by institutions such as universities, governments, and complex corporate partnerships that exist between them, that do the job of representing disability as an expense. These texts typically appear alongside appeals for more money for the producers and distributors of such facts, and serve as well as part of a plea for money for the development of more treatment and research regimens. I have selected a few ordinary examples in circulation within the public domain for analysis in order to ask, "What conception of the human do they accomplish and rely on?" In order to fully explore this question, I take up two related lines of inquiry: (1) How do mass media renderings of disability privilege cultural schemas of cost that make other meanings of disability disappear while leaving our reading of such facts typically unremarkable? (2) Can a critical analysis of such facts gesture toward the possibility of disability mattering in non-economic ways, that is, "the remainder"?

3.3 The Fact of Disability as Costly

Let us begin with a few random but exceedingly common examples of counting disability as an economic expense, in Fig. 3.1: The Facts.

The Facts

1. It can cost about $3.2 million to take care of an autistic person over his or her lifetime. Caring for all people with autism over their lifetimes costs an estimated $35 billion per year [USA]. (Harvard School of Public Health, April 26, 2006, Press release)

2. In Ontario, the direct costs of stroke are approximately $529 million a year. Add another $328 million in indirect costs and the total burden to the Ontario economy is at least $860 million a year. Left out of this estimate is the sheer human cost to the stroke patient and the stroke patient's family. (Chan & Hayes, 1998, p. S2)

3. Heart disease and stroke costs the Canadian economy more than $20.9 billion every year in physician services, hospital costs, lost wages, and decreased productivity. (Heart and Stroke Foundation, ND, 2013 "Statistics")

4. "Overweight and obesity also threaten the sustainability of our health care system. In 2009, obesity cost Ontario $4.5 billion. To create a different future, we must act now!" (Ontario Ministry of Health and Long-Term Care, 2013, p. 2)

5. Mental health problems and illnesses cost the Canadian economy at least $50 billion per year. This represents 2.8% of Canada's 2011 gross domestic product. In 2011, about $42.3 billion were spent in Canada providing treatment, care and support services for people with mental health problems and illnesses. (Mental Health Commission of Canada, 2011, Investigating in Mental Health)

6. The real financial cost of vision loss in Canada is estimated to be $15.8 billion for 2007—1.19% of Canada's GDP.
  • This breaks down to $500 for every Canadian or $19,370 for every Canadian with vision loss in 2007.
  • The real financial cost comprises two components: The indirect costs of vision loss are estimated at $7.2 billion, while direct (health-related) costs are $8.6 billion. The net cost of suffering (also known as the burden of disease) due to vision loss, over and above financial costs, is estimated to be a further $11.7 billion in 2007. (CNIB, 2009, "Cost of Low Vision")

Fig. 3.1 The facts

Whatever their differences, these statements are united in the sense that impairment is costly: "it can cost," there are "direct cost," "indirect cost," "real financial cost," not to mention the "sheer human cost" and the "net cost of suffering" to the person and their family. Of course, the cost of a condition can change over time, place, and by nation as well as in relation to impairment type and its severity. When the above statements are read as facts one thing remains unassailable—impairments and disorders are taken as the root of the fact that "disability really costs." And, *even if* these direct, indirect, or real costs are "just estimates" or merely "approximate," that there *is* a cost of disability remains beyond question.

Regardless of the condition, cost appears as if it inheres in impairment itself. Consider item 2 of Fig. 3.1—it documents the direct and indirect costs of stroke but also includes something more; namely, the "sheer human cost," which is said to be "left out of" these cost estimates of stroke (Chan and Hayes 1998, p. S2). While human cost is left out of the estimates, it is still brought in as a readily imaginable way of regarding disability. Indeed, the provision of facts on disability as if objectively given seems united with an opposite task where the reader is invited to simply imagine the "sheer human cost." This "works" insofar as the basic fact that disability-is-cost remains at every level of disability's appearance: direct, indirect, approximate, or, in the final instance, imagined. Like any other "fact," its truth claim, disability-is-cost, is "asserted at the outset," "preserved throughout," and "not essentially different" from the interpretations available in everyday life for anyone to make sense of it (Smith 1978, p. 23, 33). Notice too, that by reading cost as residing "in" a condition, there is no explicit representation of cost as a social and political interpretive relation *to* embodiment; and no social geography for a life with disability needs to be imagined, let alone measured (Chouinard 2018). Thus, at the level of cost, a disorder, condition, impairment, disability, etc., all appear interchangeable because each and every one of them is (already) imagined as costly.

Still, somehow cost is made to appear as if it is not steeped in a social imagination but based on something else. Item 6 of Fig. 3.1, for example, expresses the cost, in dollars, of vision loss, which is also depicted in relation to a percentage loss of Gross Domestic Product (GDP). GDP is an economic measure made use of around the globe, albeit in different ways (and GDP has been critiqued for the variability of its use). Nonetheless, the most basic agreed-upon meaning of GDP is as a measure of the total market *value* of all goods and services *produced* in a country in a given year. All the goods and services produced in relation to vision loss (estimated to be $15.8 billion in Canada in 2007) are counted, strangely enough, as in fact a cost. Moreover, this cost appears as a lost or unrecoverable one as the cost is itself not depicted as a valuable part of the economy; that is, the cost of vision loss is a cost *to* the GDP and is not depicted as part *of* the GDP.

Following the invocation of the GDP as one way to express the cost of vision loss, we read, "This breaks down to $500 for every Canadian…" Instead of GDP as a measure of market *value* of goods and services, we are delivered a version of goods and services that represents an economic loss; a market loss that is then further imagined as a burden to each and every Canadian. Providing such specificity as a dollar amount for each individual citizen due to the presence of vision loss also results in providing an implied "total"—in the end, disability costs us all! Yet there is something strange here even in this familiar sense of blindness as a costly loss of value. It appears that the nation is neither responsible for nor a beneficiary of this money. That vision loss financially impairs us all appears to have nothing to do with "us" except to remind us that vision loss is an unanticipated and unwanted expense. Further, it seems that "we" (non-impaired citizens?) profit not a whit from this depiction nor from the $15.8 billion of goods and services because all has vanished—null and void. In this sense, the facts on cost depict disability as pure waste and a sense of disability as a strictly negative ontology is (re)achieved (Hughes 2007; Titchkosky 2012).

Part of the way that this dis-embodied free-floating voided expense can make sense as an economic *fact* is that it appears at a time where "cost of illness" studies are a normal part of everyday life. Such studies, whose history can be traced to slave trade calculations of space, time, bodies, and death rates (McKittrick 2013, 2014), have established the normalcy of a form of perception of the human as an economic unit with inputs and outputs. In the words of a leading cost-of-illness expert, this means understanding that "a person is seen producing a stream of output that is valued at market earnings and the value of life is the discounted future earnings stream" (Rice 2000, p. 177). Indeed, the "facts" above may be read as an expression of a collective belief in "human-capital." Still, the social order that makes impairment into a "discounted future earnings stream," as well as the labor required to calculate the costs (direct, indirect, or imagined) of having an impairment, accomplished within environments that do not regard various forms of embodiment as an essential feature of daily life—all of this seems to disappear into the figure of "disability = cost." Within a social order that rarely attends to the actual labor involved in making disability appear as a cost lies a naturalized sense of their conflation. I address this conflation now as "*disability = cost*."

3.3.1 Disability = Cost

In the face of the cultural production of "facts," Dorothy Smith says that "it is clearly possible to describe behavior in such a way that people will make that definition with full confidence in its propriety" (1978, p. 26). There is a sense of propriety in imagining disability as cost, and doing so in terms of money, literally, in dollars or pounds. But as Smith suggests, assembling such a fact requires "complex conceptual work," convincingly organizing, even "forcing" the meaning of people to fit within a classification that makes any other interpretation difficult to imagine (Smith 1978, pp. 26–27). For example, the net cost of human suffering is marked by money; e.g., billions for the net cost of suffering vision loss; or millions in estimated lost wages and decreased productivity; or billions in indirect costs and the total burden to the economy. Disability can be imagined as costing approximately X insofar as *disability = cost* is a taken-for-granted Real, making any other interpretation seem difficult, i.e., not worth imagining because what would be the point? (And this too may even be costly.) In the face of an expense void, how can it make sense to imagine disability in any other way than as loss?

For these facts regarding the cost of disability to (continue to) make sense, there needs to be a transformation of the value of goods and services into an apparent economic voiding of market value. This bit of magic creates the spell of naturalizing disability as loss through and through, and further naturalizing loss as always already a cost–there is a taken-for-granted belief that what disability is *is* loss, waste, absence of function, and therefore loss of productivity. By naturalizing this sensibility, it becomes possible to read a measurement of value (GDP) as *nothing but loss* when it is associated with disability—autism costs $3.2 million; stroke costs $529 million; obesity $4.5 billion; mental health costs $50 billion; vision loss costs $15.8 billion, and so on. It is only through a critical reading of these facts that we can notice that these millions and billions of dollars or pounds *do not, and have not* vanished. There are a host of organizations and people—medical practitioners, researchers, rehabilitation workers (actual labor)—that lie between a named condition and its monetary figuration (Albrecht 1992). Turned into the currency of fact, *disability* = *cost* glosses over how the body serves as the material and imagined fodder for the production of goods and services, and such facts almost obliterate the more life-affirming sense that disability is produced, maintained, and lived as something other than a cost. *The ultimate cost that accompanies the circulation of such facts might be that their (the facts) sensibility relies on a reader who does not imagine disability as something other than a cost.*

Moving the reader far beyond the sense that disability has, *among other things*, a cost, the facts in Fig. 3.1 render costs as known-able and measurable, and thereby certain, even definitive. There is a quantifiable amount of money attributed to the presence of an impairment condition and this cost remains and is carried forward, insofar as this cost can now "stand in" for disability. Without signs of its production, *disability* = *cost* provides for and enables the propriety of further cost calculations and disability is made graspable only as such. Sylvia Wynter reminds us that in anti-black systems of classification, the map of "how things are" (1994, p. 49) is mistaken for the territory of being. I read this as a political equivalent to Garfinkel's insistence that "In indefinitely many ways members' inquiries are constituent features of the settings they analyze" (1967, p. 9). In the system of classification that understands disability as nothing but loss, the tally of expenses is mistaken for disabled people themselves since the "natural organism" is treated as if it were the "human-in-itself" (Wynter 1994, p. 49). And so, to the question "What is autism?" or "Blindness?" or "Cognitive differences?" it is made possible to answer "Expensive!" And further: "Just imagine the toll disability takes on the natural body, not to mention the national one." Conceived of as fact, *disability* = *cost* appears against the background order of the natural organism—a body of functions, capacities, abilities—doing what needs to be done to produce and consume within the equally "natural" order of modernity. Anything less than this and…well, it will cost you. Moreover, this is taken as the whole of the territory of being disabled.

Disability = *cost* is naturalized to such an extent that disability becomes an "it" and this *it* is loss. From a disability studies perspective, Mallett and Runswick-Cole suggest that attending to those moments where disability "appears, remains and proliferates as a *thing*" (2012, p. 35) is of the utmost necessity. Grounding the appearance of disability as a costly thing, is, as Goodley suggests, "deficit thinking" (2007, pp. 319, 320), which animates the marketization of impairment. While employment, volunteerism, citizenship, or even choice in services may be some of the neo-liberal promises held out to persons with disabilities (Runswick-Cole and Goodley 2015, pp. 164, 171), such promises are made on the basis of an exclusive personhood where the addition of a disability is easily rendered a void, an excessive expenditure to be eliminated with the next set of austerity measures. Without a critical disability studies perspective, readers of such facts do not need to ask, "How does a society make disability into an expense?" Nor will we ask "What other than expensive is disability?" And we may never be tempted to imagine the question: "What does disability mean for the well-being of a non-economic version of humanity?" Such questions must remain an unimagined possibility if the facts on disability are to appear as facts rather than as a bizarre form of social control that makes disability an object for the work of an economic version of "Man" who is (mis)taken as humanity itself, as Wynter (2015) suggests. Still, the critical questions remain: "What does *disability=cost* do to our collective ways of imagining bodies, minds, senses, and comportment?"

Disability = cost refers, of course, to disability as a cost, but one which is also a burden—an unexpected and an unwanted threat to the order of daily existence, including families and carers, the health care system, the economy, local governments, and nations. What autism, stroke, obesity, mental health issues, and vision loss share in common is their obvious status as an impairment circumscribed as a measurable condition that costs its bearer and its care-givers, and costs society as a whole (McGuire 2016, p. 218). This diminishment of disability is a familiar trope to those who know any of the critiques of the "medical model" of disability (Illich et al. 1977; Oliver 1996; Abrams 2015). Still, individualization and objectification of the impairment condition, mapped on to the assumption of a background order of the natural body, has consequences for conceptualizing the human-in-itself.

By economic reckoning, being ordinary pays, whereas being disabled costs—it costs the individual, the economy, and the nation. Anyone and everything calculated as exclusively a cost becomes a lost-cost, a deficit, or even an expendable expenditure. In Bauman's terms, this is the modern production of the redundant human:

> ...unneeded, of no use...The others do not need you, they can do as well, and better, without you. There is no self-evident reason for your being around and no obvious justification for your claim to the right to stay around. To be declared redundant means to have been disposed of *because of being disposable*—just like the... non-refundable plastic bottle or once-used syringe....routinely, people declared "redundant" are talked about mainly as a financial problem. (2004, p. 12)

People who are disposable remain expensive "to" others, to those who are needed to pay the price and who are expected to produce and to consume the modern order. This requires a form of figuring that makes a version of the productive functional human appear as the taken-for-granted background "natural" order against which the disabled subject is depicted and measured (McRuer 2014; Abrams 2015; Runswick-Cole and Goodley 2015; McGuire 2016).

In one sense, *disability = cost* can be read as an answer to the questions that Garland-Thomson finds lurking within cultures that orient to humans *as* economic free-agents:

> What happens to the link between virtue and work when a person's body…no longer fits the work environment? How, in short, can a culture founded upon and committed to the values of liberal individualism deal with physical disability? (Garland-Thomson 1997, p. 47)

Among other things, counting *disability = cost is* "what happens." Such accounting procedures are not only a way to indicate a problem and garner money to fix it; they are also a solution to the problem of disability defined exclusively as loss within economic systems that enforce a neo- liberal individualism that is so essential to the ongoing functioning of coloniality of power (Wynter 1994, p. 54). Thus it is normal to ask, "Just exactly how much has been lost with the advent of disability?" Behind the common practice of counting the cost of disability lies disability regarded as a cost to all forms of social life as it not only costs the citizenry but is a human cost *of* the citizenry because "it," if not fixed, no longer fits.

All of this raises the following: What does it mean to be counted as a cost to the citizenry? Or, put in Wynter's terms, how is "…securing the material well-being of the biologized Body of the Nation…within the economic logic of our present organization of knowledge…" (1994, p. 64) producing a version of the human that is stuck within the confines of the current orders, orders that make *disability = cost* sensible in the first place? Within this version of human life and its sense of the citizenry, everything, including a non-impaired body, has a cost and can be configured as such. Bauman puts it this way:

> …triumphant progress of modernization has reached the furthest lands of the planet and practically the totality of human production and consumption has become money and market mediated, and the processes of the commodification, commercialization and monetarization of human livelihoods have penetrated every nook and cranny of the globe… (2004, p. 6)

Money marks all and can be used to mediate any relation between self and other. Humanity totalized through modernization makes everyone and everything into a measurable unit of cost (but still there are some things or people that are imagined to hold a subsequent possible benefit).

Unlike the cost of raising a child or something expected of the citizenry framed by the particulars of time and place), the cost of disability is, strangely enough, rather dis-embodied, thoroughly objectified, and rendered without reference to a future or to a benefit. Recall that over their lifetime the autistic person will cost \$3.2 million; the direct cost of stroke is \$529 million; obesity costs Ontario \$4.5 billion; mental health problems cost the Canadian economy at least \$50 billion per year; vision loss in Canada is estimated to be \$15.8 billion, and all this is taken as a burden *on the citizenry*. However, given these costs of costing disability, asserting that disability should be given a future by becoming "a new citizen of the country of your [economic] vision" might only produce more of the same for the citizenry (Ellison 1952, p. 343).

This appearance of disability as an expense reveals how easy it is for a cost/benefit logic to move into a cost/cost logic where a form of life is taken-for-granted as redundant, wasted, not quite human, and not part of the over-represented version of Man required by the citizenry (Walcott 2014). Disability understood as productive lives lost to the realms of economic gain, and even more so as those lives that cost the economy and waste its productivity, are moments where we can witness the constitution of, recalling Wynter, Economic Man (mis)taken as the human itself.

3.3.2 Economic Man (Mis)Taken as the Human

As a way to continue to reveal the meaning of Economic Man, let us consider an example of his work more closely. Recall Fig. 3.1(1):

1. It can cost about $3.2 million to take care of an autistic person over his or her lifetime. Caring for all people with autism over their lifetimes costs an estimated $35 billion per year. (Harvard School of Public Health, April 26, 2006, Press release).

"It can cost" and that "it" is autism. *It* costs "about $3.2 million." What costs *is* "to take care," but… not exactly. What are counted are not care-costs nor the profit garnered for care-providers; instead, what is counted is that money for care goes into autism and makes autism into a costly thing. Agents of care, and not the figure of autism, are depicted as doing the job of producing and distributing the facts on the cost of autism. Those who care are also those who care to know the cost of autism. The activity of "care" represents a view point on the object of care as well as the perspective that can calculate the costs of caring for "it." Caring for all people with autism is done by a dis-embodied un-named over-see-er—this figure can be conceived of as Economic Man. He does things. He acts and his acts are productive. He produces about $35 billion dollars of care for all people with autism in a single year. Economic Man's function is taken as the natural state; thus, no cost analysis need be provided for him.

To "take care" is an activity that can involve a host of people and organizations. But a human agent who is engaged in caring is absented from this economic way of accounting for care. Take, for example, "It costs about $3.2 million to take care of an autistic person." Who does this caring is not accounted for. The notion of care as a form of "mutual human flourishing" is made unimaginable (Burke 2014). Instead, the facts on cost serve to depict the recipient of care, over his or her lifetime, as a kind of money pit receiving care, measured in dollars as well as in relation to "all people with autism" also depicted as a cost because they too are receiving care. Economic Man makes conditions such as autism and/or ways of being into repositories where money disappears.

"It" (autism, blindness, what have you) is associated with an individual "over his or her lifetime." The costly person is imagined with a price tag and as part of a group—"all people with autism." There are apparently a "known" number of other people who all have it and they collectively have a cost as well—"estimated $35 billion per year." Care provision, unlike autism, however, has neither an individual nor a collective life, nor does it have a price tag. The number of people who are *doing* this care need not be counted even though the fact of this care is asserted. Thus, autism and its care are depicted as opposite to one another by Economic Man.

The location of Economic Man is given as the Harvard School of Public Health, April 2006. These coordinates of organizational space and time authorize the legitimacy of the fact of care and the expense of autism. The Harvard School of Public Health has expenses; people who work there receive pay, and they may too one day become objects of Economic Man's calculations as may the Harvard business plan itself.[4] Remaining within this economic reasoning, even Economic Man's actions can disappear into the void. Confined in the imaginal space of a natural body of biological dis-function, disability is already voided, but so are almost all other collective relations to disability, even care. When Economic Man is mistaken as the human itself, all become potentially a lost cost.

Still, even within this accounting system, there are hints of a *remainder*.

3.4   Conclusion: The Possibility of a Remainder

Between being human and the cost of being so, something remains. A remainder exists between being disabled and being counted as a cost. After all, a world of interests and values exists between disability and cost. There are, for example, all sorts of organizations, such as the Canadian National Institute for the Blind, the Harvard School of Public Health, or the World Health Organization that are between anyone's life and its being accounted for in terms of cost. There are also a veritable army of individual researchers and health care practitioners between disability and its cost, not to mention friends, family, and others. Significantly, there is the figure, that is, life of disability itself that continues to be despite Economic Man's calculations to the contrary.

By critically reconsidering the facts, we can face the remainder behind these cultural practices that render *disability = cost as if it is* a reasonable way of making sense of life. This remainder can be encountered in expressions such as suffering, sheer human costs, threat, or a need for action now. That the facts of *disability = cost* come with a suggestion that the reader should imagine "sheer human suffering" means that there is something that is difficult to count as a straightforward cost. While any part of the *disability = cost* discourse can, of course, be incorporated into the profit-making economy of health care provision (cure/care/containment), a sense of a remainder nonetheless exists. Despite a powerful economic rationale, the presence of disability inserts and signifies the un-calculate-able character of life.

---

[4]For one account of such expenses, see Harvard Magazine (2014), "Harvard School of Public Health Unveils $450-Million Capital Campaign."

What remains in the face of Economic Man is that we, people, suffer ourselves as something other than an economic entity. We suffer those abnormal moments of recognition that we do not fit within the confines of the biologized version of Man that, as Wynter (1994) has shown, Modernity takes as its functional and economic version of the human. And perhaps there is some hope to be found in expanding this remainder, expanding on the sense that we cannot be totally accounted for, expanding those representations that suggest that at least some humans never add up. When we exceed cost/benefit rationality a future possibility arises peripheral to the totality of economic rationality, a peripheral potentiality for which we are, perhaps, ill-prepared. So we suffer our unimagined selves, selves that exceed the cost-counting rationality so integral to the production of these times of neo-liberal austerity.

This is why the critical disability studies work of uncovering how disability exceeds its ordinary accounting procedures might be more life-affirming than making accounting procedures more inclusive. Further inclusions will not change the fact that the human has been rendered as an economic figure, and is naturalized as a body of functions producing profit while others are seen as bodies of costs. While today conceiving of humanity in economic terms seems almost natural, the most necessary and uneasy task is to seek out and nurture the remainder, especially as Economic Man moves from cost/benefit logic to cost/cost logic, making so much and so many redundant. Rod Michalko puts it this way: "Outing the conception of the natural body as an ideology and a social construction brings disability back as a voice and an interlocutor in the conversation of the meaning of humanity" (2002, p. 71). Disability lives on despite all calculations that have already counted impairment as useless and wasted. Thus, with disability we have, knowingly or not, a cultural figure that does not tally with its counts. The remainder is important if we are to rupture the controlling hold that cost-counting wields. Even those accounting procedures that transform disability into a thing that can be defined and measured solely in terms of cost—even these practices tacitly admit that there is some uncalculable life between disability and its cost.

The counts, however, go on. And reasons to produce such counts have proliferated (if only to raise more funds, and to produce more counts). Still, there is, in the face of such counts, drawing on Michael Davidson's terms, a possibility of a *biopoetics*—which implies a "transformation of formal means—a politics of form—of thinking through the body as a discursive and institutional site" (2016, p. 5). This is not waxing poetic about a supposed pre-given biology. Instead, this biopoetics treats economic functionality (which today counts as biology) as a transformational space to re-encounter the forms of human creativity; it is to do something other than account for the cost of life; it is to make something out of the form of costs we have become that does not tally with current accounting procedures. A biopoetics of the remainder is encountered in, for example, Anne McGuire's (2016, pp. 186–224) re-counts of the murder of people with autism by those who provide care where we face the devastating cultural logics behind the *War on Autism;* a biopoetics is also witnessed in the annual March 1st Day of Mourning (http://disability-memorial. org/). A biopoetics is witnessed by Katherine McKittrict's (2013) re-counts of deaths via the Middle Passage and in *Inventory* by Dionne Brand (2006). Or consider McLaughlin's (2008, esp. 48) accounts of families, seeking to flourish with their dying and disabled children in hospice care, making life live up to death for which no economic reasoning can master. All such accounts bring the un-calculate-ability of life to the fore. Insofar as disability remains, there is the un-calculate-able that haunts economic discourse. Critical disability studies can help us to learn how we do not add up and do so as a way to resist a totalizing economic rendering of human life.

It is true, as Bauman says, every nook and cranny has been reached by an economic rationale, and it is true as Wynter (1994) and others suggest that this is rooted in the anti-black foundations of a modernity that reduced humans to capital or waste through its colonial enterprises. And yet, we suffer our non-economic ways of being and in this a biopoetics of the remainder is unaccountably invited. This chapter aimed to exemplify this possibility by regarding the factual depiction of disability as a costly thing as social action achieved through text and their circulation (Smith 1999; Titchkosky 2007, p. 11) symptomatic of current social orders, and their ongoing concerted accomplishment (Garfinkel 1967; Smith 1978; Titchkosky 2011). In showing that there is a transformation of the life of disability "into the currency of fact" (Smith 1978, p. 24) of an expense void, we can expose those powerful rationalities that organize collective taken-for-granted perceptions of what will be regarded as real. That disability can be regarded as both an expense and an expense void, and that such representations have the currency of fact circulating with ease wrapped in taken-for-granted sensibility—this was the investigative nodal point of this chapter. Hopefully, exposing the devastating ordinariness of costing people makes room for a poetic possibility of a non-economic remainder, and thus a more life-affirming relation to disability.

References

Abrams, T. (2015, June 13). Notes on the social model of disability and critical physio-therapy: A response to Mike Oliver. Retrieved from http://criticalphysio.me/2015/06/13/notes-on-the-social-model-of-disability-and-critical-physiotherapy-by-thomas-abrams/.

Albrecht, G. L. (1992). *The disability business: Rehabilitation in America*. Thousand Oaks, CA: SAGE.

Bauman, Z. (2004). *Wasted lives: Modernity and its outcasts*. Cambridge: Polity Press.

Brand, D. (2006). *Inventory*. Toronto: McClelland and Stewart.

Burke, L. (2014, July). The Alzheimer's show: Dementia and its discontents. Keynote Address at the 5th Annual Theorizing Normalcy and the Mundane Conference. Sheffield University, UK.

CBC (2007, June 22, 5:06 PM ET). "Neurological conditions cost Canada nearly $9B a year: Report. Retrieved from http://www.cbc.ca/1.677502 or http://www.cbc.ca/news/technology/neurological-conditions-cost-canada-nearly-9b-a-year-report-1.677502.

Chan, B., & Hayes, B. (1998). Cost of stroke in Ontario, 1994/5. *Canadian Medical Association Journal, 159*(6S), S2–S8.

Chouinard, V. (2018). Like Alice through the looking glass: II—The struggle for accommodation continues. In N. Hansen, R. Hanes, & D. Dreidger (Eds.), *Untold Stories: A Canadian Disability History Reader* (pp. 320–338). Toronto: Canadian Scholars Press.

CNIB [Canadian National Institute for the Blind]. (2009). *The Cost of Vision Loss in Canada: Summary Report*. Retrieved from http://www.cnib.ca/eng/CNIB%20Document%20Library/Research/Summaryreport_Covl.pdf.

Davidson, M. (2016). Missing bodies: Disappearances in the aesthetic. *Cultural Critique, 92*, 1–31. https://doi.org/10.5749/culturalcritique.92.2016.0001.

Ellison, R. (1952). *Invisible man*. New York: Random House.

Fineberg, N. A., Haddad, P. M., Carpenter, L., Gannon, B., Sharpe, R., Young, A. H., Joyce, E., Rowe, J., Wellsted, D., Nutt, J. D., & Sahakian, B. J. (2013). The size, burden and cost of disorders of the brain in the UK. *Journal of Psychopharmacology, 27*(9), 761–770. https://doi.org/10.1177/0269881113495118. Retrieved from http://www.ncbi.nlm.nih.gov/pmc/articles/PMC3778981/.

Flisfeder, M. (2013). "Debt: The Sublimated Object of Capital," Topia. 30–31: 47–63

Garfinkel, H. (1967). *Studies in ethnomethodology*. New Jersey: Prentice Hall.

Garland-Thomson, R. (1997). *Extraordinary bodies*. New York: Columbia University Press.

Ginsburg, F., & Rapp, R. (2015, May 11). Making disability count: Demography, futurity, and the making of disability publics. *Inhabitable Worlds*. Retrieved from http://somatosphere.net/2015/05/making-disability-count-demography-futurity-and-the-making-of-disability-publics.html.

Goodley, D. (2007). Towards socially just pedagogies: Deleuzoguattarian critical disability studies. *International Journal of Inclusive Education, 11*(3), 317–334. https://doi.org/10.1080/13603110701238769.

Haiven, M., & Berland, J. (2013). Introduction: The financialized imagination (In memory of Stuart Hall). *Topia, 30–31*, 7–16.

Harvard Magazine. (2014). Harvard School of Public Health unveils $450-million capital campaign. Retrieved from http://harvardmagazine.com/2013/10/hsph-celebrates-centennial-unveils-450-million-capital-campaign.

Harvard School of Public Health. (2006, April 26). Autism has high costs to U.S. society. Online press release. Retrieved from http://archive.sph.harvard.edu/press-releases/2006-releases/press04252006.html.

Heart & Stroke Foundation. (2013). Website: Statistics. Retrieved from http://www.heartandstroke.com/site/c.ikIQLcMWJtE/b.3483991/k.34A8/Statistics.htm.

Hughes, B. (2007). Being disabled: Towards a critical social ontology for disability studies. *Disability & Society, 22*(7), 673–684.

Illich, I., Zola, I. K., McKnight, J., Caplan, J., & Shaiken, H. (1977). *Disabling professions*. London: Marion Boyars.

Mallett, R., & Runswick-Cole, K. (2012). Commodifying autism: The cultural contexts of 'disability' in the academy. In D. Goodley, B. Hughes, & L. Davis (Eds.), *Disability and social theory: New developments and directions* (pp. 33–51). Hampshire: Palgrave Macmillian.

McGuire, A. (2016). *War on autism: On the cultural logic of normative violence*. Michigan: University of Michigan Press. *forthcoming*.

McKittrick, K. (2013). Plantation futures. *Small Axe, 42*, 1–15. https://doi.org/10.1215/0799053-2378892.

McKittrick, K. (2014). Mathematics Black Life. *The BLACKSCHOLAR, 44*(2), 16–28.

McLaughlin, J., Goodley, D., Clavering, E., & Fisher, P. (2008). *Families raising disabled children: Enabling care and social justice*. London: Palgrave Macmillan.

McRuer, R. (2014, July 15). Crip displacements: Voices of disability, neoliberalism, and resistance. Disability Studies Network Seminar, Liverpool Hope University, UK.

Mental Health Commission of Canada. (2013). *Why investing in mental health will contribute to Canada's economic prosperity and to the sustainability of our health care system: Backgrounder—Key facts*. Retrieved from http://www.mentalhealthcommission.ca/English/document/5210/making-case-investing-mental-health-canada-backgrounder-key-facts?terminitial=41.

Michalko, R. (2002). *The difference that disability makes*. Philadelphia: Temple University Press.

Mills, C. W. (1959). *The sociological imagination*. New York: Oxford University Press.

Oliver, M. (1996). *Understanding disability: From theory to practice.* New York: St. Martin's Press.

Ontario Ministry of Health and Long Term Care. (2013). *No time to wait: The healthy kids strategy.* Toronto, ON: Queens Printer.

Paulo F. (2017). "The Importance of the Act of Reading," Journal of Education. Vol. 165(1): 5–11. https://doi.org/10.1177/002205748316500103.

Ralph, M. (2015). Impairment. In R. Adams, B. Reiss, & D. Serlin (Eds.), *Keywords for disability studies* (pp. 107–109). New York: New York University Press.

Rice, D. P. (2000). Cost of illness studies: What is good about them? *Injury Prevention, 6,* 177–179. https://doi.org/10.1136/ip.6.3.177.

Roberts, D. (2011). *Fatal invention: How science, politics, and big business re-create race in the twenty-first Century.* New York: The New Press.

Runswick-Cole, K., & Goodley, D. (2015). Disability, austerity and cruel optimism in big society: Resistance and 'the disability commons'. *Canadian Journal of Disability Studies, 4*(2), 162–186.

Schutz, A. (1970). *On phenomenology and social relations.* Chicago: University of Chicago Press.

Smith, D. E. (1978 [1976 German]). 'K is mentally ill': The anatomy of a factual account. Sociology, 12, 23–53.

Smith, D. E. (1999). *Writing the social: Critique, theory and investigations.* Toronto: University of Toronto Press.

Thomas, W. I. (1971 [1923]). On the definition of the situation. In M. Truzzi (Ed.), Sociology: The classical statements (274–277). New York: Random House.

Titchkosky, T. (2007). *Reading and writing disability differently: The textured life of embodiment.* Toronto: University of Toronto Press.

Titchkosky, T. (2011). *The question of access: Disability, space, meaning.* Toronto: University of Toronto Press.

Titchkosky, T. (2012). The ends of the body as pedagogic possibility. *The Review of Education, Pedagogy, and Cultural Studies; special issue: Health, Embodiment, and Visual Culture, 34*(3–4), 82–93.

Titchkosky, T., & Aubrecht, K. (2015). Who's mind, whose future? Mental health projects as colonial logics. *Social Identities, 21*(1), 68–94. doi.org/10.1080/13504630.2014.996994.

Walcott, R. (2014, April 9). Zones of black death: Institutions, knowledges, and states of being or funk: A black note on the human. Antipode: Florida. http://antipodefoundation.org/2014/04/02/the-2014-antipode-aag-lecture/.

WHO. (2006). *Neurological disorders: Public health challenges.* Geneva: WHO Press. Retrieved from http://www.who.int/mental_health/neurology/neurological_disorders_report_web.pdf.

WHO. (n.d.) *Metrics: Disability-adjusted life year (DALY): Quantifying the burden of disease from mortality and morbidity.* Retrieved December 19, 2019, from http://www.who.int/healthinfo/global_burden_disease/metrics_daly/en/.

Wynter, S. (1994). No humans involved: An open letter to my colleagues. *Forum: N.H.I.: Knowledge for the 21st Century: Knowledge on Trial, 1*(1), 42–73.

Wynter, S. (2015). On Being Human as Praxis. Edited by Katherine McKittrick Durham, NC: Duke University Press. https://doi.org/10.1215/9780822375852.

Chapter 4
Theorising Disability and Humanity

Dan Goodley

4.1 The Question of the Human

What does it mean to be human? This question is, of course, hardly a new one. It is a query humankind has always asked of itself. And it is an inquiry that I have found myself really occupied with in recent times for a number of reasons. Let me pick out a few. The first is thanks to the Canadian sociologist and disability studies scholar *Tanya Titchkosky*. The seminar that she organised in Toronto, Canada, in June of 2013, to which I contributed, was entitled *Ableism and the Question of the Human.*[1] Her work since that time (and before that to be fair) has always contemplated what disability brings to the party. Titchkosky asks us to think about what disability reveals about human selves, subjectivities, social worlds, and our relationships with others. For example, in *The Question of Access* she makes a simple but not simplistic point: *When disability demands inclusion in social and educational spaces, then it also reveals the exclusionary nature of those spaces.*[2] Access is unveiled as a site in which to deliberate about the ways in which societal contexts invite some human beings into those places whilst leaving others on the outskirts, the borderlands, and the periphery. These are all very human moments of contemplation.

The second reason for thinking about the human is the influence of the work of the postcolonial scholar *Sylvia Wynter*.[3] Her analysis makes clear that the colonisation of the Americas and other parts of the globe erroneously termed the "New World" led inevitably to a split between dominant Ethnoclass Man and the rest of

---

[1] http://www.newcollege.utoronto.ca/event/able-ism-and-the-question-of-the-human-a-seminar/.

[2] Titchkosky (2011).

[3] Wynter (2003). And I also have to thank Tanya again and Rinaldo Walcott—both at the University of Toronto—for turning me on to this work.

D. Goodley (✉)
University of Sheffield, Sheffield, UK
e-mail: dgoodley@sheffield.ac.uk

© Springer Nature Switzerland AG 2020
L. Ware (ed.), *Critical Readings in Interdisciplinary Disability Studies*, Critical Studies of Education 12, https://doi.org/10.1007/978-3-030-35309-4_4

the empirical human world engaged in human struggle. White, capitalist, coloniser man came to understand what it means to be a valued human being (read: profitable active member of the rapidly expanding global bourgeois order) not only in terms of his own ontological, cultural, and economic preferences but also in terms of conceptualising the Other as less than human (and in contrast to the demands of capitalism). To risk seriously simplifying Wynter's work, her analysis makes clear that to secure the narrow humanness of white bourgeois order requires dehumanising those that sit or stand in opposition to that order. And those members of the empirical human world would include poor, black, non-European, and, I would add, disabled people. Wynter's work has troubled me. It makes me wonder if the category of human is actually worth keeping hold of, especially in light of its genealogy. Should we retain a category that is inherently so racist and disablist? Who would not want to invite excluded others into the category of human recognising the historical fights of many of the world's population for human recognition? But who is actually doing the inviting? And what does this reveal about those who feel comfortable in owning the category whilst others do not even get a foot in the door? This human phenomenon is an unsettling thing.

The third reason to ask about the human is *Frantz Fanon*; in particular *Black Skin, White Masks*, and especially a striking sentence of his text that reads, "The black man does not exist".[4] This is an incredible thing to read from a pioneer of the decolonising movement. But what does he mean? To say that a black person does not exist is to recognise the whiteness of the symbolic imaginary, cultural order, and dominant alterity of society. Fanon seeks to expose the damaging impact of a colonising discourse that secures its potency (originally gained through genocide, the stealing of land, and economic oppression) through a further colonisation of the black psyche by white alterity. At the heart of being oppressed is a feeling of belittlement, worthlessness, and self-negation. The early days of colonisation were maintained through a psychical colonisation to the extent that the original owners of land are urged to view themselves as less than human by those who have taken their land by force. Similarly, recognising that the disabled person does not exist in the dominant ableist imaginary raises similar concerns about dehumanisation. Fanon reveals himself as a student of Lacan here, echoing the latter's claim that we all become alienated by our immersion in language and culture. This is particularly the case for those of us who are denounced as Other by the dominant semantics of symbolic culture. Culture and language shape humankind. Language matters. So do words. And words are unsettling.

The fourth is, perhaps unsurprisingly in a volume such as this, *disability*. Critical disability studies scholarship has consistently evidenced the ways in which disabled people are routinely dehumanised. And this dehumanisation involves a cyclical pulling in of a number of economic, cultural, social, and political moments of disablism. Disabled people just never seem to be included in the normative order of things: and this we might define as disablism. The emergence of the United Nations

---

[4] Fanon (1993).

(hereafter, UN) Convention on the Rights of Disabled People (The Convention) is testimony to the many ways in which disabled people are not afforded the same opportunities and access to community living, education, work, sexual health, and parenting as their non-disabled peers. The very fact that the Convention had to be written in the first place is an exposition of the varied ways in which disabled people are already excluded from everyday, mundane, and ordinary activities associated with being a human being in the world. Disability acts not simply as a cultural vent for some of the discriminatory acts of society. It also provokes an intervention: a need to question, contest, and understand why disability is excluded from the normal or normative workings of everyday life. Just as with the decolonising work of Fanon and the postcolonial writing of Wynter, disability comes to ask some troubling questions about the common ways in which humanity has been understood. Disability is indeed unsettling.

The fifth reason is *iHuman*. Since 2013 I have been working with a number of colleagues at the University of Sheffield to pull together an interdisciplinary research centre that feeds on research from the humanities, social sciences, and STEM disciplines (Science, Technology, Engineering and Medicine). One goal is to produce trans-disciplinary conversations and communities to theorise how we are or might understand the human in the twenty-first century. Conversations have occurred, for example, with colleagues in robotics about the possibilities for using technology to think about how we think of support and personal assistance. We have engaged with colleagues in law about the legalistic tensions produced by practices associated with human enhancement. We have also listened to the work of humanities colleagues that bring together histories of colonialism and disablism in order to understand the ways in which identifying citizens in terms of disability and able-bodiedness was crucial to discourses of nation building. And we are exploring with colleagues in architecture how migration patterns through Europe shift not only the boundaries of countries and permeate national borders but also trouble the contemporary marking of the human as entrepreneurial labourer and consumer. Migrants and refugees have questionable humanities, at least in terms of how they are disavowed by national governments and local communities. In June 2014, The *UN High Commissioner for Refugees* (UNHCR) reported that the number of people displaced by bloody conflict and persecution had exceeded 50 million for the first time since the post-World War II era. Contemporary conflicts are exacerbating the problems of displacement. And we know from the *2011 World Report on Disability* by the World Health Organization (WHO) that where there is conflict, war, poverty and displacement then there is often disability. What it means to be human is increasingly up for grabs in these deep interconnections of culture, economy, human movement, and technology. The refugee crisis was only becoming more pronounced at the time of writing.

The sixth reason is *the post-human*. Here I am referring to the work of feminist scholars such as Donna Haraway and Rosi Braidotti,[5] who have each, in their own inimitable ways, brought some serious questions to bear upon the human. Haraway's

---

[5] Braidotti (2006, 2013) and Haraway (1991).

work on the blurring of human and technological worlds has been very powerful, especially to those of us in disability studies who are interested in the impact of prosthetics, technological, and assistive devices; the support of people by animals (and vice versa); and the support of other people. Donna Reeve[6] has recently expressed concerns with some of the more uncritical proponents of technological advancement, critically appraising the input of Haraway and suggesting that techno-logical input is neither a panacea for the access dilemmas of disabled people nor necessarily a benevolent offering. There is a fine line between human enhancement and the technological erasure of impairment. Braidotti's work builds on Haraway's ideas in some very interesting ways. At the heart of Braidotti's thinking is, I believe, an interesting disavowal of the human. On one hand, she is clear that the human is an incredibly helpful phenomenon to appeal to as a political strategy. Human rights are but one consequence of the discourse of humanism that disabled people cite in an attempt to be recognised by a dominant alterity that has hitherto failed to recog-nise them as human beings. But on the other hand, like Wynter and Fanon, Braidotti is troubled by the human, as it tends to be defined in narrow humanistic ways (a definition that has relied heavily on racist human distinctions and anthropocentric segregation of humans and non-humans). Furthermore, pointing to advances in technology, spirituality, migration, and environmental politics, it might make better sense to think of our contemporary times as post-human. To be post-human affirms our expansiveness with other humans, the environment, and technology. The disper-sal of our subjectivities and communities through the internet and social media, the nomadic movements of people and their cultural footprints through migration pat-terns and forced displacement, and the growing environmentalist connections between animals and human beings are just some of the ways in which we are living in a time that we might deem post-human. This frame of reference has gained grow-ing kudos in the field of disability studies, not least because the notion of expansive fits well with disability's relationship with assistive technologies, support of others, and distributed forms of competence. Braidotti opens up, then, a contradictory rela-tionship with the human: a category to be used as a moment of recognition and a category to be dissolved in favour of the post-human. But I do not view this contra-diction as a problem. Indeed, I reckon that contradiction can be very helpful. We know too that contradiction can be unsettling.

This leads me to a seventh reason why I have been considering the question of the human and that is in relation to an intellectual and political project that I have been working on with Rebecca Lawthom, Kirsty Liddiard, and Katherine Runswick Cole, namely the *DisHuman*.[7] Embracing the ambivalence that Braidotti, Wynter, Fanon, and Haraway have towards the human (not least in terms of the dominant ways in which this category has been shaped and morphed in modernity), our DisHuman project seeks to disavow the human. Our project has been fashioned, in particular, by learning from disabled activists, especially those with the label of

---

[6] Reeve (2012).

[7] Goodley et al. (2014a, b), Goodley and Runswick Cole (2016), and Goodley et al. (2015).

intellectual disabilities. Indeed, self-advocacy politics posits that the human is (1) a sign through which social recognition can be gained and (2) a classification requiring extension. An under-girding argument of the chapter is that people with intellectual disabilities are already engaged in what we might term a post-human politics from which all kinds of human can learn. Hence, for the remaining parts of this chapter we will expand upon the politics of people with intellectual disabilities and illuminate the ways in which their activism might be understood in terms of DisHuman activism. And a DisHuman positionality should unsettle.

4.2   Four DisHuman Encounters with Disability

I have been lucky enough to be involved for over 20 years with the politics of intellectual disabilities. This has involved research with people so-labelled as well as the opportunity to work as a voluntary supporter and advisor to a self-advocacy group in Huddersfield in the North of England. Empirical work for my doctoral study involved me spending ethnographic time with a number of self-advocacy groups dotted around the country.[8] And more recently, with colleagues, I have had the opportunity to work alongside researchers with intellectual disabilities to capture their experience of community living, work, and leisure for a recent research project.[9] Over the 15 years since my book on self-advocacy was published the theoretical and activist landscape has shifted enormously in relation to the politics of intellectual disability. For a start, disabled people with intellectual disabilities have had their activism, ambitions, and lifeworlds more readily acknowledged by the mainstream disability studies community. The self-advocacy movement has been more overly accepted too into the fold of the disability movement. People with intellectual disabilities have fought alongside their physically impaired peers for their human rights. Alongside this growing representation there have been major developments in terms of how disability has been theorised. Whilst disability remains broadly conceptualised in terms of theories of social oppression (building on the foundational work of the social model), disability has increasingly been reframed in terms of possibility and disruption. Crip desires have produced new forms of agitation, organisation, and relationships to the study and politics of disability. Many of us can now state with confidence that disability does not just signify discrimination, tragedy, or social inequity. Disability denotes affirmation. Disability is something to be desired because it broadens what we understand as being human. This harks back to Titchkosky's work in which she foregrounds disability as an interpretivist moment and a phenomenologically rich entity through which to contemplate our humanity. So, let us now unpack some very human

---

[8] Goodley (2000).

[9] https://bigsocietydis.wordpress.com/.

elements and disability's place in desiring but also redefining these elements: a position we might think of DisHuman (disability's disavowal of the human).

The first element is that of *support*. Rather than viewing support as something that a human needs when they are found lacking, we might instead recast support as a marker of humanity. Specifically, an invitation to be supported is an indicator of human vulnerability. To require support is to be human. To be human is to need others. And without others we would not be human. Disability acts as a mirror to humanness: to reflect back interdependence and mutuality as necessary human characteristics that sadly often get lost in a contemporary society that attaches far much significance to individual achievement, isolated self-sufficiency, and economic gain. Disability affirms human vulnerability and in so doing reaffirms what it means to be human. In reflecting on the development of disability studies (especially in relation to the inclusion or not of intellectual disabilities), I have witnessed the emergence of a bifurcated complex in relation to disability: a heightened awareness of oppression alongside a growing cognizance of the affirmative work done by disability to the world. The question is what is to be done with such an apparently conflict-ridden realisation? One response is to live with the tension. And when one has learnt to live with it perhaps we can work the tension in some interesting and helpful ways. Furthermore, we would also want to find out if this working of the tension is already being enacted in the world. My sense is that disabled people and their allies have always found themselves in this frictional working of what Rod Michalko calls the difference that disability makes[10] alongside a desire to be deemed as humanly normal (and normally human) as anyone else. Disability calls to be known as human whilst also pursuing a politics of diversity that rubs up against taken-for-granted normative ideas of being human. Let me give an example. Think of the naming of self-advocacy politics (People First Groups) and the slogans that are used (Label Jars Not People). The message here is clear: people with intellectual disabilities are people, just like anyone else, and labels can be damaging and limiting. Labelling people risks denying their personhood. And the humanity of the members of self-advocacy groups is clawed back from disabling society through the naming of People First. This is a form of politics that simultaneously recognises sameness *and* normality: that people with intellectual disabilities are people nonetheless. In distancing oneself from a label—a sticky tag to be added to a jar—self-advocacy recaptures a relationship with the everyday normality of being a person. To be seen as a person requires a rejection of the pathologising totality of psychologising discourses associated with diagnosis. These discourses create a vision: a pathological category, a psychopathological phenomenon, and a misreading of people that seems to be so very far away from the idea of being a member of the human race. In contrast, when one engages with the workings and details of self-advocacy groups we find a very interesting relationship with humanity. Most groups are supported by people without the label of intellectual disabilities and these advisors work with group members to enhance the politics of self-advocacy. These working

---

[10] Michalko (2002).

relationships are deeply sophisticated as human relationships usually are. Advisors work hard to make sure that their views, ambitions, and perspectives do not direct members of the groups. Advisors seek to find ways of supporting that feed into a politics of self-advocacy that contest the centrality of disability labels. And self-advocates (the term used by people with intellectual disabilities who populate the groups) are moved and shaped by the support networks around them (and they too shape their networks). Hence, in order to be recognised by the normative register of humanness—a Person First—then self-advocacy groups construct very nuanced forms of collective work and action. And these toned forms are made available through the presence of this phenomenon termed intellectual disability. This disability category brings together people in the first place and provides a platform from which to collectively claim, through support, a seat at the humanist table. To sit together as People First. Disability affirms interdependencies that define us as human beings. And the presence of intellectual disability also brings with it a number of innovative demands of (and invitations to) support. In this sense, then, disability and the human rub together in a moment of support that, when they work, are truly [mutually] humanising.

The second element is *frailty*. Many people with intellectual disabilities and their supporters would struggle with my choice of word. They would find this term too deficit-making, worrying that it could be used to assign a passive position of dependency and negation. Frailty is a term seemingly miles away from the uber-competent and self-aggrandising individual of our contemporary times. Recently I have argued that we live in a time of neoliberal-ableism where the privatisation of the self, the marketisation of everyday life, and justification for austerity politics are enshrined in a belief that global citizens will work and shop themselves into positions of self-sufficiency that no longer require the support of government nor the services of the welfare system.[11] In these competitive and individualistic times, why would anyone want to claim frailty as something that stigmatises them? My sense is that self-advocacy politics have always held this phenomenon in play with the work that they do. The British self-advocate and someone I had the pleasure to work with for a number of years, Joyce Kershaw, once told me just before she died that "we all having intellectual disabilities". By this she was not simply placing us all on some new spectrum of human variegation but, instead, alerting us to the ways in which everyone fails to match up to the high standards and augmented ideals associated with human health and well-being. We all have difficulties. Being human is precarious. But she was also clear about the power of people with intellectual disabilities and their collective durability to work against a disabling society. She spoke to me about Huddersfield People First's success in getting the local council to stop using the term mental retardation in their policies. I witnessed her take apart numerous professionals in day centres and group homes when she felt that they were preventing service users and residents of homes from becoming involved in Huddersfield People First. This was a show of strength by Joyce and her comrades against the

---

[11] Goodley (2014).

pathologising gaze of professionals and services. It was also a mark of the muscle and vigour of disability activists. But the point, so often for Joyce in her work, was the simple notion that she and her comrades could not do their work alone. Individually they would struggle. Together they were powerful. Frailty demands collectivity and necessitates the interventions of others. And this sense of a shared frailty as a meeting point for activism harks back to long-held debates in feminism, especially around an ethics of care as a response to human vulnerability.[12] Recently, this work has been built upon by the queer theorist Jaspir Puar. In introducing herself to the disability studies field, she has reclaimed debility as a political and human commons on which we can find comradeship.[13] I welcome any theorisation of vulnerability when it captures the ways in which the human body risks being rendered vulnerable, worked to death through its engagement with neoliberal capitalism. My own opinion, though, is that the distinction between humanness and disability (the latter category a dominant signifier of being very much Other than human) is very much alive and well in our late capitalist society. In collapsing this binary—in calling out to debility—we risk ignoring the very material, immaterial, and phenomenological ways in which disabled people are excluded from the rigid humanist human category and, perhaps even more importantly, bypasses the radical work done by disability to the human world. The horizontal appeal of a term such as debility—whilst welcome as a political strategy of bringing disability together with other transformative identities associated with queer, feminist, and postcolonial thinking—risks erasing the political potency of disability politics, a politics that has often not touched the sides of political debate (historically ignored by Marxist, feminist, and postcolonial thought, to name but a few transformative arenas who can be accused of being at the very least disability-lite in their work). The politics of self-advocacy as we have seen is very much capable of working the formations of disability and the human. And it is this interplay I want to keep in tension.

The third is *capacity*. In current debates about debility as a trope around which to organise politically and theoretically, one wonders what might be left of the notion of capacity. When this term is evoked it recalls synonyms such as aptitude, faculty, and competence. And these synonyms quickly become wrapped up in the language of neoliberal-ableism and humanism: as abilities owned by some and not by others. For people with intellectual disabilities it has been paramount to keep hold of these concepts in order to demonstrate their capacities as human beings, whether it be in relation to living in the community, holding down a job, continuing to parent children in the face of professional surveillance, or offering rational responses to questions about the value of life and death. Yet in order to demonstrate capacity this, like support, has required imaginative means and methods. Disability has always been post-human in the ways in which it has displayed capacity, demanding forms of human expansion through connections with human and non-human others including technology and animals. Disability deconstructs capacity as an

---

[12] Kittay (2007).

[13] Puar (2009).

individual asset and opens up capacity is as being relational and materially realised through a host of networks, assemblages, and connections. Capacity is not simply something we own but an entity enacted with other humans and non-humans. Capacity is something that emerges through the presence of a person in the world. And this phenomenological complexity, as we all know and feel, makes us human.

The fourth is *desire*. What do we desire in these neoliberal-able times? Post-human literature has asked some searching questions about what we are doing to the human in a time of technology, globalisation, and militarisation. What kinds of human enhancement are we wanting to produce and endure? What is it about the human we want to enhance? Disability, I feel, asks us to think again about the objects of our desires. Let us take two examples: having enough money (or credit cards) to spend and working hard (to demonstrate one's worth), two practices valorised by society. But these are two practices immediately contested by disability and, equally, two practices desired by disability. People with intellectual disabilities have long held out in their politics their desire to work, to earn, to hold a position of employment that they would value. In rich-income nations the benefits trap is one that has been bastardised by right-wing debate. The benefits trap might be reframed as the inflexibility of welfare to permit people to work (sometimes) and keep hold of welfare entitlements that support people to live in their own homes, with support, often with families. Living with family is often a necessity because welfare never goes far enough in supporting people to live interdependently with a community. And we know that communities are becoming ever more harsh places for those not deemed to be earning their keep. Many disabled people have reminded us of the inflexible ways in which work is supported by governments and desired as the only meaningful contribution to society. Disability can also go further in flattening a desire to work or spend as the only ways of exhibiting one's human competence. How might we understand a person with complex needs and their contribution to society? How might we include a person that cannot work? On one hand such individuals create jobs for others to support them. [Not to mention entire networks of agencies that also exist in their bureaucracy-heavy entities. I think there is good work to be done to figure out how such places can "flip" their structures in response to DS critiques.] A person with profound impairments produces labour for a number of people. So they ironically fulfil a crucial role in increasing job opportunities (albeit a rather passive role). At the same time, people with complex needs demand us to ponder the rigidity of valuing paid work. Those who cannot work do not have this activity as an individual skill to highlight to others. Being a non-worker is often associated with idleness, dependency and inactivity: which is, ironically, a rather lazy response. These people who some might deem as non-workers urge us to think again about what we desire in human beings and as human beings. This reframing of desire is so important. And it should be linked too to consumption. How much of human activity is directed to consuming those material and immaterial—real and virtual—objects that we lack? How might we think of consumption of other entities: relationships, ways of living, new community spaces, reorganisation of spatial and temporal arrangements with other human beings (and non-humans) in search of new humanities? One of the few positives of living in austerity Britain, so it seems, is a replenishing of activism and collegiality amongst many people, witnessed in the recent choice of a new Labour party leader with the most socialistic of ideals. Another observation relates to the growth in Global South disability studies scholarship that has, at its epicentre, a critique of neoliberal capitalism and a re-engagement of hybrid traditional-modern forms of community activism. These are very real human desires, desires that are pushed away from a narrow obsession with labour and shopping and a more generalist interest in collective belongings and becomings.

4.3   Conclusions

At a recent conference in the home of the Beatles—Liverpool, England—the sociologist, disability studies scholar, and writer of fiction Rod Michalko[14] expressed his worries about the impact of disability studies on the rest of the normative world. Whilst appreciative of disability studies scholarship and activism Michalko expressed this concern: Has disability studies really disrupted anything? He carefully laid out in his paper the seductive power of the normal world, the normative register ingrained in a social world transfixed by sameness and the recuperative capacity of a cultural ideology of normalcy. He reminded the conference of normality's inbuilt durability to reproduce its centrality and its reach. Indeed, when I think of the ubiquitous nature of neoliberal-ableism I know where Michalko is going with this one. Has disability studies really disrupted and usurped normalcy? And when we think of normative notions of the human (against which disability is found lacking), has disability studies or the politics of disability really made inroads into redefining these normative ideas and ideals? My answer to Michalko is this: I fear that disability studies has not disrupted nor radically overhauled normalcy, nor strict normative notions of the human. The reason? Advanced capitalism (of course), but also a contemporary commitment to human enhancement that risks casting off disability as the Other described by Fanon when he wrote about blackness in a world owned by whiteness. When Fanon wrote that all this "whiteness blinds me", one is reminded too of Michalko's argument that sighted society (as an example of normalcy) blinds those that sit outside of the normative register.[15] But my sense is that disability has, at the very least, unsettled normative ideas of the human. The human being, at least as it is held up in Western Europe and North American, continues to display its colonial, racist, and capitalist origins. It is endlessly evoked as something to desire, commensurate with societal development and economic progress. It is tied to civil and social rights as the primary means of ensuring recognition. But it is also a category that disability messes with, subverts, revises, reassesses, and troubles. Most importantly, disability has worked hard at the normative centre, evidenced by the activism of people with intellectual disabilities described in this chapter. Whether

---

[14] Michalko (2015).

[15] See, for example, Michalko (1998).

or not this is radical enough is open to question—and a question we should always keep open. And in these times of globalised ableism, one wonders what is really to be done. Perhaps, at least by creating some friction and tension, disability has shaken if not stirred one element of the normative centre. And in thinking of the human, disability always has a chance of being a little bit unsettling—and this potential to unsettle seems to me to be very human.[16]

References

Braidotti, R. (2006). Posthuman, all too human: Towards a new process ontology. *Theory, Culture & Society, 23*(7–8), 197–208.

Braidotti, R. (2013). *The posthuman*. London: Polity.

Fanon, F. (1993). *Black skins, white masks* (3rd ed.). London: Pluto Press.

Goodley, D. (2000). *Self-advocacy in the lives of people with learning difficulties: The politics of resilience*. Maidenhead, England: Open University Press.

Goodley, D. (2014). *Dis/ability studies: Theorising disablism and ableism*. London: Routledge.

Goodley, D., Lawthom, R., & Runswick Cole, K. (2014a). Posthuman disability studies. *Subjectivity, 7*(4), 342–361.

Goodley, D., Lawthom, R., & Runswick Cole, K. (2014b). Dis/ability and austerity: Beyond work and slow death. *Disability & Society, 29*(6), 980–984.

Goodley, D., & Runswick Cole, K. (2016). Becoming dishuman: Thinking about the human through dis/ability. *Discourse: Studies in the Cultural Politics of Education, 37*, 1–15.

Goodley, D., Runswick Cole, K., & Liddiard, K. (2015). The DisHuman child. *Discourse: Studies in the Cultural Politics of Education, 37*(5), 770–784. https://doi.org/10.1080/01596306.2015.1075731.

Haraway, D. (1991). *Simians, cyborgs and women: The reinvention of nature*. London: Free Association Books.

Kittay, E. (2007). A feminist care ethics, dependency and disability. *APA Newsletter on Feminism and Philosophy, 6*(2), 3–7.

Michalko, R. (1998). *The mystery of the eye and the shadow of blindness*. Toronto: University of Toronto Press.

Michalko, R. (2002). *The difference that disability makes*. Philadelphia: Temple University Press.

Michalko, R. (2015, July 1–2). *Decentering the disruptive education of disability*. Paper presented at disability and disciplines: the international conference on educational, cultural, and disability studies, Centre for Culture and Disability Studies, Liverpool Hope University.

Puar, J. K. (2009). Prognosis time: Towards a geopolitics of affect, debility and capacity. *Women & Performance: A Journal of Feminist Theory, 19*(2), 161–172. Retrieved from http://www.socialtextjournal.org/periscope/2010/11/ecologies-of-sex-sensation-and-slow-death.php.

Reeve, D. (2012). Cyborgs, cripples and iCrip: Reflections on the contribution of Haraway to disability studies. In D. Goodley, B. Hughes, & L. J. Davis (Eds.), *Disability and social theory: New developments and directions* (pp. 91–111). London: Palgrave Macmillan.

Titchkosky, T. (2011). *The question of access: Disability, space, meaning*. Toronto, ON: University of Toronto Press.

Wynter, S. (2003). Unsettling the coloniality of being/power/truth/freedom: Towards the human, after man, its overrepresentation—an argument. *CR: The New Centennial Review, 3*(3), 257–337.

---

[16] Big thanks to T and R for commenting on this chapter and offering support along the way.

Chapter 5
The Metaphor of Civic Threat: Intellectual Disability and Education for Citizenship

Ashley Taylor

5.1 Introduction

The philosophical study of the role of schooling in preparing democratic citizens has tended to presume an able-minded learner. Indeed, dominant philosophical and theoretical models of democratic education consider neither the civic preparation of individuals with perceived intellectual disabilities in particular, nor the presumptions of able-mindedness that are built into theorizing about democracy and citizenship. As a result, democratic citizenship aims are frequently conceptualized according to an unevaluated assumption that civic preparation requires a particular level and display of intellectual ability, communicative competence, social independence, and behaviour. This unevaluated assumption parallels the presumed incompetence of individuals with perceived intellectual disabilities in other areas of education, a phenomenon that has been well documented by scholars of disability studies. Theory and research in Disability Studies in Education (DSE) and other areas of critical educational studies challenge this assumption by showing that the ability to reason effectively and to develop, exercise, and display intellectual abilities is highly contextualized and dependent on multiple factors, including access to education and the opportunity to benefit from it (e.g., Kliewer et al. 2015; Rubin et al. 2001; Schalock 2011). A number of scholars (e.g., Baglieri and Shapiro 2012; Kliewer et al. 2015) have concluded that because the demonstration or exhibition of intellectual ability is highly contextualized and dependent for its measurement on subjective factors of assessment and inferences based on behaviour or communication, there is a question of whether it makes sense to continue to refer to "intellectual disability" as a discrete phenomenon having material basis. For example, in their recent article "At the End of Intellectual Disability", Kliewer et al. (2015) argue that:

A. Taylor (✉)
Colgate University, Hamilton, NY, USA
e-mail: ataylor1@colgate.edu

© Springer Nature Switzerland AG 2020   53
L. Ware (ed.), *Critical Readings in Interdisciplinary Disability Studies*, Critical
Studies of Education 12, https://doi.org/10.1007/978-3-030-35309-4_5

> Intellectual disability (and its immediate categorical antecedent, *mental retardation*) is no
> more objectively real than the label *witch* imposed by male authorities onto some unfortu-
> nate women to explain and control their supposedly disturbing and troubling behaviour …
> Intellectual disability does not exist independently of the observer but is, in fact, always an
> inference made by those in positions of power and control over those accused. (p. 22)

In what follows, I take up what Kliewer, Biklen, and Peterson refer to as the "metaphor" of intellectual disability, the sense in which "We do not literally see mental
retardation; we infer its existence" (Kliewer et al. 2015, p. 22). This metaphor
emerges within the context of citizenship education in particular and troubling
ways. *We do not see intellectual disability; we infer its existence through manifestations of non-citizenship.* As I will discuss, intellectual ability—and disability—is
actively constructed by and through gendered and racialized attachments to the
notion of the ideal citizen. Individuals who are perceived to manifest undesirable
differences in cognition, behaviour, communication, or performance appear to
threaten notions of civic well-being, of nationhood, and of social reciprocity. In this
sense, intellectual disability becomes a metaphor for civic threat. Consequently,
educational theorizing around democratic citizenship education advances the metaphor of intellectual disability through a process of negation: the citizen is that which
the person with intellectual disability is not *or* intellectual disability is that which is
not citizenship.

This chapter begins with a broad discussion of the place of dis/ability, implicit
and explicit, within educational theorizing about citizenship aims. As I discuss in
the first section, the future citizen is constructed as an able-minded learner. I then
describe how people who are considered to have questionable cognitive status are
positioned as non-citizens often in virtue of undesirable traits perceived through
gendered and racialized norms of civic worth. More specifically, I develop the
notion that intellectual disability is a metaphor for civic threat. Finally, I consider
the deconstruction of the discourse of civic threat, paying particular attention to the
dearth of *imaginative* possibilities for citizenship.

5.2   The Future Citizen as Able-Minded Learner

The aspiration that schools be places where democratic citizens are created or
shaped is foundational to public schooling in the USA, Canada, and other Western
countries (although certainly not exclusively). Scholars of all educational sub-
disciplines and stripes have written about the role of education in preparing young
people for active engagement in their national polity and, increasingly, in the global
world. Scholarship and research in DSE and inclusive education are no exception;
indeed, a foundational argument for inclusion that has emerged from these fields is
that all children receive better civic preparation when they learn together, regardless
of ability level. Says Minow (2013), "Integration in the context of disability holds
promise for enhancing social understanding and the sense of 'we' among all students" (p. 52). While many philosophers and theorists of education share the view

of the importance of diversity and inclusivity for democracy, few outside of DSE explicitly address disability as one such instance of diversity. Yet if being a good citizen involves being exposed to a diversity of perspectives and experiences, then it follows that schools should endeavour to facilitate cross-positional learning. When students are educated together, citizenship can be enacted in the classroom through the development of understanding, patience, empathy, respect, and belonging—at least this is the aspiration. Thus, the school as an institution and the classroom community can be regarded as unparalleled environments for incubating civic knowledge, skills, and virtues that are attentive to ability differences.

Many scholars in the field of philosophy of education have shared this view of the relationship between schooling and the civic preparation of diverse groups of students, albeit with different manifestations.[1] Nevertheless, considerations of the full inclusion of young people with significant disabilities have not emerged as clearly (Terzi, 2008 is a notable exception). For the most part, and whether they are more concerned with the reproductive dimensions of citizenship or with the transformative dimensions thereof, philosophers of education have focused on the extent to which democratic decisions are made and community is created within conditions of interest plurality and identity difference, with strong emphasis on socioeconomic, religious, cultural, linguistic, and racial identities in particular. Nevertheless, questions within these discussions about the capabilities and dispositions that students need to engage effectively and cooperatively in democratic politics across even extreme differences in worldview are always questions about the "ability expectations" (Wolbring 2012, p. 156) that potential or developing citizens must have in order to do so. Frequently, students judged capable of democratic citizenship education are framed as possessing, or possessing the potential for, particular abilities that correspond to desirable skills, knowledge, and dispositions or character (see Biesta 2006). This is especially so within, although not exclusive to, the liberal democratic philosophical tradition in philosophy of education (see Erevelles 2002, for discussion). The delineated capacities usually include high (although not usually specified) levels of cognitive ability, economic or civic reciprocity of a particular level and kind, intellectual and social independence, a disposition towards respecting democratic values, and normalized communication and behavioural expressions. As I will explain, these presumed capacities or ability expectations create significant challenges for envisioning people with disabilities, and perhaps especially people with intellectual disabilities, as future citizens. This is so not only because these capacities correspond to expectations of ability based on normalized constructs of human functioning, but also because they promote a view of the citizen as primarily cooperative and unfettered by an existing history of distrust for civic norms.

According to Wolbring (2012), ability expectations are the developed capabilities (and sometimes innate capacities), dispositions, behaviours, and virtues that are desired and sometimes even expected within a particular contextualized frame-

---

[1] Certainly John Dewey is of particular noteworthiness here, as Danforth has pointed out (2001).

work of education (see also Biesta 2006; Hehir 2002); they "influence the very meaning of citizenship" (Wolbring 2012, p. 156) and are shaped by a dominant view of what citizenship requires. Some ability expectations are benign, even beneficial; for example, the expectation that individuals have the ability to be free from oppression and social marginalization. However, others function as prescriptions of the *necessity* of abilities that might otherwise be considered merely *desirable*. Such a move can rise to a form of ableism[2] when and because those abilities considered normal and therefore socially desirable are instead promoted as necessary. For example, it may be desirable for civic participation that a person is able to read, but making literacy a requirement of citizenship has historically amounted to oppression, promoting a view of the citizen as a white, property-owning male (Kliewer et al. 2004).

The slide from desirable to necessary can be seen in the frequent and perhaps dominant emphasis on deliberation or some variation of dialogic civic exercise within liberal democratic philosophical conceptions of democratic participation. According to Gutmann and Thompson (2004), deliberative democracy is "a form of government in which free and equal citizens (and their representatives) justify decisions in a process in which they give one another reasons that are mutually acceptable and generally accessible, with the aim of reaching conclusions that are binding in the present on all citizens and open to challenge in the future" (p. 7). The deliberative model of citizenship is quite demanding of citizen participants: the democratic person is one who is motivated to engage in public discussion with others whose views or interests are conflicting; she is open to listening to others and to being persuaded to change her position; she is able to engage in reasoned debate, presenting reasons to support her position and listening to the reasons of others; and she is capable of autonomous decision-making, acting independently and freely in giving reasons and forming consensus or disagreement. These ability expectations would seem to pose significant problems for people labelled with intellectual disabilities (although not only this group). In fact, Clifford (2012) charges that deliberative democracy is "implicitly coded as able-boded" (p. 218). I would add that it is also coded as able-minded, in that it places a strong emphasis on reasoning abilities and on independent decision-making. Moreover, deliberation relies on "communicative reciprocity" (Clifford 2012, p. 221), implicitly—or at least by omission—marked by normatively valued or understood modes of communication. Individuals who experience significant limitations in communicative ability—who do not communicate verbally, whose speech is slow or hard to decipher, who use assistive devices to communicate and so on—are significantly disadvantaged by deliberative democracy. This is because verbal communication (as a privileged form of communication) is presented as not merely *desirable* but actually *necessary* for one's inclusion in civic activities.

---

[2] The term "ableism" has been used in many different ways. Here I define ableism as the systematic privileging of those abilities considered normal within a particular social context as well as the systematic marginalizing of individuals perceived as disabled or as having undesirable ability characteristics.

Presumptions about communication, as well as behaviour and cognitive and social independence, are woven as invisible and invisibilized threads into the fabric of deliberative theory. The emphasis on communicative reciprocity is particularly problematic as a foundational component of an aspirationally inclusive civic society. Indeed, people with intellectual disability labels and other disabilities affecting communication or comprehension are left on the margins of citizenship, to borrow Alison Carey's (2010) apt terminology, by the deliberative model. Importantly, it is not just expectations of capacity that contribute to this marginalization but also the emphasis on norms of reasonableness, dispassionate dialogue, open-mindedness, and "civic magnanimity" that "other" people with disability labels (see McGregor 2004, p. 95). Some educational scholars, and feminist scholars in particular, have pointed out how democratic deliberation, contrary to its inclusive and transformative intentions, may actually place unfair demands on those who lack power or undermine the authority of those whose lived experiences differ from dominant norms (Ellsworth 1989; Jones 1999; Levinson 2003; McGregor 2004). According to Levinson, for example, deliberation calls for "social trust" among parties in a dialogic exchange (2012, p. 37). The problem of social trust can be seen as particularly troubling for people labelled with intellectual disabilities as individuals and as members of a group. As frequent recipients of care, of external life management, and of decision-making support or substitution, such individuals are frequently positioned in situations where, as adults, they must place a great deal of trust in caregivers, teachers, service professionals, and so on—often of necessity. Yet, these relationships of personal trust are required despite a long history of abuse, exploitation, and social marginalization and exclusion that people labelled with intellectual disabilities have experienced. It isn't clear why or how one can be expected to develop personal trust given this history, and it would be perfectly reasonable in many cases for individuals so labelled to experience a great deal of social *dis*trust.

For both these reasons, namely that dominant conceptions of citizenship reflect the necessity of capacities that do not reflect all individuals' abilities and because they ignore important social histories, feminists and critical race theorists have critiqued the reliance on Westernized individualism in conceptualizing citizenship more generally. Philosophers, and especially feminist philosophers of disability, have moved this discussion into the realm of dis/ability, especially through the critique of discourses of independence and reciprocity as foundational to citizenship (e.g., Erevelles 2002; Kafer 2013; Kittay 2001). For example, Nirmala Erevelles (2002) writes that, "notions of autonomy and rationality are, in fact, closely tied to the historical and material conditions of capitalism where certain definitions of reason and autonomy become more plausible than others" (p. 13). For Alison Kafer (2013), civic and other forms of belonging are always tied to a notion of expected futurity, wherein a person's actual civic worth is tied to their potential growth and development towards an expected vision of future contribution. Kafer writes, "Ideas about disability and disabled minds/bodies animate many of our collective evocations of the future; in these imaginings, disability too often serves as the agreed-upon limit of our projected futures" (2013, p. 27). As I will explain in the next section, worries about the future—the future of the nation, the future of the citizen, the future of the family—have historically dominated discourses of citizenship in ways that position some individuals, by virtue of their embodied alterity, as threats to civic well-being and growth.

5.3   The Construction of the Civic Threat

Notions of able-bodiedness and able-mindedness are the backdrops against which the ideal citizen is imagined and against which schooling practices and processes are measured. Built into any notion of citizenship is the construct or image of the *good* citizen; it is a normative assessment. This normative assessment corresponds to dominant views of the social good, socially desirable behaviour, and socially desirable embodiments. Thus good citizenship is also a binarized construct, depending on its social "other"—the socially undesirable other—for description and assessment. In this section, I will discuss how the racialized and gendered positionality of *civic threat* forms the foil to the good citizen and positions intellectual disability as a metaphor for civic unfitness.

Disability studies scholars have documented how the linking of able-mindedness to potential or actual civic status is a highly racialized and gendered process. This process is perhaps most clear and familiar within examples of the construction of the concept of feeblemindedness, what James Trent (2004) calls a "catch-all" term for people considered not only mentally/intellectually deficient but also morally defective and of questionable civic worth. Writes Trent:

> What made this new image [of the feeble-minded] so threatening and ensured acute concerns and shrill warnings was the increasing insistence in the first and second decades of the new century that mental defectives, in their amorality and fecundity, were not only linked with social vices but indeed were the most prominent and persistent cause of those vices. Graduating from being merely associated with social vices to being their fundamental cause, mental defectives became a menace, the control of which was an urgent necessity for existing and future generations. (2004, p. 141)

The construction of feeblemindedness as a metaphor for civic threat was disproportionately damaging for new immigrants and poor women, especially those perceived as racially impure. New immigrants arriving at Ellis Island were screened for apparent markers of physical and mental disability through medical inspections and intelligence testing (Baynton 2013). A suspect screening could be readily used to disqualify them from seeking residency in the United States. Importantly, it was taken as self-evident that individuals who exhibited markers of disability would be excluded from entry, a position buttressed by the twin notions of heredity and contagion linked to disability.

Figure 5.1 demonstrates the linking of undesirable race, gender, and sexuality in the construction of the civic threat. The image, titled "Inheritance of 'Mongolian' Deficiency", appears in *Applied Eugenics*, a 1918 textbook (Popenoe and Johnson 1920). It depicts a woman and a child in separate side-by-side photographs. The woman is unsmiling and appearing of darker complexion. Her race or ethnicity is

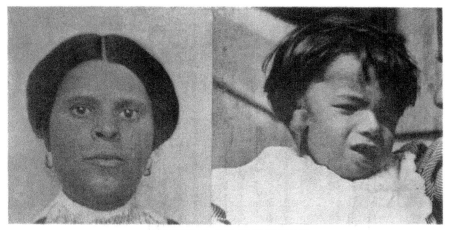

INHERITANCE OF "MONGOLIAN" DEFICIENCY.

A common type of feeble-mindedness shows external indications by a type of feature which is called "mongoloid," because of a certain resemblance to that of some of the Mongolian races. The woman at the left has this appearance, yet the tests showed that she was normal mentally. She was admitted as an immigrant, and by a normal husband gave birth to the child at the right, which not only had the mongolian characteristics exaggerated, but was a pronounced imbecile. The child was deportable, and the mother of course went with him. There is nothing in the immigration laws at present to prevent the entry of such women as these, if they themselves can pass the mental tests, although it is evident from many such cases as this, that they transmit feeble-mindedness to their offspring, even though they themselves may seem to be normal. (Frontispiece.) (See page 122.)

Fig. 5.1 Inheritance of 'Mongolian' Deficiency (1918)

not explicitly identified but it is clearly referenced. The child appears to be a toddler with a full head of dark hair, a wide forehead, and what might be considered a "deformed" ear. The caption reads:

> A common type of feeble-mindedness shows external indications of a type of feature which is called "mongoloid" because of certain resemblance to that of some of the Mongoloid races. The woman at the left has this appearance, yet the tests showed that she was normal mentally. She was admitted as an immigrant, and by normal husband gave birth to the child at right, which not only had the Mongolian characteristics exaggerated, but was a pronounced imbecile. The child was deportable, and the mother of course went with him. There is nothing in the immigration laws at present to prevent the entry of such women as these, if they themselves can pass the mental tests, although it is evident from many such cases as this, that they transmit feeble-mindedness to their offspring, even though they themselves appear to be normal (Popenoe and Johnson 1920, p. 174).

In this image, disability is presented as both a heritable trait and a contagion, transmissible through parentage as well as through the suspect sexuality of the questionable and racialized motherhood. This woman's child "outs" her as parentally and civically unfit because she is linked to the child's supposed feeblemindedness, itself exemplified by the child's racialized ("mongoloid") characteristics. This woman's status as a citizen is called into question by her relationship to apparently feebleminded offspring, thus solidifying the contradiction between citizenship and disabilities of the mind.

In addition to policies and practices that aimed to prevent putatively deviant individuals, and especially women, from procreating, eugenics authorities promoted a system of education designed to encourage the socially and civically desirable to procreate, and to become vigilant about the undesirable elements of society. Ideals of whiteness, desirable gender behaviour, and mental health and ability were linked together as social—and educational—goals to which citizens ought to aspire. Indeed, many of these eugenics narratives became public lessons of civic responsibility displayed in textbooks, at state fairs, and through public health pamphlets and circulars (Ferri and Connor 2006). The creation of the notion of feeblemindedness solidified a binary notion of citizenship that depended on the exclusion of some to uphold the membership of others. The increased public awareness and vigilance allowed individuals to retain their civic membership through working towards ideals of able-mindedness.

It may be tempting to consider this cultural artefact and these stories as confined to the past; indeed, doing so not only allows us to distance ourselves from these disturbing histories, but also situates responsibility for their perpetuation squarely with individuals who are long since gone. But the notion of civic threat and the fact of contemporary complicity remain strong in our contemporary world. Policies and statutes governing public health and political activity continue to concern themselves with the cognitive or mental health status of individual members of society. One need only look as far as recent voter ID laws in some US states that disproportionately limited the voting opportunities of poor African Americans and Latinos (Childress 2014), or discourses about immigrants and refugees as national threats and contagions, for example, Chavez (2013); see also Schweik (2011). An image from a recent public health campaign in NYC is likewise a striking example of the discourse of civic threat. The campaign, which involved a series of subway and bus posters with messages about the dangers of teen pregnancy, positioned teenaged mothers as contributing to and even responsible for the potential ill health of the polity through their "choices" to bear children into situations of poverty, lowered educational opportunities, and single-parenthood. For example, Fig. 5.2 shows a toddler, who has light skin and ambiguous racial and ethnic identity features and who is crying. The caption reads, "I'm twice as likely not to graduate high school because you had me as a teen", followed by a slightly more detailed statistical statement putatively confirming this caption (Taylor 2015). The campaign not only appeared to attribute the perpetuation of systemic social conditions—of poverty, lack of education, and so on—to individual women, but also positioned children born to such women as problems. Here civic competence—and incompetence—is presented as inherent to the individual.

While these examples implicitly reference ability and ability expectations of citizens—often by negation—other policies and practices pertaining to nationhood, social reciprocity, or civic well-being are more explicit in their management of dis/ability. For example, legal statutes governing the political activity of individuals perceived as having lowered cognitive status are especially illustrative of the continuance of the discourse of civic threat or liability in the contemporary period. At present all but 11 states have laws that can restrict the voting rights of people with disabilities, usually because of their assessed intellectual abilities or mental health status. Additionally, many states outright bar individuals who are placed under guardianship from voting (14 in 2012, according to Pan 2012). Such restrictions

Fig. 5.2   NYC Teen Pregnancy Prevention campaign poster (2013)

continue despite the fact that guardianship restrictions have been widely criticized as oppressive by the disability community and beyond (see Rood et al. 2015). Legal guardianship, which is ostensibly about an individual's ability to make decisions on their own behalf, therefore becomes equated with and indeed enacts a loss of civic status, as I will explain.

The legal process of guardianship involves a court appointing an individual or individuals to make decisions for and on behalf of an individual who is deemed incapable of making those decisions for herself or of acting in her own best interests. As Rood, Kanter, and Causton (2015) argue, guardianship processes are based in and promote a particular view of disability that is aligned with the presumption of incompetence rather than a presumption of competence; a disability is considered "*synonymous* with an inability to make decisions in one's own best interests" (Rood et al. 2015, p. 319; emphasis in original). The presumption of guardianship for individuals with intellectual disabilities therefore demonstrates the reliance on the idea that certain people globally lack competence by virtue of their cognitive status. Thus, while many alternatives exist, including formal and informal supported decision-making, person-centred planning practices, and limited guardianship, full guardianship dominates (Rood et al. 2015). These legal impositions can occur even when the individual in question exhibits high levels of social, political, and personal competence. Such a paradox is evident in the recent case of Jenny Hatch, a young woman in her early 20s who had a rewarding job, a happy living arrangement, and an active role in local politics when she was placed under the legal guardianship of her parents and removed to a group home living arrangement that she did not desire and that limited her social activities (Vargas 2013). In an unprecedented demonstration of competence, and with the support of friends, Hatch undertook and won a legal battle petitioning for the right to choose her guardians (Vargas 2013). Here we see an example of how supporting relationships, when harnessed as competence-facilitating rather than competence-impeding, can produce opportunities for civic exercise (in this case a legal challenge over rights).

When one is placed under guardianship, however, one's access to civic opportunities is reduced, whether as a matter of overt and/or non-overt political consequences (e.g., overt denial of political opportunities like voting or potential denial of access to information necessary to take advantage of those opportunities). The logic of political restrictions for those under guardianship appears to be that individuals either lack competence to engage in such political activities because they lack competence to make decisions on their own behalf or that they cannot justifiably take part in political practices like voting because they are at risk of being coerced by their guardians. Certainly the latter worry—of manipulation and abuse in decision-making—is real and concerning. However, it is curious that this should motivate further restrictions on individuals under protection rather than motivate further inquiry into safeguarding against coercion, manipulation, and abuse in civic practices. Indeed, restricting the rights and opportunities of labelled individuals as a result of such risks situates the threat to political power as within those individuals. Why should the individuals who experience the restrictions be situated as *threats* and bear the consequences thereof? The case of Jenny Hatch, alongside other instances of guardianship restrictions, illustrates how states of dependency and lowered cognitive status can be confused with, and perhaps even naturalized, as a lack of civic potential. Such a confusion can be seen as continuous with the historical positioning of the socially undesirable as threats to the civic well-being.

5.4   Deconstructing the Metaphor of Civic Threat: Potentialities of Imagination

Despite Kafer's (2013) critique about the lack of (civic) futurity that is projected onto individuals with significant disabilities and that can be seen in the failure to conceptualize disabled citizenship, some educational practices do in fact quite overtly consider the future of individuals with intellectual disabilities. So what kind of civic future is envisioned and enacted through these practices? Unfortunately, the answer is often one that corresponds to norms of able-bodiedness and able-mindedness. One example that I will discuss is legally mandated transition planning, which is part of the individualized education planning process for adolescents with identified disabilities in the USA. As I will explain, this educational mandate, aimed at advancing the social, economic, and political opportunities of labelled individuals, nevertheless bumps up against dominant notions of civic participation that are able-bodied and able-minded.

The democratic or civic potential of many of the educational practices that are *nominally* aimed at advancing the democratic inclusion and participation of individuals with intellectual and developmental disabilities can actually function as programs of social regulation, exacerbating the gap in political opportunities that labelled individuals experience. For example, Peterson (2009) illustrates how practices of self-determination in schools can devolve into narrow expectations of close-ended performance standards. In this context, learning aimed at democratic inclusion can instead play out as a practice of normalization rather than autonomy-facilitation within transition planning in schools (Cowley and Bacon 2013; Peterson 2009). Peterson (2009) offers the example of Shana, whose nominal self-determination process involved not only the ignorance of her true preferences, but also highly circumscribed opportunities for "choice". Peterson observes that "a great schism existed between self-determination as a democratic ethos and the reality that ensued when attempting to support self-determination" (2009, n.p.). This example illustrates how education for citizenship, when confronted with the able-bodied and able-minded norms of the schooling context, can become a mandated program rather than a democratic process, practice, or experience (Leake 2014; Powers 2005; see also Cowley and Bacon 2013). However, it is not simply the encounter with the schooling context that can render civic education practices as circumscribed programs. Rather, the very definition of citizenship tied to a dominant ideal of independence and autonomy can permeate practices ostensibly aimed at emancipation. In fact, as Aspis (1997, 2002) points out, self-determination and self-advocacy discourses and practices appear to support a narrative of citizen that is highly individualistic, despite originating from a tradition of social research tied directly to significant disability. While ostensibly aimed at developing students' abilities to become citizen participants or civic agents—to make decisions and act on their own behalf, and to turn that decision-making outwards towards political action—the democratic dimensions of these frameworks are lost amongst the fog of programmatic and standardizing practices.[3]

It is certainly clear that a problem exists where frameworks of social inclusion and political participation that have transformative potential—like self-advocacy— simply reinforce the status quo of alienation, regulation, and social control of people labelled with intellectual and developmental disabilities. We might look at how this co-option of self-advocacy can reaffirm individuals' social distrust of care providers, service-professionals, educators, and so on, rather than enhancing opportunities for civic valuation and participation. How does a lack of attention to the *methods* of support itself impede opportunities for citizenship? Is it individual incapacity or external power that prevents civic growth and agency?

---

[3] It is important here to distinguish between the self-advocacy movement as a whole and the experience of self-advocacy as institutionalized within educational and service contexts. I am decidedly *not* making an argument that self-advocacy work necessarily fails as a civic project.

These questions are especially pertinent in considering how the need for sometimes-significant support is taken as a threat to a person's ability to exercise political agency. This double-bind is seen in Jenny Hatch's experience. In a discussion of the need for increased legal and policy emphasis on supported decision-making (in contrast to guardianship), Hatch's lawyer, Jonathan Martinis, describes how when Hatch asks for help it disqualifies her from being independent, whereas when a non-labelled person asks for help it can be taken as *evidence* of independence ("Introduction", 2014). Says Martinis:

> Think about the way you [non-labelled person] make decisions in your life. Think about the things you do every day. If you have a big decision that you have to make, do you just make it with your gut all the time? No, you do research. You ask people for information. You go out and get the support and information that you need to make the best decision that you can. And when you do that people tell you that you're smart. People tell you that you're making an informed and intelligent decision. ("Introduction", 2014, p. 8)

Hatch's existing label/diagnosis as intellectually disabled means that she is already held suspect. Certainly this double-bind illustrates the necessity for a sustained conversation on prejudice against individuals labelled with intellectual disabilities— indeed, for a sustained conversation on ableism in general. Yet even if educators, support people, and others fully understand this prejudice against the capacities of individuals with intellectual disabilities, they may not correspondingly understand the bias *towards* a particular view of citizenship that permeates—namely that citizenship is expressed through normalized displays of communication, behaviour, and cognition. And here we see the complexity: that challenging the able-minded presumption of citizenship involves challenging the very notion of citizenship itself—perhaps most importantly the idea that civic participation is precluded by the need for complex support, by a limitation in or lack of verbal communication, or by the presence of socially devalued behaviour.

A view of citizenship as based in able-bodied and able-minded norms will fail to be *relevant* to the lives of such individuals. For individuals labelled with significant disabilities, and perhaps especially those for whom reasoning, decision-making, and communication are highly dependent on others, any notion of citizenship that privileges cognitive and communicative independence will also fail to be inclusive. It will privilege the capabilities of those already in positions of dominance within the educational sphere, reinforcing the chasm that already exists in civic opportunities.

Disability activist Simone Aspis (2002) has argued that the self-advocacy movement must involve attention to the problem of social power if it is to be transformative. Others diagnose the problem of self-advocacy co-option as in part emerging because the people who are intended to support and empower labelled individuals are themselves frequently socially, economically, and culturally disenfranchised (Powers 2005, p. 169).[4] Disenfranchisement compounds disenfranchisement. These

---

[4] Eva F. Kittay has made the argument that just caring for individuals labeled with significant disabilities requires justice in (gendered) caring relations, including attention to the social, economic, and political positions of caregivers. See Kittay (2001).

material conditions that jeopardize civic status should certainly be the focus of critical work on civic inclusion and beyond. I would propose, however, that such critical work also requires an understanding that the problem of the civic exclusion of individuals with intellectual disabilities, both from within theorizing and within concrete social policies and educational practices, is also a profound problem of imagination. This vacuum of imagination persists in the failure to imagine significant disability tied to meaningful citizenship—or indeed to imagine citizenship otherwise than able-minded or able-bodied. As Maxine Greene so eloquently puts it, "Imagination alters the vision of the way things are; it opens space in experience where projects can be devised, the kinds of projects that may bring things closer to what ought to be" (Greene 2009, p. 141). Imagining citizenship otherwise involves asking: What does civic participation look like for individuals with significant intellectual and other disabilities? What does civic agency look like? Imaginative answers to these questions are urgent. Without such imaginative answers a clear reinforcement of the discourse of vulnerability and incompetence prevails, buttressed by highly racialized and gendered historical narratives of civic unfitness. Without such answers "intellectual disability" will continue to operate as a metaphor for civic threat.

References

Aspis, S. (1997). Self-advocacy for people with learning difficulties: Does it have a future? *Disability & Society, 12*(4), 647564.

Aspis, S. (2002). Self-advocacy: Vested interests and misunderstandings. *British Journal of Learning Disabilities, 30*, 3–7.

Baglieri, S., & Shapiro, A. (2012). *Disability studies and the inclusive classroom: Critical practices for creating least restrictive attitudes.* New York: Routledge.

Baynton, D. C. (2013). Disability and the justification of inequality in American history. In L. Davis (Ed.), *The disability studies reader* (4th ed., pp. 17–33). New York: Taylor & Francis.

Biesta, G. J. J. (2006). *Beyond learning: Democratic education for a human future.* Boulder, CO: Paradigm Publishers.

Carey, A. C. (2010). *On the margins of citizenship: Intellectual disability and civil rights in twentieth-century America.* Philadelphia, PA: Temple University Press.

Chavez, L. R. (2013). *The Latin threat: Constructing immigrants, citizens, and the nation* (2nd ed.). Stanford: Stanford University Press.

Clifford, S. (2012). Making disability public in deliberative democracy. *Contemporary Political Theory, 11*(2), 211–228.

Cowley, D. M., & Bacon, J. K. (2013). Self-determination in schools: Reconstructing the concept through a disability studies framework. *PowerPlay, 5*(1), 463–489.

Danforth, S. (2001). A Deweyan perspective on democracy and inquiry in the field of special education. *Journal of the Association for Persons with Severe Handicaps, 26*(4), 270–280.

Ellsworth, E. (1989). Why doesn't this feel empowering? Working through the repressive myths of critical pedagogy. *Harvard Educational Review, 59*(3), 297–325.

Erevelles, N. (2002). (Im)Material citizens: Cognitive disability, race, and the politics of citizenship. *Disability, Culture and Education, 1*(1), 5–25.

Ferri, B. A., & Connor, D. J. (2006). *Reading resistance: Discourses of exclusion in desegregation & inclusion debates.* New York: Peter Lang.

Greene, M. (2009). Teaching as possibility: A light in dark times. In S. L. Macrine (Ed.), *Critical pedagogy in uncertain times: Hope and possibilities* (pp. 135–149). New York: Palgrave Macmillan.

Gutmann, A., & Thompson, D. (2004). *Why deliberative democracy?* Princeton, NJ: Princeton University Press.

Hehir, T. (2002). Eliminating ableism in education. *Harvard Educational Review, 72*(1), 1–32.

Introduction to Supported Decision-Making [Transcript]. (2014, April 30). The Jenny Hatch project. Retrieved from http://jennyhatchjusticeproject.org/sites/default/files/043014_transcript.pdf

Jones, A. (1999). The limits of cross-cultural dialogue: Pedagogy, desire, and absolution in the classroom. *Educational Theory, 49*(3), 299–316.

Kafer, A. (2013). *Feminist, queer, crip.* Bloomington, IN: Indiana University Press.

Kittay, E. F. (2001). When caring is just and justice is caring: Justice and mental retardation. *Public Culture, 13*(3), 557–579.

Kliewer, C., Fitzgerald, L. M., Meyer-Mork, J., Hartman, P., English-Sand, P., & Raschke, D. (2004). Citizenship for all in the literate community: An ethnography of young children with significant disabilities in inclusive early childhood settings. *Harvard Educational Review, 74,* 373–403.

Kliewer, C., Biklen, D., & Peterson, A. J. (2015). At the end of intellectual disability. *Harvard Educational Review, 85*(1), 1–28.

Leake, D. W. (2014). Self-determination requires social capital, not just skills and knowledge. *Review of Disability Studies: An International Journal, 8*(1), 34–43.

Levinson, M. (2003). Challenging deliberation. *Theory and Research in Education, 1*(1), 23–49.

Levinson, M. (2012). *No citizen left behind.* Cambridge, MA: Harvard University Press.

McGregor, C. (2004). Care(full) deliberation: A pedagogy for citizenship. *Journal of Transformative Education, 2*(2), 90–106.

Minow, M. (2013). Universal design in education: Remaking all the difference. In A. S. Kanter & B. A. Ferri (Eds.), *Righting educational wrongs: Disability studies in law and education* (pp. 38–57). Syracuse, NY: Syracuse University Press.

Pan, D. (2012, November 5). Protecting the voting rights of people with mental disabilities. *Mother Jones.* Retrieved from http://www.motherjones.com/politics/2012/11/voting-rights-mental-disabilities.

Peterson, A. J. (2009). Shana's story: The struggles, quandaries and pitfalls surrounding self-determination. *Disability Studies Quarterly, 29*(2).

Popenoe, P. & Johnson, R. H. (1920 [1918]). *Applied eugenics.* New York: The MacMillan Company.

Powers, L. E. (2005). Self-determination by individuals with severe disabilities: Limitations or excuses? *Research & Practice for Persons with Severe Disabilities, 30*(3), 168–172.

Rood, C. E., Kanter, A., & Causton, J. (2015). Presumption of incompetence: The systematic assignment of guardianship within the transition process. *Research & Practice for Persons with Severe Disabilities, 39*(4), 319–328.

Rubin, S., Biklen, D., Kasa-Hendrickson, C., Kluth, P., Cardinal, D. N., & Broderick, A. (2001). Independence, participation, and the meaning of intellectual ability. *Disability & Society, 16*(3), 415–429.

Schalock, R. L. (2011). The evolving understanding of the construct of intellectual disability. *Journal of Intellectual and Developmental Disabilities, 36*(4), 227–237.

Schweik, S. (2011). Disability and the normal body of the (native) citizen. *Social Research, 78*(2), 417–442.

Taylor, K. (2015, March 6). Posters on teenage pregnancy draw fire. The New York Times. Retrieved from http://www.nytimes.com/2013/03/07/nyregion/city-campaign-targeting-teen-age-pregnancy-draws-criticism.html?_r=0

Terzi, L. (2010). *Justice and Equality in Education: A Capability Perspective on Disability and Special Educational Needs.* London: Continuum.

Trent, J. W., Jr. (1994). *Inventing the feeble mind: A history of mental retardation in the United States*. Berkeley, CA: University of California Press.

Vargas, T. (2013, August 2). Woman with Down syndrome prevails over parents in guardianship case. *The Washington Post*. Retrieved from https://www.washingtonpost.com/local/woman-with-down-syndrome-prevails-over-parents-in-guardianship-case/2013/08/02/4aec4692-fae3-11e2-9bde-7ddaa186b751_story.html.

Wolbring, G. (2012). Citizenship education through ability expectation and "ableism" lens: The challenge of science and technology and disabled people. *Educational Sciences, 2*, 151–164.

Chapter 6
Complex and Critical: A Methodological Application of the Tripartite Model of Disability

David Bolt

6.1 Introduction

A few of years ago I was invited to contribute a paper to David Mitchell's panel at the Society for Disability Studies Conference, Minneapolis, 2014,[1] entitled *Non-Normative Positivisms: Towards a Methodology of Critical Embodiment*, the SDS panel to which I refer throughout this chapter also included work by Stephanie Kerschbaum and the late Tobin Siebers. The premise was that the concept of non-normative positivisms would open up a space from which we could sketch out an alternative ethics about why and how disabled lives matter (Mitchell 2014). Though appreciative of the salient assertion that disabled people must be allowed to pursue our lives much as non-disabled people pursue their lives, the panel set out to argue that in practice this ethical trajectory is defined by limitations and serves to bolster the desirability of the normate subject position. At the time of this invitation I was completing a book that explored distinctions between ableism and disablism (Bolt 2014a), which I pondered with the theme of the panel in mind and came up with the idea of the tripartite model of disability.

---

[1] I introduced the tripartite model of disability at the SDS Conference before exploring it in a couple of keynote presentations at the University of Liverpool in 2014 and Lancaster University in 2015, organised by Maryam Farhani and Alan Gregory, respectively. Since then, based on the model, I have had an article accepted for publication in *Disability & Society*; another is under consideration with the *Journal of Further and Higher Education*; and my partner Heidi Mapley and I have completed a chapter for the forthcoming InVisible Difference book that focuses on the intersection of dance, disability, and law.

D. Bolt (✉)
Centre for Culture and Disability Studies, Liverpool Hope University, Liverpool, UK
e-mail: boltd@hope.ac.uk

© Springer Nature Switzerland AG 2020   69
L. Ware (ed.), *Critical Readings in Interdisciplinary Disability Studies*, Critical Studies of Education 12, https://doi.org/10.1007/978-3-030-35309-4_6

6.2   The Tripartite Model of Disability

The tripartite model follows a number of important models that are explored in disability studies. Most obviously, there is the social model of disability, with which the SDS panel explicitly engages (Siebers 2014), thereby chiming with more recent approaches that encompass individual, collective, and cultural positivisms, where it is emphasised that disabled people can lead full, satisfying, and even exemplary lives (Swain and French 2000; Kuppers 2009; Mitchell and Snyder 2015). In accordance with the affirmative model, for example, positivity about both impairment and disability may be asserted. To affirm a positive identity around impairment is to repudiate the dominant value of normality, so this model offers more than a transformation of consciousness about disability; it facilitates an assertion of the value and validity of the lives of people who have impairments (Swain and French 2000). Furthermore, if a rhizomatic model is invoked, disability becomes a site of richness and artful living (Kuppers 2009; Allan 2011). The tripartite model follows these approaches because they help to recognise that disabled people can often find the best way forward by transcending the norms to which we are meant to aspire.[2]

Fundamental to my foundation of the tripartite model is the acknowledgement of various forms of prejudice. There is no uniformly accepted term for discrimination against disabled people (Harpur 2012), a form of prejudice sometimes referred to as the nameless apartheid (Goggin and Newell 2003). Nevertheless, a couple of Anglophone terms have emerged in the shape of *ableism* and *disablism*. *Ableism* is more widely used around the world, while *disablism* is favoured in the UK (Ashby 2010), which suggests that the two terms have emerged because of the distinction between person-first and social model language (Harpur 2012). This being so, *ableism* is associated with the idea of ableness, the perfect or perfectible body, and *disablism* relates to the production of disability, in accordance with a social constructionist understanding (Campbell 2008). In founding the tripartite model, I follow work that appreciates the respective merits of the two critical terms (Campbell 2008, 2009; Harpur 2012; Goodley 2014), and proceed on the basis that, whereas ableism renders non-disabled people supreme, disablism is a combination of attitudes and actions against the rest of us.

My proposition in this chapter is that the tripartite model can be instrumental in the methodology of textual analysis. This proposition resonates with the SDS panel, which argues that when considered in terms of non-normative positivisms it becomes evident that qualitative research methodologies must be *disabled*—or enabled in a way that is profoundly informed by disability (Kerschbaum 2014). Accordingly, I assert that ableism and disablism can be understood as normative positivisms and non-normative negativisms, respectively, both of which should be explored, but that consideration should also be given to non-normative positivisms.

---

[2] I have sensory and physical impairments as a result of retinitis pigmentosa and psoriatic arthritis, meaning I am generally and easily identified as a disabled person. This is my rationale for the way in which I employ the pronoun *we* when referring to disabled people throughout the chapter.

In keeping with the overarching theme of the book, then, the chapter is interdisciplinary insofar as it bridges the social sciences and the humanities. That is to say, I draw on education, sociology, and psychology, among other things, in order to define the model that I apply to a work of fiction.

In accordance with my contribution to the SDS panel, the work of fiction in question here is a relatively unknown novel that nonetheless has much to say about disability. First published in 1987, *Happiness Is Blind* is one of a number of works by George Sava that draws on medical insights gained from his career as a surgeon. Within the novel, Anthony Street is a test pilot who sustains a facial injury that leaves him, as the book's jacket description terms it, "hideously disfigured." As a result, unable to find employment and shunned by his friends, he falls into a life of crime. He breaks into a flat but is interrupted by the owner, Helen Bourne, who, again as the jacket description puts it, "lives alone despite the fact that she has been blind since birth." This ostensibly unfortunate meeting marks the beginning of a romantic relationship that results in the two characters getting married and having a child together. Though loaded with problematic tropes, the story illustrates how the tripartite model can be applied to unveil a complex representation of disability.

6.3 From Normative Positivisms to Non-normative Negativisms

Marked by ableism, the first part of the tripartite model pertains to normative positivisms—by which I mean the affirmation of socially accepted standards. *Ableism* has been defined as a political term that calls attention to assumptions about normalcy (Davis 1995); it can be traced back to *handicapism*, a term coined nearly four decades ago to denote not only assumptions but also practices that promoted the unequal treatment of people because of apparent or assumed physical, mental, and/or behavioural differences (Bogdan and Biklen 1998; Ashby 2010). The concept of ableism, however, has been societally entrenched, deeply and subliminally embedded in culture, and is rampant throughout history, widely used by various social groups to justify their elevated rights and status in relation to other groups (Campbell 2008; Wolbring 2008). That is to say, whatever we call it, ableism is an age-old concept that runs deep in society.

There are many variants of ableism. Cognitive ableism, for instance, is a bias in favour of the interests of people who actually or potentially have certain cognitive abilities (Carlson 2001); lexism is an array of normative practices, assumptions, and attitudes about literacy (Collinson 2014); sanism is the privileging of people who do not have so-called mental health problems (Prendergast 2014); and ocularcentrism is the dominance of visual perception to which I return in a moment (Jay 1994). This list of critical terms could be far longer, for there has been a proliferation of normative positivisms in modernity.

A thing to remember is that when non-disabled people endeavour to occupy the subject position of ableism, they buy into a myriad of normative assumptions but often do so without premeditation or intent: they do so by acquiescence. After all, ableism is a deeply rooted, far-reaching "network of beliefs, processes, and practices" that produces a "corporeal standard," a particular type of mind and body, which is projected as the perfect human (Campbell 2001, p. 44). This network of notions about health, productivity, beauty, and the value of human life itself, represented and perpetuated by public and private media, renders abilities such as productivity and competitiveness far more important than, say, empathy, compassion, and kindness (Rauscher and McClintock 1997; Wolbring 2008). Indeed, so pervasive is this network that not only non-disabled people but also disabled people are likely to pick up a highly detailed working knowledge of ableism via acculturation alone (that is, through the gradual absorption of ideas that results from continual exposure to the values of another group).

Whatever the intent, the widespread endorsement of ableism has dire consequences for society. Many bodies and minds are constructed and positioned as Other, meaning that many people fall outside the dominant norms of bodily appearance and/or performance and thus face social and material exclusion (Ashby 2010; Hodge and Runswick-Cole 2013). From this perspective, impairments are necessarily negative: they must be improved, cured, or else eliminated altogether; they certainly cannot contribute to a positive identity (Campbell 2008). Ableism, in effect, becomes a combination of discrimination, power, and prejudice that is related to the cultural privileging of non-disabled people; it oppresses people who have so-called mental health problems, learning difficulties, physical impairments, sensory impairments, and so on (Rauscher and McClintock 1997; Eisenhauer 2007). The normative positivisms of ableism, therefore, indirectly result in the exclusion, victimisation, and stigmatisation of disabled people.

Yet despite its dramatic effects, ableism has been referred to as a nebulous concept that evades both identification and definition (Hodge and Runswick-Cole 2013). What is more, the term has been deemed limited in content and scope on the basis that it should not allude exclusively to disability, but should be used as an umbrella term (Wolbring 2008), a call for specificity that is answered to some extent by the term to which I now turn, *disablism*. After all, although ableism itself is often obscured, the value it places on certain abilities leads to disablism (Wolbring 2008; Hodge and Runswick-Cole 2013). My point at this juncture is that the normative positivisms of ableism result in the non-normative negativisms of disablism.

Marked by disablism, the second part of the tripartite model pertains to non-normative negativisms—by which I mean problematised deviations from socially accepted standards. The term *disablism* is derived from the social model of disability, whereby the everyday practices of society perpetuate oppressive structures on those of us who have biological impairments (Madriaga 2007). Discriminatory, oppressive, and/or abusive behaviour arises from the belief that we are somehow inferior to non-disabled people (Miller et al. 2004). As so-called less able people we are discriminated against, and different abilities become defined as disabilities (Thomas 2004; Wolbring 2008). Disablism, then, involves not only the "social imposition of restrictions of activity" but also the "socially engendered undermining" of "psycho-emotional well-being" (Thomas 2007, p. 73). It is arguably a more profound, targeted, and specific development of ableism.

This specificity aside, disablism is not necessarily explicit. Adapted from aversive racism theory, the term *aversive disablism* has been coined to denote subtle forms of prejudice (Deal 2007). Like aversive racism, aversive disablism is often unintentional, meaning that the perpetrators may recognise the problems of disablism without recognising their own prejudice (Deal 2007). Given these subtleties, my point here is that ableism and disablism might be critically conceptualised on an ideological continuum that moves from normative positivisms to non-normative negativisms.

In applying the tripartite model to Sava's *Happiness Is Blind*, then, one might begin by recognising how this ideological continuum can be illustrated with reference to, among other things, social and cultural constructs of visual perception. Ocularcentrism, as noted, is the dominance of visual perception that is a fact of life for most people in most societies and as such becomes manifest in countless normative positivisms. A consequence of this variant of ableism is that people who do not perceive by visual means are necessarily Othered. Moreover, ocularcentrism predicates what I have elsewhere designated ocularnormativism (Bolt 2014b), whereby the senses of touch, hearing, smell, and so on, are culturally and socially problematised. The normative positivisms thereby become non-normative negativisms as non-visual means of perception are judged in visual terms and thus found wanting.

While focusing on the first and second parts of the tripartite model, it should be acknowledged that, given the ubiquity of ableism and disablism, it is hardly surprising that positivity tends to be obscured in representations of disability. Professional and public discourses about disability and rehabilitation are predominantly negative, for instance, although many potentially positive discursive and narrative factors are hidden beneath ableist if not disablist ways of knowing, being, acting, and describing in academic, policy, and practice settings (Sunderland et al. 2009). Accordingly, the initial thing to note about *Happiness Is Blind* is that it contains massively problematic representations of disability. If social stereotypes become tropes in textual representation (Garland-Thomson 1997), then Sava's novel is underpinned by much in the way of stereotyping. Beauty and the beast, blindness-darkness synonymy, and the fifth-sixth sense are just a few of the recurrent tropes that are utilised in the work (Bolt 2014b). One illustration of this problematic representation is offered when Helen becomes a mother:

> I want to see. I want to look on the sunshine. I want to see my child. All these years I've been happy and content in my darkness and now, when I've got something to be really happy about, I feel miserable for the first time (Sava 1987, p. 176).

Illustrated here, in the terms of the tripartite model, is the way in which normative positivisms lead to non-normative negativisms. For one thing, the normative positivisms of ocularcentrism render motherhood a fundamentally visual experience. For another thing, the non-normative negativisms of ocularnormativism dictate that vision is a necessary condition of the enjoyment if not the very success of motherhood, thereby exempting women who do not perceive by visual means.

Given the proposed conceptual continuum from normative positivisms to non-normative negativisms, a relatively complex understanding of disability is encouraged by the first and second parts of the tripartite model. Key, here, is the social model from which the term *disablism* is derived. However, this understanding becomes still more complex when further informed by the ethos of the SDS panel. The panel clearly recognises that proponents of the social model set out to identify and remove barriers, to save disabled people from the objectification of medicalisation by shifting the focus to the environment. Yet one important contention is that, consequently, disabled people become identified by our inability to fit into the environment, that robbed of bodies and agency we come to be objectified in a different way (Siebers 2014). This being so, in order to appreciate a more complex form of embodiment, I contend that it is necessary to cut across the conceptual continuum from normative positivisms to non-normative negativisms.

6.4 Non-normative Positivisms and Complex Embodiment

Informed explicitly by the focus of the SDS panel, and departing dramatically from ableism and disablism, the third part of the tripartite model pertains to non-normative positivisms—by which I mean affirmed deviations from socially accepted standards. It is not enough to recognise disability along a continuum of difference that defines human variation; it is important to consider the ideology of neoliberal inclusiveness (Jordan 2013). After all, thanks to neoliberalism, disability is in some ways more present than ever, a state of affairs that, in part, has resulted from tolerance that can be thought of as inclusionism (Mitchell and Snyder 2015). This means that opportunities may well have opened to formerly excluded groups, which must be commended, but for inclusion to become truly worthwhile it must involve recognition of disability in terms of alternative lives and values that neither enforce nor reify normalcy. There is a need for non-normative positivisms because the fight for equality is both limited and limiting in its very scope, while empowering and progressive potential is offered by the profound appreciation of Peripheral Embodiments (Mitchell and Snyder 2015). In other words, inclusion may well be paramount but can become transformative and more comprehensively productive when disability is recognised as a site for alternative values.

The continuum of normative positivisms and non-normative negativisms that the tripartite model disrupts is resonant with the medical model of disability. This medicalisation is underpinned by normative positivisms, a preoccupation with which renders paramount the very idea of cure. This being so, if and when the third part of the tripartite model is illustrated, it seems possible if not probable that the representation will depart from the medicalisation of disability, from the idea that people who identify as disabled are "merely patients waiting in line for their proper cure" (Kuusisto in Savarese 2009, p. 199). In other words, a representation that recognises non-normative positivisms is more likely to be appreciative of the fact that "no one needs to be cured to achieve a life of dignity and purpose" (Kuusisto in Savarese

2009, p. 199). The tripartite model, then, implies a logic in which positive identity and disability can coexist without the presence or promise of cure.

It is perhaps surprising, given the various medical aspects of the work, that the implied logic of the tripartite model is illustrated recurrently in Sava's novel. For instance, cure is not sought by Helen from the outset—although it does become so when she has a child. Ironically, the curative operation is rendered unsuccessful because Helen is so keen to see her child in the sunlight that she removes her bandages prematurely: "And then came the sudden blackness—an awful hot blackness. She almost dropped Victor Anthony to the floor with the pain of it. The sunshine was gone" (Sava 1987, p. 189). In this moment Helen's ocularnormative longing peaks, meaning she subsequently appreciates perception in non-visual ways that depart from medical preoccupations with cure. That is to say, this representation challenges preconceptions about disability in its disruption of the notion that cure is a necessary preliminary of positivity. After all, the assumption tends to be that, for disabled people, medical intervention holds the key to our positive identity—if that is a possibility at all.

This positive identity is exemplified by the SDS panel, especially in the paper about returning the *social* to the social model (Siebers 2014). Here the term *social* refers to what disabled people know about society as a result of the complex ways in which we embody it. This complex embodiment changes the identification of disabled people. Rather than being identified by biological or environmental unfitness (as in the medical and social models), we are recognised by our embodied epistemology (Siebers 2014). That is to say, disability becomes a complex and critical body of knowledge on which all can draw.

In this vein, the reader of *Happiness Is Blind* is informed that Helen is unique *because* rather than *in spite* of her blindness, that she has "found the secret of turning disability into a source of strength" (Sava 1987, p. 163). Resonant with the constructive reframing of hearing loss as Deaf Gain (Bauman and Murray 2009), as well as the subsequent reframing of disability loss as disability gain (Garland-Thomson 2013), this transformation is illustrated when Helen persuades Tony to discuss and recognise virtues in his so-called ugliness:

> "You are easier to talk to than most people," she remarked, as they sipped their coffee. "Easier for me to talk to, perhaps, I should say. You see, so many people talk with their faces as well as their voices that I lose half their meaning. You have got to put all your meaning into your voice" (Sava 1987, p. 156).

Here the idea is that, because of his facial injury, Tony's mode of communication becomes focused on the verbal, an audible form that is particularly pertinent to Helen, given that she does not perceive the visual cues of body language. Moreover, with allusion to the rhizomatic model of disability, it might be said that there is comfort in the company of people whose impairments may be different, but whose experiences chime together (Kuppers 2009). These considerations once again lead me back to the SDS panel, which returns the *social* to the social model by theorising embodiment, but not at the expense of subjectivity (Siebers 2014). A premium is thereby placed on disabled people precisely because of the knowledge we acquire as long-term inhabitants in a non-disabled society (Siebers 2014). Thus, non-normative positivisms can be identified not only in the meeting of Sava's two disabled characters but also as a result of the embodied knowledge they share.

For all that, it must be acknowledged that the whole identification of non-normative positivisms may raise concerns about compensatory powers, a notion widely problematised in relation to cultural representations of visual impairment (Monbeck 1973; Kirtley 1975; Kleege 1999; Bolt 2014b). Nevertheless, a close reading of *Happiness Is Blind* reveals a number of departures from ocularnormativism. For instance, music and poetry are said to bring Helen beauty, as does the touch of silk, fur, and so on. She goes on to explain that "normal people" know little of such beauty but it is present for those who wish to appreciate it (Sava 1987, p. 157). This comment on aesthetics, that the "resources of life are infinite to those who know how to draw on them," (p. 157) diminishes connotations of compensatory powers. After all, the resources to which Helen refers must be engaged with actively, meaning that impairment is neither necessary nor sufficient as a condition of ability. The thing to stress is that normative compensatory powers involve, say, being able to *see* with one's hands or ears, whereas non-normative positivisms value the senses in and on their own terms.

All in all, although *Happiness Is Blind* contains problematic representations that may be categorised as normative positivisms and non-normative negativisms, it redeems itself on many counts. Helen goes through the ocularnormative phase of longing to see, but the eponymous state of happiness is ultimately found when the eye surgery is unsuccessful. She brings the novel to its conclusion by critiquing the sighted majority for looking on blindness as an affliction: "You do not know what it is to be blind, and you naturally think that without eyes our lives must be incomplete and denied most of the things you cherish. It is not true" (Sava 1987, p. 192). The key point, for me, is that these moments of happiness are not rendered legitimate by ocularnormative representation. Helen owns the means of perception that are available to her; she does not find her own way of seeing. For this reason it can be argued that the novel departs from ableism and disablism, that it ventures beyond ocularnormativism and recognises the complex potential of non-normative positivisms.

6.5   Conclusion

This chapter outlines the tripartite model of disability and illustrates how it can be applied in the critical analysis of literary representation. Consideration is thereby given not only to normative positivisms and non-normative negativisms but, in the spirit of David Mitchell's SDS panel, also to non-normative positivisms. The result is a critique of the representation of disability in Sava's novel that benefits from understandings of fruitful alternatives to the dominance of visual perception, as well as awareness of ocularcentric assumptions and ocularnormative discrimination. In these terms, the novel illustrates that the continuum of normative positivisms and non-normative negativisms can be disrupted by the recognition of non-normative positivisms, that the tripartite model becomes tee-shaped in its conceptual form. Accordingly, the often swift and imperceptible regression from ocularcentrism to ocularnormativism can be blocked. This whole approach resonates with a point made in the SDS panel, that complex embodiment renders the social model episte-mological, dependent on disabled people who are defined by our ability to produce and share knowledge (Siebers 2014). In this vein, my conclusion is that the tripartite model of disability helps to reveal the great complexity of experiential knowledge from which those who engage in literary criticism can draw.

References

Allan, J. (2011). Complicating, not explicating: Taking up philosophy in learning disability research. *Learning Disability Quarterly, 34*(2), 153–161.

Ashby, C. (2010). The trouble with normal: The struggle for meaningful access for middle school students with developmental disability labels. *Disability and Society, 25*(3), 345–358.

Bauman, H.-D., & Murray, J. M. (2009). Reframing: From hearing loss to deaf gain. *Deaf Studies Digital Journal, 1*(Fall), 1–10.

Bogdan, R., & Biklen, S. (1998). *Qualitative research for education: An introduction to theory and method.* Boston: Allyn and Bacon.

Bolt, D. (2014a). *Changing social attitudes toward disability: Perspectives from historical, cultural, and educational studies.* Abingdon: Routledge.

Bolt, D. (2014b). *The metanarrative of blindness: A re-reading of twentieth-century Anglophone writing.* Ann Arbor: University of Michigan Press.

Campbell, F. K. (2009). *Frontiers of ableism.* Australia: Palgrave Macmillan.

Campbell, F. K. (2008). Exploring internalized ableism using critical race theory. *Disability and Society, 23*(2), 151–162.

Campbell, F. K. (2001). Inciting legal fictions: Disability's date with ontology and the ableist body of the law. *Griffith Law Review, 10,* 42–62.

Carlson, L. (2001). Cognitive ableism and disability studies: Feminist reflections on the history of mental retardation. *Hypatia, 16*(4), 124–146.

Collinson, C. (2014). "Lexism" and the temporal problem of defining "dyslexia". In D. Bolt (Ed.), *Changing social attitudes toward disability: Perspectives from historical, cultural, and educational studies* (pp. 153–161). Abingdon: Routledge.

Davis, L. J. (1995). *Enforcing normalcy: Disability, deafness and the body.* London: Verso Books.

Deal, M. (2007). Aversive disablism: Subtle prejudice toward disabled people. *Disability and Society, 22*(1), 93–107.

Eisenhauer, J. (2007). Just looking and staring back: Challenging ableism through disability performance art. *Studies in Art Education: A Journal of Issues and Research, 49*(1), 7–22.

Garland-Thomson, R. (2013). *Disability Gain.* Liverpool: Address to Avoidance in/and the Academy: The International Conference on Disability, Culture, and Education.

Garland-Thomson, R. (1997). *Extraordinary bodies: Figuring physical disability in American culture and literature.* New York: Columbia University Press.

Goggin, G., & Newell, C. (2003). *Disability in Australia: Exposing a social apartheid.* Sydney: University of New South Wales Press.

Goodley, D. (2014). *Dis/ability Studies: Theorising disablism and ableism.* Abingdon: Routledge.

Harpur, P. (2012). From disability to ability: Changing the phrasing of the debate. *Disability and Society, 27*(3), 325–337.

Hodge, N., & Runswick-Cole, K. (2013). "They never pass me the ball": Exposing ableism through the leisure experiences of disabled children, young people, and their families. *Children's Geographies, 11*(3), 311–325.

Jay, M. (1994). *Downcast eyes: The denigration of vision in twentieth-century French thought.* London: University of California Press.

Jordan, T. (2013). Disability, able-bodiedness, and the biopolitical imagination. *Review of Disability Studies, 9*(1), 26–38.

Kerschbaum, S. L. (2014). Accessing Non-Normative Positivisms: Disabling Research Interviewing. Non-Normative Positivisms SDS 2014 Panel [online]. *The Society for Disability Studies in Minneapolis, MN.* Accessed July 28, 2015, from https://nonnormativepositivisms. wordpress.com/.

Kirtley, D. D. (1975). *The psychology of blindness.* Chicago: Nelson-Hall.

Kleege, G. (1999). *Sight unseen.* London: Yale University Press.

Kuppers, P. (2009). Toward a rhizomatic model of disability: Poetry, performance, and touch. *Journal of Literary and Cultural Disability Studies, 3*(3), 221–240.

Madriaga, M. (2007). Enduring disablism: Students with dyslexia and their pathways into UK higher education and beyond. *Disability and Society, 22*(4), 399–412.

Miller, P., Parker, S., & Gillinson, S. (2004). *Disablism: How to tackle the last prejudice.* London: Demos.

Mitchell, D. T. (2014). Panel Introduction. Non-Normative Positivisms SDS 2014 Panel [online]. *The Society for Disability Studies in Minneapolis, MN.* Accessed July 28, 2015, from https:// nonnormativepositivisms.wordpress.com/.

Mitchell, D. T., & Snyder, S. L. (2015). *The biopolitics of disability: Neoliberalism, ablenationalism, and peripheral embodiment.* Ann Arbor: University of Michigan Press.

Monbeck, M. E. (1973). *The meaning of blindness: Attitudes toward blindness and blind people.* London: Indiana University Press.

Prendergast, C. (2014). Mental disability and rhetoricity retold: The memoir on drugs. In D. Bolt (Ed.), *Changing social attitudes toward disability: Perspectives from historical, cultural, and educational studies* (pp. 60–68). Abingdon: Routledge.

Sava, G. (1987). *Happiness is blind.* London: Robert Hale Ltd.

Savarese, R. J. (2009). Lyric anger and the Victrola in the attic: An interview with Stephen Kuusisto. *Journal of Literary and Cultural Disability Studies, 3*(2), 195–207.

Siebers, T. (2014). Returning the Social to the Social Model. Non-Normative Positivisms SDS 2014 Panel [online]. *The Society for Disability Studies in Minneapolis, MN.* Accessed July 28, 2015, from https://nonnormativepositivisms.wordpress.com/.

Sunderland, N., Catalano, T., & Kendall, E. (2009). Missing discourses: Concepts of joy and happiness in disability. *Disability and Society, 24*(6), 703–714.

Swain, J., & French, S. (2000). Towards an affirmation model of disability. *Disability and Society, 15*(4), 569–582.

Thomas, C. (2007). *Sociologies of disability, "impairment," and chronic illness: Ideas in disability studies and medical sociology.* London: Palgrave.

Thomas, C. (2004). Developing the social relational in the social model of disability: A theoretical agenda. In C. Barnes & G. Mercer (Eds.), *Implementing the social model of disability: Theory and research* (pp. 32–47). Leeds: The Disability Press.

Rauscher, L., & McClintock, M. (1997). Ableism curriculum design. In M. Adams, L. Bell, & P. Griffin (Eds.), *Teaching for diversity and social justice: A sourcebook* (pp. 198–230). New York: Routledge.

Wolbring, G. (2008). The politics of ableism. *Development, 51*, 252–258.

Part II
Disability Representations in Juxtaposition

Chapter 7: *Unexpected Anatomies: Extraordinary Bodies in Contemporary Art—* Ann M. Fox, Davidson College. Fox probes complex embodiment through her presentation across various strands of disability and visual culture. Fox was among the early career scholars who participated in the institute and has over the years developed analyses that consider disability and drama, disability and the arts and most recently she curated two museum shows that featured disability and art. Her chapter opens with questions for the reader: *How might we render our imagination of the body more expansive in an age where it seems we already can look at it in every conceivable manner, through means medical and media-driven? How might we imagine disabled bodies anew when, paradoxically, the most vulnerable bodies among us remain invisible?* In response, Fox invites the readers to consider Garland-Thomson's notion of "disability gain" which originated within the Deaf community (Bauman and Murray 2014). Fox further considers the question, *what do works about bodily difference, by disabled and nondisabled artists alike, show us about the lived experience of disability?* Although these questions inform her analyses as a disability studies scholar, she is quick to remind that understanding disability in terms of "gain" remains "largely unfamiliar territory for art historians, curators, and dealers."

Chapter 8: *The Names of Physical Deformity: A Meditation on the Term Disability and Its Recent Uses—*Melania Moscoso Pérez, Universidad del Pais Vasco/Euskal Herriko Unibertsitatea. Perez explores use of the term "disability" in its current usage, contrasted to that which emerged in the sixteenth century. In juxtaposition to the analyses offered by Fox and Bolt set in twenty-first century, readers will find analyses of the historical tradition that gave us the very terms that today we find so offensive—and more as Perez provides visual examples that augment her argument. That many of these works can be found in galleries around the world today underscores the importance of understanding how disability was read over the centuries. Readers are likely aware of the early use of "monstrosity" tracing back to Ambroise Parre (1582) and familiar as well, with Henri-Jacques Stiker's A History of Disability (1982), Perez probes, through the use of recognized works of art images, how the monster and the jester became the social markers of difference in the example of disability. It is with careful unfolding of beliefs and language that she contends that disability evolved to the bio-political category which "designates all of us with non-normative bodies".

Chapter 9: *"Once Big Oil, Always Big Oil": Disability and Sustainability in Pixar's Cars 2*—Shannon R. Wooden, Department of English, Missouri State University. Popular Pixar films, according to Gooden, are "neither acclaimed nor notorious" for disability representations. As the author notes, it was not until the 2016 premier of "Finding Nemo" and Nemo's "lucky fin" that over disability connections were made, while deeper disability issues were not addressed. In this chapter, Gooden explores the myriad ways that Pixar films rely upon physical impairment narratives, and how this inevitably underscores the assumption for "anthromorphic hypermasculinity" as a related theme in this chapter. Troubling the intersection of these critiques further asks readers to further connect the dots to capitalism, national identity, and anti-environmentalism as real-world beliefs that merit "scrutiny" rather than continued reification through media.

Chapter 10: *"I'd Prefer Not To": Melville's Challenge to Normative Identity in Bartleby, the Scrivener*—Natalie M. Fleming, University of Buffalo. In her treatment of the canonical refrain, "I'd prefer not to," Fleming points to a contemporary conversation on the viability of the claim that Herman Melville's character, Bartleby would be diagnosed today, as autistic. Recognizing a bounty of prior diagnoses and claims to the rationale for the character's peculiar behavior—and whether Melville intended the ambiguity to drive the reader's inability to understand Bartleby—Fleming hones in on changing attitudes that reflect the medical field. The question of whether a diagnosis of autism can be considered today to explain behavior in an era when the actual definition of autism did not exist, leads Fleming to unpack a critical analyses for disability studies and the "limits of normal." Borrowing from the disability studies scholar, Michael Rembis, Fleming unbraids the influence of culture and medical discourse that result in the construction of hegemonic normativity. Revisiting this well-known novel through a disability studies lens offers a very clever meandering on the effective pull toward the demand for normalcy.

Chapter 11: *Co-Constructing Frames for Resistance: Reflections on Disability by a Daughter and Her Mother*—Suzanne Stolz, University of San Diego. This chapter follows early and on-going negotiations over disability lived, across multiple strands of meaning in the lives of Stolz, a disability studies scholar and her mother. Crafted through emails, journal entries, and phone conversations with her mother, the chapter captures meanings over four decades of shared disability representations and its inevitable juxtapositions. In many ways, the conversation captured here travels across disability tropes—as they played out within a family and a rural community—with the reach that is both intimate and predictable. It is a courageous exchange that leads Stolz to celebrate the value of her move "away" from the family home—and her mother, to trust in the value of resistance that was always, and remains to this day a value that comes into focus with those who live with disability. The chapter serves as a compliment to several in this book that leave readers richer for knowing.

Chapter 7
Unexpected Anatomies: Extraordinary Bodies in Contemporary Art

Ann M. Fox

7.1 Introduction

How might we render our imagination of the body more expansive in an age where it seems we already can look at it in every conceivable manner, through means medical and media-driven? How might we imagine disabled bodies anew when, paradoxically, the most vulnerable bodies among us remain invisible? They only exist in the popular imagination, it would seem, as diagnostic exemplars, sentimentalized images of inspiration porn scrolling across our Facebook feeds ("The Only Disability in Life Is a Bad Attitude!"), or transhumanist fantasies of bodily enhancement and genetic manipulation. Disability in the visual arts remains a powerful, vital means to imagine human variation beyond memes or mimesis. The works I will discuss in this brief essay, examples of the intersection between disability and art, invite a more intense look at how disabled bodies compel creation, and how we view them. These imagined anatomies are indeed unexpected as the matter makers and the made matter of art.

I am an English professor who loves working at the intersection of disability studies and visual representation. My professional life started as a scholar of modern and contemporary drama, but once I began to understand my subject through the framework of disability studies, I was led to consider more wide-ranging examples of visual representation. Not only was the visual landscape rich with examples of disability hiding in plain sight; because representation creates reality, bringing those examples forward is an essential part of disability studies work. The stakes of interrogating representation, as Michael Bérubé reminds us when he writes about the depiction of intellectual disability in literature, are high, "because the stakes are ultimately about who is and who is not determined to be 'fully human' and what is to be done with those who (purportedly) fail to meet the prevailing performance

A. M. Fox (✉)
Davidson College, Davidson, NC, USA
e-mail: anfox@davidson.edu

© Springer Nature Switzerland AG 2020
L. Ware (ed.), *Critical Readings in Interdisciplinary Disability Studies*, Critical
Studies of Education 12, https://doi.org/10.1007/978-3-030-35309-4_7

criteria for being human" (2016, p. 192). And so, over time, I have transformed into someone who teaches about disability and visual culture. I teach classes about disability and drama, graphic novels and disability, and have co-curated three shows on disability and art: *RE/FORMATIONS: Disability, Women, and Sculpture* (Cooley & Fox 2009a); a show entitled *STARING* (Cooley & Fox 2009b) based on Rosemarie Garland-Thomson's 2009 book, *Staring: How We Look;* and *Re/Presenting HIV/ AIDS* (Fox et al. 2014).[1] As a curator, I continually ask: what do works about bodily difference, by disabled and nondisabled artists alike, show us about the lived experience of disability? How do these works dissect what we think we know about the body, and how we replicate and recirculate those beliefs? Given what these works do to raise such questions, can we then move to see disability in visual art as yet another example of what Garland-Thomson calls "disability gain"—that is, evidence of disability as a force for creativity and the generation of new ways of imagining the world and our bodies within it?[2]

7.2   The Intersection of Disability and Art

Understanding disability in this way is something that is still largely unfamiliar territory for art historians, curators, and dealers. In the country in which I write, teach, and curate, a good part of the problem is that American society still does not generally understand disability as an identity and a culture; indeed, disability metaphors that reinscribe ableism are often deployed in other fights for social and political progress. This, despite the fact that the Americans with Disabilities Act is three decades old, despite the fact that disability has been a lived presence in our country before its founding and an activist presence as far back as the nineteenth century.[3] Stigma, shame, medicalization, and the individuated experience of disability have all contributed to this resistance.

Where the relationship between disability and art does exist in the public, historical, and curatorial imaginations, it follows some very highly determined models.

[1] The online catalogue for *RE/FORMATIONS: Disability, Women, and Sculpture* can be viewed at http://academics.davidson.edu/galleries/reformations/index.html.

[2] I first heard Garland-Thomson use the phrase "disability gain" in a 2013 conference talk at the Avoidance in the Academy Conference, Centre for Culture and Disability Studies, Liverpool Hope University, Liverpool, UK. In it, she expanded upon the concept of Deaf Gain, one itself discussed at great length by H. Dirksen Bauman and Joseph J. Murray, editors, in *Deaf Gain: Raising the Stakes for Human Diversity* (University of Minnesota Press, 2014).

[3] For an overview of disability history, good introductory sources include Joseph Shapiro, *No Pity: People With Disabilities Forging a New Civil Rights Movement* (Three Rivers Press, 1993); Kim Nielsen, *A Disability History of the United States* (Beacon Press, 2012); *Encyclopedia of Disability,* ed. Gary L. Albrecht (Sage Publications, 2006); and the *Encyclopedia of American Disability History,* ed. Susan Burch (Beacon Press, 2009). I should note that disability activists point out the important reminder that the history of disability, as well as the resistance to ableism, goes further back than what has been documented by scholars.

My collaborator and fellow curator, Jessica Cooley, offers her own taxonomy for understanding this frame of reference in a talk we initially presented together as a conversation about disability in art (Cooley & Fox 2016). She first identifies the therapeutic model, which is a kind of art that "perpetuates a medical model of disability and doesn't engage the cultural and social aspects that we find most compelling." This is not to deny the salutary effects of art as therapy, or to suggest that there is no place for creativity or self-expression within it. One problem comes in public perceptions of such art as inherently inferior (akin to outsider art). Another is the presumption that disabled people would only create art for therapeutic purposes, and that the art they create is only the result of therapeutic workshops or interventions. Therapy should not be dismissed—after all, one could legitimately make the point that a good deal of art has a therapeutic quality to it for the creator and/or audience—but neither should it be seen as the only place where disability and art intersect.

The second disability/art intersection Cooley details is critics using "a historical lens that uses art to reveal and also critique the way that disability was understood in different places and at different times." This visual historiography of disability is useful, and can tell us a great deal about the social perception of illness and impairment. Re-assessing history also compels us to understand how an artist's disability might have influenced the creation of their work. For example, we might ask what it means to re-read Matisse through the lens of disability; how did his surgery for abdominal cancer and resulting wheelchair use, which necessitated the turn to his famous cut-outs, inform the creation of a new aesthetic? We might also ask what it means to re-read French-American artist Niki de Saint Phalle through the lens of disability studies. As I argue elsewhere, her feminist interventions into the body created over the course of her career depend on disability. For example, her "skinnies," figures created later in her life, were created to allow air to pass through. Because they were catalyzed by the breathing problems that plagued Saint Phalle after a lifetime breathing in the fiberglass fibers of her early sculptures, they suggest creative innovation spurred by disability.[4] We do have to exercise caution in applying this historical perspective, however. Paintings are constructions of reality, and depending on them to diagnose an age's view of illness has to be approached with some care. Similarly, when we acknowledge an artist's disability, we need to be careful not to simply use the work to either diagnose them or point to the magnificence of their work because it was accomplished "in spite of" their impairment.

The third intersection between disability and art which Cooley details is "the activist model where artists push back against the prevalence of medical and pathological imaging." Artists might reimagine disability things, question the normate, retort against medical interventions, or "[create] art that opens up to embrace the complex, vibrant, and meaningful lives of disabled people, their families, and their friends." So, for example, we might consider the accompanying painting by North

---

[4] For a more extended discussion of disability aesthetics in the work of Niki de Saint Phalle, see my 2016 essay "Peeking Under the Veil: Niki de Saint Phalle's The Bride and/as Feminist Disability Aesthetics," *Journal for Religious and Cultural Theory*, 15.2 (n. p.), jcrt.org/archives/15.2/fox.pdf.

Carolina artist Beverly McIver of herself and her sister Renee, entitled *Sisters* (2016, Fig. 1). Renee McIver, who is intellectually disabled, was the subject of a 2011 documentary, *Raising Renee*, about her move to live independently after their mother died. The painting places Renee McIver at the center, with Beverly McIver purposefully pushing herself to the side. There are several things to delight in here: the solidity of both figures and their relationship; the open, joyful expression of affection; the representation of intellectual disability that neither sentimentalizes nor stereotypes it. But I am also intrigued by the brace on the arm that Beverly McIver has flung around her sister. Is this perhaps a suggestion that disability binds them both—not as Renee McIver's state of being to which her sister reacts, but as a mutually shared identity? This is not to suggest McIver is appropriating her sister's disability, but rather subtly underscoring it as a point of connection between them. Disability is a shared identity between these sisters, who have not only negotiated what Renee's disability means for their lives, but who both live, as all humans do, in contingent, variable bodies.

The fourth and final place Cooley locates a disability/art intersection is the work to understand the concept of disability aesthetics, as put forward by the late disability studies scholar Tobin Siebers. In *Disability Aesthetics* (Siebers 2010), he points out that disability, rather than being avoided in modern art, has actually undergirded it; the rejection of the symmetrical and idealized forms of classical and Renaissance ideals fully depends on disrupting the normate. And so one cannot understand modern and contemporary art without understanding that disability is integral to creating what we find beautiful within it: fragmentation, distortion, and the disruption of static bodily ideals as a source of pleasure. Cooley avers that according to Siebers:

> ...we don't see disability broadly in art history because we have limited our gaze to look for visibly recognizable disabled people as opposed to the aesthetic, or perhaps even style, of disability. In this way, disability is opened up to the expansive possibilities of recognizing the broken brushstroke of Picasso as embodying, both physically and affectively, a disability experience.

An attention to disability aesthetics therefore prompts us to value art that reconfigures our understanding of how we look at the extraordinary or different.

These last two models, the activist and aesthetic, are where disability in art is least generally appreciated; yet they are for me, as a curator and critic, the most exciting places in which to work. My own curating has sought to find disability presence in work beyond what is simply visible at first glance. Art has had a long-standing preference for attending first to physical impairments and their supposed costs, with disability marking diminished identity. But following the lead of discourses of disability aesthetics foregrounded by scholars like Siebers, I find myself greatly interested in disability presence in art. And in actuality, some of the most interesting examples of this presence can be found in works that seek to circumvent typical narratives, images, and rhetorical discourses about disability and extend our discussion of the creative possibilities present in disability aesthetics beyond mimetic representation. In this chapter, I want to offer some more ways in which disability activism and aesthetics can be seen as being made manifest in a playful and diverse way in contemporary art by considering anatomies in art that are particularly unexpected in subject, approach, and appearance. Empowered by the imaginative possibility of disability, these works look at the body slant, disrupting habitual, overdetermined ways of looking. As a way of advancing this discussion, I want to highlight three strategies I see operant in some contemporary and intriguing work on disability. The strategies I mention are not necessarily new ways to shape a reconsideration of the body in art; nor are they the only ways for the body to be refigured. But they are compelling patterns that take on renewed and heightened significance when they intersect with disability.

7.3   Operant Strategies in Disability and Art

7.3.1   Harriet Sanderson

One strategy creates an absent presence of the extraordinary body. This, on its surface, would seem to contravene the very notion of representing the disabled body: don't we need it before us? Shouldn't we be working to make it more visible? Yet the residues of the body, when so looked at, can speak powerfully. For example, consider Harriet Sanderson's photo collages that use the residues bodies leave behind on mattress pads: they suggest a body in repose because of long-term illness. Sanderson embodies an experience literally put out of sight elsewhere, illustrating how time is experienced by a body requiring long periods of bed rest. *In her collages,* imprints on a mattress pad suggest a body that has lived and aged in that bed, leaving behind the residue not only of movement, but of shed oils, dirt, and skin cells: someone was here. Those imprints, figured in both black and white, are not so black and white in clarifying the emotional life of that body. Did that person feel anger, boredom, or restlessness? Does the curve of the residue suggest a body curved into the fetal position, in perhaps pain, or self-protection? Or was the time of rest a period of creativity and reflection? Or perhaps both realities exist at once? Sanderson plays connect-the-dots on her images; in *Biding time: playing the numbers* (2012a), she joins different points on a mattress pad, while in a similar work called *Unravelling time* (2012b), she connects the pores from her own skin, digitally reworked to overlay the image of the mattress pad.[5] In linking the points, whether on stitches or on skin, Sanderson literally shows our impulse to "connect the dots," to make and impose meaning on the body; her new paths alternately trace meandering trails and geometric shapes on the surface of the body-sized prints. Sanderson's new forms overlie extant patterning, underscoring our ability, like hers, to break old

---

[5] *Biding time: playing the numbers* can be viewed at harrietsanderson.com/portfolio/uneasylandsc apes2012/?p=uneasyimg&i=05Biding.jpg. *Unravelling time* can be viewed at harrietsanderson. com/portfolio/uneasylandscapes2012/?p=uneasyimg&i=04UnravellingTime.jpg.

ways of knowing apart to be then reshaped. This landscape is both contracted and expansive, where a mattress pad, or a small patch of skin, can become an investigation of the social construction of the body.

7.3.2   Laura Splan

Laura Splan uses absent presence of a disabled body in *Host* (2014), a work she created for *Re/Presenting HIV/AIDS*.[6] In an e-mail to me (2013), Splan described the genesis point for the installation: in the late 1980s,

> my uncle showed up at our quaint home with his boyfriend who was dying of AIDS. The memory of his frail, weak, wasting body in our lavender and lace decorated guest room left an indelible impression on me. Since then, my family has barely spoken of my uncle's visit or of his partner's illness… It quietly announced itself in the hollowed face that stared up at us, the same face of so many dying men staring out of our television sets during the latest news stories about the still very taboo topic.

The recreated guest bedroom that is simultaneously not a bedroom suggests many things: the absence of the man who is now long gone, gaps in disclosure, and a dawning awareness of HIV/AIDS at the time. It simultaneously expresses the incompleteness of memory; knowledge of who that man was, and of what his life consisted, has long since faded away. Even a moment that vividly lives on in Splan's memory is impossible to fully recreate. In the installation, the entire bedroom is evoked through fragments of a bedpost, side table, curtain, and torn pillow with an indentation on it. All these details are carefully realized even in their incompleteness—except for the very body that was simultaneously highly scrutinized and politely glanced away from. Originally from Memphis, Tennessee, Splan notes the Southernness of the piece in the way the domestic runs up against biomedical reality; this is most clearly displayed in this suggestion of a window made up of six "panes" (pieces of paper) on which doilies have been imprinted with her own blood. The patterns—dainty, dark, and round—seem to float outside the room as menacing viral shapes. Indeed, they are overlaid with biomedical and other HIV-related imagery such as molecular structures, dissected HIV, vaccines and hypodermic needles, a torn-open condom, a bacteriophage, and an intravenous solution bag. The installation thus speaks to the way HIV/AIDS was and still is rendered invisible in the South: it is an idea made all the more important by the fact that that the Southern United States remains a place where new infection rates are disproportionately high, particularly among people of color.[7] The material reality of the virus and the bodies it inhabits is rendered invisible by social conventions of nicety, economic inequity, racism, sexism, homophobia, and transphobia.

---

[6] *Host* can be viewed at laurasplan.com/host/.

[7] For a more extensive discussion of the current state of HIV/AIDS in the southeastern United States, see http://www.cdc.gov/hiv/statistics/overview/geographicdistribution.html.

7.3.3 Shan Kelley

Besides this notion of absent presence, another way in which contemporary artists deploy the extraordinary body is by revising the representation of the body's anatomy. We are now far beyond the anatomical illustrations of Vesalius or Gray's; in such recasting, as in Sanderson's work, the anatomical becomes transformed: scale is inverted, relationships within the body are upended, and bodily structures and experiences are conveyed in an unexpected manner. In the case of artist Shan Kelley, perforated parchment paper in his 2013 *Disclosures* series seems completely removed from the anatomical. Kelley creates a series of works spelling out truisms he has said or heard as an HIV+ man: "I really don't want you to be afraid of me" and "I'm not afraid of you I'm afraid of it" (2013a, b).[8] *Disclosures III* (Kelley, 2013c) states: "She pushed the AIDS pamphlets aside before climbing on top of me once again," in a retort to the notion that someone diagnosed with HIV cannot be sexual. It also subtly suggests the disparity of class, race, and economics among those with HIV; who, it subtly asks, has access to prevention? Indeed, who has privilege, prior knowledge, access to treatment, and sexual agency enough to push those pamphlets aside? It is the creation of these works and how they recast the body of someone living with HIV that I find to be of particular interest, however. Close up you can see that Kelley formed each letter from multiple needle perforations on parchment paper. Certainly the perforations suggest the social experience of HIV/AIDS, evoking the death by a thousand stabs that stigmatizing statements cause. Those pricks (which reference a sexual pun) have a metaphorical but also a literal reference; that parchment, close up, begins to look like skin that has been pierced with a thousand needle sticks. What are we meant to recall here? The experiences of transmission through sexual contact or drug use? Testing? Blood draws for medical procedures? These pricks replicate, embodying the virus that has brought them into being and in their repetition suggesting a kind of obsessiveness with the lived and physical dimensions of HIV. The skin embodied in this way cannot help but also evoke the body as in *Peeled* from Sanderson's series *Cured* (Sanderson 2000), where she does something similar to Kelley.[9] Her square of paper with scattered and seemingly random pinpricks is meant to refer to those in pharmaceutical trials. Random medical testing of this kind, we are reminded, makes itself visible on the skin of the subject. *Peeled* honors their endurance under these trials over time, placing as much value, if not more, on their embodied experience over the medical knowledge that was the end result.

---

[8] Shan Kelley's *Disclosures I, II, and III* can be viewed at shankelley.com/disclosures.

[9] *Peeled* can be viewed at harrietsanderson.com/portfolio/cured/?p=curedimg&i=5peelc.jpg.

7.3.4 Carol Chase Bjerke

I first encountered Carol Chase Bjerke's *Misfortune Cookies* (2005) in *Humans Being II*, a 2013 disability arts exhibition.[10] The exhibition was curated by artist Riva Lehrer, a Chicago-based portraitist and painter who has long created and curated art about disabled subjects and the disability experience, both her own and others'. Bjerke's installation consists of dozens of small, stoma-shaped red polymer clay "misfortune cookies," arranged in a larger, stoma-shaped circle. The shape, and the daily short reflections about this disability experience stamped on small pieces of paper inserted into the cookies, gives voice to living in a body radically reshaped by ostomy surgery after colorectal cancer:

> You will have a secret.
>
> It will not matter how fastidious you are. You will still have messes to clean up.
>
> You will observe that medical people are uncomfortable when you ask questions about your ostomy.
>
> You will consider not eating as an alternative.
>
> You have experienced a great loss.
>
> You will observe that support group publications are sweetness-and-light stories about what people do in spite of their ostomies. They never show or tell the truth about the ostomy itself.
>
> You will wonder who might come up with a better solution to the problem and how you might connect to him or her.
>
> You will find that no one wants to hear or talk about your predicament anyway.
>
> You will become annoyed with answering the same thoughtless and inane questions every time you reorder supplies.
>
> You will be sick to DEATH with being preoccupied with your own excrement.
>
> You will be sick to DEATH of wearing your pouch.
>
> Your stoma will bleed.
>
> You will think you are being very careful but you will get feces on your floor anyway.
>
> You will learn that the nurses whose job it is to help you in caring for your stoma are nurses who specialize in the care of wounds.
>
> You will observe that medical people treat you as though you are weak and unstable because you ask questions about your ostomy.

These "fortunes," sprouting over and over again from the multiple clay openings, call to mind the intersection of the physical embodiment and lived experience of the patient who has had a colostomy. Graphic yet not graphic, realistic yet not realistic, these smaller versions of the larger stoma they constitute suggest the anatomy of disability while resisting photorealism or medicalized documentation too easily subject to voyeurism or revulsion.

The final way in which I think the artists in whom I am interested create meaning through unexpected anatomies is through emphasizing variability and flux, shifting emphasis from the notion of disability as a static state of being to an emphasis on the instability inherent to disability. We have seen human variability honored in

---

[10] Examples of the "misfortune cookies" can be seen at carolchasebjerke.com/public/display_images.php?u_id=48.

images that depict disabled people using the visual rhetorics of portraiture and classical sculpture, in works by artists such as Doug Auld and Riva Lehrer.[11] For example, Auld has painted burn survivors in his 2016 *State of Grace* series, showing his subjects in their new embodiment after a long process of healing and recovery. Their scars are recreated in vivid colors and impressionistic brushstrokes, even as those who have those differences gaze out from their portraits calmly, meeting our gaze with unflinching dignity.

7.3.5   Riva Lehrer

Lehrer's *Risk Pictures* (2014–2018) offer us one way in which that variability can be engaged conceptually. In them, Lehrer's subjects can respond to her drawings of them by amending or changing them in any way they like, taking ownership of and responsibility for the work and their own self-representation within it. While Lehrer herself is a disabled artist and has documented important figures in disability culture through her work, it is impossible to tell whether all the subjects of *Risk Pictures* have a disability. The focus, at least in part, turns to the relationship between the painter and her subject. Lehrer gives up some of her privilege as an artist to define her subjects in a way that models a kind of mutuality and exchange distinctly different from the top-down power dynamics to which disabled people are more typically subject. Her yielding of privilege grants power to her subject in a way that acknowledges that attention must be paid: to their voice, their vision, their sense of self. The attention subjects give to their portrait may not always fully align with Lehrer's artistic vision. Indeed, it may be an uneasy fit; their changes may even "disable" the picture, making it unsalable or undercutting its original aesthetic. The body of the picture remains in flux beyond the moment Lehrer is ostensibly done with it; in that lies the eponymous risk. It seems paradoxical for an artist to embrace this right for her paintings to fail by giving over some control to others. And yet this act becomes a symbolic articulation of how disability pushes us to claim the variability of bodies, vulnerability, interconnectedness, and the right to risk—and perhaps in so doing, fail. What might be read in a different context as the defacing of Lehrer's work instead creates a more complex manner in which we can say disability is embodied in contemporary art.

---

[11] For a more extensive discussion of how visual rhetorics of disability are used by artists to refigure how we see disability, see Rosemarie Garland-Thomson, "Picturing People With Disabilities: Classical Portraiture as Reconstructive Narrative," in *Re Presenting Disability: Activism and Agency in the Museum* (Routledge, 2010), edited by Richard Sandell, Jocelyn Dodd, and Rosemarie Garland-Thomson. The works of Doug Auld can be viewed at dougauld.com; the works of Riva Lehrer can be viewed at rivalehrerart.com.

7.3.6 Beverly McIver

This emphasis on variability also reflects the experience and knowledge extant within diverse states of "wellness." As we have seen, Beverly McIver depicts members of her family with various physical disabilities. The paintings *Double Amputee* (2013a, Fig. 2) and *Sharon in the Hospital* (2013b, Fig. 3) show her cousin Sharon's figure in repose after surgery, imagined in a private moment; drainage tubes crisscross her body. Where does she end and they begin? This apparatus of recovery, humble as it is, is a part of her shifting self; it, and her present embodiment, are worthy of depiction. These images create a tension for us as viewers; what does it mean that we are looking on someone in such a moment of extreme vulnerability? We are made aware of our own proclivity to look by the discomfort that ensues. The portraits also, however, honor a moment of Sharon's embodiment, underscore the notion that disabled bodies are no more static, no more prone to change, than nondisabled bodies. Disability, in this sense, is our common identity.

7.3.7 Chun-Shan (Sandie) Yi

Chun-Shan (Sandie) Yi's *Re-fuse Skin Set* (2011) also confronts our voyeurism as she approaches the results of surgery in a more critical way—but not in a manner the viewer might expect.[12] Yi insists on instability as a way to imaginatively reverse the ways her body was made more typical, and in so doing, challenges our obsession with the whole, cohesive, normalized being. In a series of photographs, Yi imagines her body back to a place before the trauma of surgical intervention used to normalize it. In one, we see her only from the waist down, wearing latex underwear that evokes a second skin. There are cuts into that "skin" through which we can see scars from past surgeries. Yi holds her differently formed hands in front of her; digits that were once separated have now been re-fused with pieces of the latex "skin." We are invited to study her body not as aberrant or in need of fixing, but as an anatomy still in flux. How we define pathology and cure are inverted; in recovering the refuse of that surgery, Yi refuses to acquiesce to her body as deviant. Rather, in making her body unruly, Yi compels us to make a study of our own understanding of deviation. As in other photographs (such as a series of fashion photographs in which she wears gloves specially made to fit her extraordinary hands, or shoes that themselves have imaginative protrusions), she adorns and celebrates her own difference from the typical.

---

[12] *Re-fuse Skin Set* can be viewed at cripcouture.org/re-fuse-skin-set.html.

7.4 Conclusion

The strategies I have delineated are merely the start; it is exciting for me to contemplate how, in the coming years, artists and critics will continue to discover the means through which disability presence in art can enhance our understanding of the experience of bodily variation. Audiences are used to highly determined—and ableist—ways of looking; I have watched spectators impose tales of misery and woe onto disability portraits that to me were anything but. During *RE/FORMATIONS*, in campus tours passing through the Davidson College art galleries, hearing this was a disability art exhibition, some visitors asked: "Where are the wheelchairs?" To this day, it delights me that the expectations of those who have visited my exhibitions were confounded, that disability art in its more full sense moved them in unexpected directions past the iconography to which they had assigned disability in their minds. And indeed, the unexpected anatomies of disability in art flip the old adage, for good or for ill. Here, for ill is for good, as disability art, unexpectedly but importantly, connects us to the lived experience of disability, and by extension, to the bodily contingency and vulnerability at the heart of all our humanity.[13]

References

Auld, D. (2016). "State of Grace Project." *Doug Auld: Paintings & other work, 2005–2016.* Retrieved from dougauld.com.

Bérubé, M. (2016). *The secret life of stories: From Don Quixote to Harry Potter, how understanding intellectual disability transforms the way we read.* New York: New York University Press.

Bjerke, C. C. (2005). *Misfortune cookies.* [Mixed media with polymer clay.]

Cooley, J., & Fox, A. M. (January 16–February 27, 2009a). *RE/FORMATIONS: Disability, women, and sculpture.* Van Every/Smith Galleries, Davidson College, Davidson, NC.

Cooley, J., & Fox, A. M. (October 16–December 9, 2009b). *STARING.* Van Every/Smith Galleries, Davidson College, Davidson, NC.

Cooley, J., & Fox, A. M. (5 March 2016). "*RE/FORMATIONS: Disability, Women, and Sculpture.*" Lecture. Gothenburg Konsthall, Sweden.

Fox, A. M., Gardner, R., Newman, L., & Wessner, D. (August 25–October 5, 2014). *Re/Presenting HIV/AIDS.* Van Every/Smith Galleries, Davidson College, Davidson, NC.

Garland-Thomson, R. (2009). *Staring: How we look.* Oxford: Oxford University Press.

Kelley, S. (2013a). *Disclosures I.* [Needle-perforated parchment and printed paper.] Van Every/Smith Galleries, Davidson College, Davidson, NC.

Kelley, S. (2013b). *Disclosures II.* [Needle-perforated parchment and printed paper.] Van Every/Smith Galleries, Davidson College, Davidson, NC.

Kelley, S. (2013c). *Disclosures III.* [Needle-perforated parchment and printed paper.] Van Every/Smith Galleries, Davidson College, Davidson, NC.

Lehrer, R. (May 10–June 20, 2013). *Humans being II.* Woman Made Gallery, Chicago, IL.

Lehrer, R. (2014–2018). "The Risk Pictures." *Riva Lehrer,* rivalehrerart.com. Accessed December 5, 2016.

---

[13] I wish to thank my colleagues who offered helpful feedback on this essay: Suzanne Churchill, Gabriel Ford, Randy Ingram, and Ben Mangrum.

McIver, B. (2013a). *Double amputee.* [Oil and collage on canvas.]
McIver, B. (2013b). *Sharon in the hospital.* [Oil and collage on canvas.]
McIver, B. (2016). *Sisters.* [Oil on canvas.]
Raising Renee. (2011). Directed by Jeanne Jordan and Steven Ascher. West City Films.
Sanderson, H. (2000). *Peeled.* [Digital print.]
Sanderson, H. (2012a). *Biding time: playing the numbers.* [Archival digital print.]
Sanderson, H. (2012b). *Unravelling time.* [Archival digital print.]
Siebers, T. (2010). *Disability aesthetics.* Ann Arbor: University of Michigan Press.
Splan, L. (2014). *Host.* [Porcelain, plastic, blood.]
Splan, L. (2013). Re: Image reproduction rights. Received by Ann Fox, October 23, 2013.
Yi, C.-S. (2011). *Re-fuse skin set.* [Latex, rubber, plastic, and black thread.]

Chapter 8
The Names of Physical Deformity: A Meditation on the Term Disability and Its Recent Uses

Melania Moscoso Pérez

Mucho es lo que tienen en común los monstruos y esos seres efímeros y espectrales que habitan en los espejos. Tanto unos como otros son escurridizos e imposibles de fijar" Luis Peñalver De soslayo: una mirada sobre los bufones de Velázquez.

8.1 Introduction

Disability is commonly used to refer to a wide array of physical impairments, either congenital or acquired, that impair typical physical or intellectual development. The person's ability to live independently and to fully participate in social life can ultimately be affected. As such, it is an umbrella term that encompasses a range of conditions ranging from organic disorders to individual personality disorders that have been identified as deviations from the norm. The term "disability" was coined early in the nineteenth century to address the predicament of the war veteran that came back mutilated from the battlefront. It was also readily applied to polio survivors in this same period, and to children with developmental disorders such as CP or Down Syndrome, who were also known by other names such as spastics and retarded. The recent interest in disabilities in the humanities (disability studies) and social sciences has led to speculation about applying the term to people with different embodiments who lived prior to the nineteenth century. An example of this is the recent "Mujeres con discapacidad" [*Women With Disabilities*], edited by Maria Ángeles Cózar in 2011, in which she includes, under the rubric of disabled people, Ana de Mendoza y de la Cerda, the Duchess of Pastrana and an active schemer in the Court of Philip the Second (sixteenth century) (Cózar Gutiérrez 2011).

M. Moscoso Pérez (✉)
Instituto de Filosofía, Consejo Superior de Investigaciones Científicas (CSIC),
Albasanz 26-28, Madrid 28037, Spain
e-mail: melania.moscoso@cchs.csic.es

© Springer Nature Switzerland AG 2020   93
L. Ware (ed.), *Critical Readings in Interdisciplinary Disability Studies*, Critical
Studies of Education 12, https://doi.org/10.1007/978-3-030-35309-4_8

Much earlier, and undisputedly one of the best studies on corporal difference in the humanities, is the work of Henri-Jacques Stiker (1982), *Corps infirmes et sociétés*, which has been translated into English under the title *A History of Disability*.

Stiker contends in this book that a society's attitude to people with different embodiments attests to its capacity for inclusion relative to diversity. Stiker's neat use of the term disability within the frameworks of the late nineteenth through to the early twentieth century did not prevent the English version, which outsold the original, from carrying the word *Disability* in the title.

My purpose in this chapter is to reflect on the use of the word disability among people who lived prior to the nineteenth century. I suggest that using this term to define people with non-normative embodiment who lived in earlier times which characterized difference with its own distinct description distorts the experiences lived by these individuals and conceals the contemporary nature of the cultural patterns we use to make sense of body difference.

With the aim of casting doubt on the use of *disability* to describe the people who lived in the inceptions of modernity (fifteenth to sixteenth centuries), I will devote the first section to the notion of monster, which at the time was the most consistently used category to address anatomical deformity. In the second section, I will focus on the Court Jester with the aim of exploring a unique cultural location for body difference in sixteenth-century Spain, so as to explore the ways in which a category devised to address social oppression in the twentieth century misleads the cultural reality of body difference in the Baroque period. This is due to convenience and personal inclination, as the Spanish Courts were one of the few places where records of people were kept. From an anthropological standpoint, exploring jesters necessitates a return to Victor Turner's concept of liminality and Michel Foucault's historicism to guide our reflection.

8.2   Between the Horrific and the Hilarious: Physical Deformity from the Fifteenth to the Seventeenth Centuries

It was in the year 1496, when a scale-covered human-like creature with the head of an ass was spotted on the banks of Tiber River, near Rome. The event was recounted by Philip Melanchton and Martin Luther in 1523 in a famous pamphlet. The two Reformers considered such a creature to be an unequivocal admonition of the impending Apocalypse as described by Daniel, who included political satire in his account. According to Davidson (1991):

> … the pope-ass, according to Melanchton, is the image of the Church of Rome; and just as it is awful that a human body should have the head of an ass, so it is likewise horrible that the Bishop of Rome should be the head of the Church (37–38).

Closely related to hurricanes and storms, monsters encompassed a broad category that included fantastic creatures from medieval bestiaries and travel logs, which in the fifteenth century still belonged to the realm of prodigy (Daston and Park 1998).

Fig. 8.1 *The Ass-Pope.* Martin Luther (1523). Source: https://commons.wikimedia.org/wiki/File:Bapstesel.png

What was completely new was the fact that the Ass-Pope became an issue under scientific consideration, something which was previously unheard of, as Martin Luther noted in a letter dated 1523. Prodigies of nature had been considered divine admonitions by both Protestants and Catholics, who took them as warning signs to take sides in the European religious wars. The radical novelty of the pamphlet was that the appearance of the Ass-Pope was deemed to be a reaction against the abominations of Papacy (Fig. 8.1).

At the end of the sixteenth century[1], eschatological explanations did in fact coexist with nascent scientific or proto-scientific reflection on the origin of monstrosity. In 1575, Catholic surgeon Ambroise Paré (1571/1982), regarded monsters as a result of the "Wrath of God" (Paré 1571/1982, p. 5).

Thus it is understood that blindness serves no purpose other than to testify to the power of Christ through miraculous cures, as is narrated in the Gospel According to John, or that "demons find a thousand ways to transform themselves into different creatures and get inside men, especially into a woman's womb, giving rise to monstrosities" (Paré 1571/1982, pp. 4–5). Nevertheless, and despite admitting that such apparitions always foretold disastrous events, Paré introduced an important

---

[1] Italics are mine

Fig. 8.2 *Prodigies and Monsters*. Ambroise Paré (1571). Source: BIU Santé (Paris). http://www.biusante.parisdescartes.fr/histoire/images/?cote=009830

distinction between these creatures. On one side were the prodigies, "things opposing the natural order, such as when a woman gives birth to a snake or a dog" (Paré 1571/1982, p. 2) and monsters, "things which *appear* to be outside the natural order" (Paré 1571/1982, p. 2), such as the birth of "a baby with two heads or with more or fewer limbs than normal," which is possible in the natural world (Paré 1571/1982, p. 3). Paré distinguished 13 causes, of which at least ten were "natural" and could be grouped into three categories. The first was that relating to excess or defect, and this included Siamese twins, multiple births in general, and *polydactylism*, all these being considered the result of an excess of seed. Secondly was the lack of or malformation of one or various limbs, known today as *amelia or phocomelia*, attributed in this case to insufficient seed. Finally, there are those who, due to the mother having adopted indecorous postures or having been exposed to blows or unpleasant emotional impressions, were born hunchbacked, with inverted legs, or, in the case of a mother with a particularly feverish imagination, with hair all over their face (Paré 1571/1982, p. 5). It is worth noting that while Paré was already pointing out some causes which are today well recognized by modern medicine, such as hereditary diseases, or infections during pregnancy, the concern about the theological significance of such malformations still lived side by side with his proto-scientific attitude (Paré 1571/1982, p. 85) (Fig. 8.2).

Shortly after Ambroise Paré wrote *On Monsters and Marvels*, Philip the Second wrote to his daughters from Lisbon:

> Madalena is feeling very lonely today, since her son-in-law left, although I think she does it out of compliance. And she was very angry with me for taking her to task over some things she had done in Bethlehem and in the galleys. And with Luis she was very bad tempered for the same thing[2] (Moreno Villa 1939, p. 25).

Madalena Ruiz served in Felipe II's court from 1568 to 1605 [Illustration 3], and according to Moreno Villa "was fond of bullfighting, dance and liquor" (Moreno

---

[2] Letter dated May, 2nd, 1581. Source; Moreno Villa (1939).

Villa 1939, p. 141). The detailed chronicle of the intrigues between a servant of the King's Palace and a jester serving daughter Isabel Clara Eugenia, written by the Holy Emperor, comes as a surprise. Unlike Germany, where people with physical abnormalities would occasion passionate debates on creation and the legitimacy of the Pope, in the Spanish court of the Habsburgs they were involved in the pleasant domesticity of the Royal Palace. It has been estimated that the Habsburg dynasty had a total of 201 dwarfs at court, which amounts to one per year of rule since Carlos V became the Holy Roman Emperor (Moreno Villa 1939).

It is clear that Madalena Ruiz, Nicolaso Pertusato, or Mari Bárbola (the two dwarfs that appear in *The Meninas*) would now be regarded as disabled, yet they belonged to the court precisely because of their corporeal form. We wonder, then, if the category of disability, coined in the nineteenth century, can accurately be applied to people who lived in the sixteenth century or to mythological characters. My point is that while people whose physical impairments would qualify them as disabled have always existed, extending this category to the past may not be justified.

Dwarfs looked after children, kept the Maid's honor safe until marriage, and took care of administration, but their main function was to be decorative: their main task was to amuse (Bernand 2001, p. 121). Having a fool, a buffoon, man of amusement, or a dwarf "is like having ripples in a stone doorway or in one's hair, on a coat of arms or in items of clothing" (Moreno Villa 1939, p. 34). The court jester was not only amusing because of his ingrained wittiness; his bodily build made him an asset as a laughing stock (Welsford 1961, p. 56). The king would spare no expense on providing jesters with as many commodities as they might fancy. Moreno Villa refers to the case of the jester Guzman who, in the period of a year, had 95 pairs of shoes.

Philip de Valois spent large amounts of money on covering his jester's bed with leather and providing him with luxury. Ledgers at *Monasterio del Escorial* attest to how Queen María Luisa de Orleans made sure that Bernarda Blasco, her dwarf attendant, would always have four pounds of snow in summer and an adequate supply of coal in winter, in addition to fabric for blouses, doublets, and silk dresses; pillows; and handkerchiefs. Still, Hidalgos and low noblemen regarded them as a debased standard of humanity in which they found some comfort, (Southworth 1998, p.1)[3] and authorities were only forgiving to a certain extent when it came to overly defiant jokes and jesters (Fig. 8.3).[4]

Sebastián de Covarrubias (1539–1613), Spanish lexicographer and best known for having written the first monolingual dictionary of the Spanish language, *Tesoro de la lengua castellana o española* (1611), defined jester as "a Tuscan word, meaning a rogue, coarse, a fool" ((Covarrubias 1611/1979, p. 243). Covarrubias also suggested hypothetical etymologies for the word, derived from Latin *bufo-bufonis,* *"venomous toad or frog,"* Covarrubias 1611/1979, p. 243) that resemble the jesters

---

[3] This seems to be also true in the English court. According to John Southworth (date?), The Jester "was someone on whom the king could bestow his favour without giving rise to any of the jealousies or counterclaims on the part of competing court factions that normally accompanied the exercise of Royal patronage" (p. 1).

[4] This is only true when it comes to the "favourite Jesters," Jon Southworth (1998) says.

Fig. 8.3 *La infanta Isabel Clara Eugenia y Madalena Ruiz.* Sánchez-Coello (1586). Museo del Prado, Madrid. https://es.wikipedia.org/wiki/Retrato_de_la_infanta_Isabel_Clara_Eugenia#/media/File:Alonso_S%C3%A1nchez_Coello_001.jpg

in that "they pour shameful impudence from their mouths with which they entertain the stupid and indiscreet" Covarrubias, [1611] 1979, p. 243) "por estar echando de su boca desvergüenças, con que entretienen a necios e indiscretos" and from *farce*, a pointless thing "void of substance and full of wind" (translated). Finally, the scholar draws our attention to the fact that the Tuscan word *bufa* means scuffle or brawl "because the jester fights with everybody and everybody fights him" (Covarrubias 1611/1979, p. 243). Luis Peñalver distinguishes between fools, low-witted jesters, and people with physical deformities, and knaves and lowly people like the improvisation actor Pablo de Valladolid. The slow-witted ones or people with disabilities were allowed to tell the truth as if they were an oracle of sorts amidst the legion of flatterers and sycophants that surrounded the King in the con-strained environment of the Royal Court. Knaves, on the other hand, were accused by moralist writers of being ingratiators, hated by the people because of their close-ness to the King and their privileges (Peñalver 2005).

According to German Jestbooks, Jesters performed in all kinds of social situa-tions. They were not taken seriously, but because their physical or mental limita-tions granted them compassion, they could afford to speak the truth (Zijderveld 1982). The *rascals* or *rogues* that populated the court of Philip IV were creatures of the limen; they inhabited an intermediate world between the ordinary people of Spain and the refined world of the court and the clergy. Under the cloak of amusement, they could be painfully truthful about the harsh economical realities of an Empire in decline in ways that were not allowed to the court members. This intermediate world of "ambiguity and paradox"[5] was built on the social subordination of the Ancient Regime, but free at the same time both from the strictures of court and from the scarcity of the *pueblo llano,* the lay people of Spain.

As Victor Turner would put it, the *sabandijas* or *truhanes,* Jesters, dwarfs, and other people of amusement inhabit a place of "ambiguity and paradox," and are liminal creatures (Turner 1965, p. 245). They take part in court life by being its antithesis. They are the underside of Royal protocol; their life in Palace embodies the communitarian base of life, that of domesticity as opposed to the hieratic Royalty: "The figures, representing the poor and the deformed appear to symbolize the moral values of the *communitas* as against the coercive power of supreme political rulers" (Turner 1977, p. 110). Jesters are included because of their exclusion, they lurk on the threshold, inside and outside at the same time. They belong to society, but also depend on it.

But the feudal stratified society also depended on the jester. Jesters are the institutionalization of liminarity. It was they who objected to the theological legitimacy of a political power whose divine origins were questioned by everyday life. As Gluckmann puts it, "... in a system where it was difficult for others to rebuke the head of the political unit, we might have here an institutionalized joker, operating at the highest point of the unit" (Gluckman 1965, p. 103). Enid Welsford writes about Claus Narr, a slow-witted jester who lived in the German vicinity of Randstat and who amused the repartee with this story.

> The first wonder is that barefooted monks who have no money at all build magnificent houses, when everybody else needed to pay bricklayers. The second wonder, said Claus, is that preaching orders in Leipzig daily acquire so much corn that they have become very wealthy, yet never in my life have I seen them doing any agricultural work (Welsford 1961, p. 234).

Welsford quite correctly makes the point that Luther's theses were not so daring but he was nevertheless prosecuted (Welsford 1961, p. 234). The jester would serve as a valve to the social pressures of the *Anciéne Regime,* but the kind of rebellion they carried out could only take place within farce. However, the suspicion that the jester raised in rulers and diplomats alike proves that farce was not completely harmless. As Bakhtin put it, the jester opposes "lies, flattery and hypocrisy" (Bajtin 1998, p. 87), destructing power because it reveals its truth. The jester communicates the Royal palace with the Commoner and relates the rigid hierarchy of the feudal society with the *communitas.* It is the explicit acknowledgment of the following: "... liminality implies that the high could not be high unless the low existed and he who is high must experience what it is like to be low" (Turner 1977, p. 97). The glaring contrast between their Highnesses the Infanta Isabel Clara Eugenia and King Felipe IV and their "Lownesses" Madalena Ruiz and Diego de Acedo does not preclude that the latter knew they belonged to a common world (Fig. 8.4).

---

[5] Turner, V. (1979). Betwixt and between: The luminal period in rites of passage. In W. A. Lessa, E. Z. Vogt, & J. M. Watanabe (Eds.), *Reader in Comparative Religion: An Anthropological Approach.* 4th ed. New York: Harper & Row, p. 236.

Fig. 8.4 *El bufón Diego de Acedo* (1644). Diego Velázquez da Silva. Museo del Prado, Madrid.
https://es.wikipedia.org/wiki/El_buf%C3%B3n_don_Diego_de_Acedo,_el_Primo

Already known in antiquity, buffoons and jesters were part of the banquets and courts during the Middle Ages. A source of entertainment, they were also known as "men of amusement" and were also called upon at banquets and on whichever occasion a loosening of the strictures of court life was needed. Jesters, as Welsford said,

> … are a source of entertainment, their company is welcome, good stories about them accumulate and if they have little conscience and no shame, they often manage to make a handsome profit out of their supposed irresponsibility (Welsford 1961, p. 3).

Buffoons and jesters appear profusely in the Royal court chronicles from the eleventh to the thirteenth century, but they did not reach the spotlight of court life until the fifteenth—sixteenth century, in the historical twilight between the end of the Middle Ages and the brink of modernity. As the main empire of its time, the Spanish court of the Austrians had plenty of buffoons,[6] as the royal correspondence revealed. However, out of all the kings of his dynasty Philip IV was most fond of them. Philip the IV, at once "moody and frivolous,"[7] was one of these men, "of whom Erasmus tells us in his Praise of Folly that without their fools they can neither eat nor drink nor while away a single hour. These fools are inseparable from him appearing in the theatre at festivities and public audiences by his side and having free access everywhere."[8]

---

[6] Moreno Villa, J. (1939) *Locos, enanos, negros y niños palaciegos; Gente de placer que tuvieron los Austrias en la corte española desde 1563 a 1700*. Editorial Presencia, Mexico. 37.

[7] Justi, C. (2006). *Velázquez and his times*. New York: Parkstone International. 436.

[8] Ibid.

Philip IV was not only fond of buffoonery, but also a dedicated protector of the arts, who had the good fortune of having his prime minister recruit for him one of the most talented court painters ever, Diego da Silva Velázquez, who made the most of his friendship and patronage.

During Antiquity through to the Baroque period, people with physical anomalies were recruited to join the Courts or occupy positions of social prestige, or else could find their place in society within a theologically legitimized charity system. It was not until the period between the last part of the eighteenth century and the very end of the nineteenth century, what Foucault terms "The Classical Age," that people with deviant bodily builds were segregated or classified into bio-political categories. Foucault himself points out how, during the eighteenth century, there appears a then-unheard-of "utilitarian analysis of poverty" (Foucault 1999, p. 93), which aims to substitute the "global enshrinement of the poor" (Foucault 1999, p. 93), charac- terized by the Old System. It is in this context of making work compulsory that the handicapped becomes an avatar of the deserving poor. As opposed to the buffoon or the blind man who went from village to village singing ballads, the handicapped (not yet disabled) is the one who is incapable of productive work.

8.3   The Monster Enters Natural History

The word *monster* comes from Latin through its vulgar form *monstruum,* which at the same time derives from the Latin verb *monere,* "to warn." Monsters were there- fore considered to be creatures of ill omen. According to mythologist Rene Girard (2005), monster characters in Greek tragedy display monster-like features to warn about the impending return of original violence in times of peace. The monster addresses what erupts out of normalcy, what strikes the understanding and the senses alike, akin to the prodigies which during the Middle Ages referred to hurri- canes or to any phenomena that resisted explanation, as well as to the creatures deemed to bear a preternatural meaning or admonition. It was not until the eigh- teenth century that Kaspar Friedrich Wolff ended his *Objecta Meditationem Theoria Monstruorum* with a categorical "Monsters are not the work of God but of Nature." (Roe 1981, p. 29). By then they had already lost their links with both God and the Devil; the question concerning their meaning had given way to that of their place in the creation. There was an overlapping between theological inquiry and the nascent sciences of life. This "disenchantment of the monstrous," as Michael Hagner (1999, p. 35) likes to term it, started in the Renaissance and extended well into the eigh- teenth century. The display of Monsters in *Wunderkammers* was the first step in the secularization of horror.

During the eighteenth century, the monster becomes a natural phenomenon. Monsters enter natural history, which is, as Foucault defined it, "the description of the visible" (Foucault 1982, p. 134). Monsters become interesting for natural history in that they contest Linnaeus's system of classification for animals as he presented it in *Systema Naturae:* form, quantity, magnitude, and relative disposition of elements in space. Monsters have to be classified according to these features. There is a conceptual limit to monstrosity, which helps to consolidate Ambroise Paré's distinction between monsters and prodigies. The brand-new science, teratology, studies those living creatures that do not fit into Linnaeus's classification. As Canguilhem (1976) would put it, they show the *hiatus* in the system of classification:

> Monsters had been treated as substitutes for the crucial experiences capable of deciding between two systems concerning generation and the development of plants and animals: Preformationism and Epigenesis. They had been used to provide the great chain of being theory with the argument of transitional forms, or as Leibniz said, of middle species. As they appeared especially ambiguous, monsters ensured the passage from one species to another. Their existence provides the spirit with the concept of continuity: *Natura non facit saltus, non datur hiatus formarum* (p. 210).

Monsters became a brand new category for exceptionality in living beings: as Canguilhem points out: "there is no mineral monster" (1976, p. 201). However, as late as 1706, Louis Lémery (1738) wrote in *Mémoire sur les monstres*:

Any animal born with a structure that defies the natural order, or very different to that one of the animal species he belongs to, and I do not mean to a light and shallow difference: anything that does not cause genuine awe does not deserve to be called a monster" (1738, np. https://archive.org/details/mmoiresdelacad00acad).

The definition still evokes the horror of Melanchton's pamphlet, but the monster appears in Lémery as something against Nature, rather than a preternatural admonition.

The monster addresses a kind of infraction of natural normativity, a *ratio* u *ordo rerum*. In the eighteenth century there is an attempt to make distinctions through taxonomy and classification, as opposed to the Middle Ages and Renaissance, when, as Canguilhem put it, "… the mad and the sane lived within society and monsters lived among the normal people" (Canguilhem 1976, p. 209). Diderot and Robinet were interested in embryological specimens showing what medicine now recognizes as disability-causing conditions. This was the case of many of the "monstrous births" collected in Ruysch's *Thesaurus Anatomicum,* in which Siamese twins and supernumerary limbs were abundant and prominent. Bought in 1717 by Tsar Peter the Great of Russia, it is now in the *KunstKamera Museum,* which also holds the Tsar's personal collection, including hermaphrodite twins captured in a farm in Siberia, and bicephalic fetuses, confiscated from the midwives by the royal favorites. Peter the Great of Russia banned the burial of fetuses with physical deformities, sending the Royal Guard to fetch any creature worthy of forming part of his collection, vested as he was by the moral authority in the fight against superstition.

Still, many now labeled as disabled would be excluded from both the *Thesaurus Anatomicum and* Peter the Great's collection because they do not challenge Linnaeus's classification system.

With a long historical tradition, the monster addressed the wondrous, the preternatural—that which was *praeter naturam*, beyond nature. Only in the eighteenth century does it begin to be used as a term for natural creatures, referring to the living; the aim of collecting them was no longer to amaze, but to educate and prevent superstition. From then on, monster became a category of the living: again, as Canguilhem says, "There is no mineral monster" (Canguilhem 1976, p. 140).

In the twentieth century, monstrosity was the biological correlative to the concept of biological normalcy. In 1989, Pere Alberch (1989) published an article entitled *The Logic of Monsters: Evidence for Internal Constraint in Development and Evolution*. The text, which would become the foundation of the *Evo-Devo* theory in biology, shows how monsters had their own logic, namely how developmental abnormalities make developmental laws evident.

Unlike previous expressions like "handicapped" or "maimed," disability "is co-extensive with rehabilitation and their extension in time" (Stiker 1999, p. 128). Rehabilitation is then not only a set of procedures, but also an ideology that aims to include people with disabilities under the paradigm of assimilation. In the attempt of including a group in society lies the assumption that they are in fact excluded. As Stiker (1999) notes: "… the disabled, henceforth of all kinds, are established as a category to be reintegrated and thus to be rehabilitated" (p. 134). Disability singles out a group to be cared for or healed. Disability is there to consolidate the norm. The rehabilitation culture of "as if" diversity was accepted conceals it twice. The theological legitimization of hierarchy designated people with non-normative constitutions as creatures, either of God or of the Devil. They were there to awe, without any attempt to domesticate their alterity. I am not idealizing a society in which death was too often the destiny for non-conforming people, but wish to draw to the reader's attention the fact that there were approaches other than rehabilitation and its double concealment. The transformation of prodigy in personal tragedy demanding the intervention of medicine and social services is recent and has increased life expectancy and quality of life for many people, but subjecting them to what Foucault (1982) termed "medical power," which made a social destiny of exclusion out of diagnostics.

8.4 Conclusion

What do Sebastian de Morra and the two-headed fetuses of Ruysch's *Thesaurus Anatomicum* have in common? What do Siamese twins and the jesters that appeal to us from Velázquez's portraits have in common? If Peñalver is right in the quote that heads this text, both are "elusive, hard to capture," what then is the slippery surface in which they are rooted? Monsters seem to elude the strictures of the *ordo rerum*. As Foucault (1971) points out, "… the monster ensures the emergence of difference. This difference is still without law and without any well-defined structure. The monster is the root stock of specification" (p. 171). With the consolidation of natural history in the eighteenth century, the monster anticipates the science of the relation of the individual with his type. The monster is thus the *raison d'être* of Kantian critical distance: the proof that phenomenical evidence is never conceptualized to its full plurality. The jester, on the other hand, addresses the *communitas* of Court life, the human link without which Court life could not exist. The monster and the jester are the two faces of Janus: sinister and hilarious. They look to opposite directions: to the end and to the new beginning while inhabiting the threshold. The monster shows the precariousness of our concepts about the living. As Canguilhem said, monsters belong to the imagination—"Nature is poor in monsters" (1988, p. 137). The jester, on the other hand, is the ambassador of the grotesque and the Carnival. Where the monster makes evident the irreducibility of the living, the jester is the institutionalization of liminarity. Opposed to both monsters and jesters, disability is this bio-political category which designates all of us with non-normative bodies.

- This article was published the by *Encrucijadas: Revista Crítica de Ciencias sociales* under the title "Nombrar de la deformidad física: breve reflexión en torno al término discapacidad y sus usos recientes." I am indebted to Patxi Lanceros, Ana Romero de Pablos, and Jesús Rodríguez Velasco who read previous versions of the manuscript. The link to the original article in Spanish is http://www.encrucijadas.org/index.php/ojs/article/view/216/176

References

Alberch, P. (1989). The logic of monsters: Evidence for internal constraint in development and evolution. *Geobios, 22*(2), 21–57.

Bajtin, M. M. (1998). *La cultura popular en la Edad Media y en el Renacimiento: El contexto de François Rabelais*. Madrid, Spain: Alianza.

Bernand, C. (2001). *Negros esclavos y libres en las ciudades hispanoamericanas*. Madrid, Spain: Fundación Histórica Tavera.

Canguilhem, G. (1976). *El conocimiento de la vida*. Barcelona, Spain: Anagrama.

Covarrubias, S. (1611/1979). *Tesoro de la lengua castellana o española*. Madrid, Spain: Turner.

Daston, L., & Park, K. (1998). *Wonders and the order of nature, 1150–1750*. New York: Zone Books.

Davidson, A. I. (1991). The horror of monsters. In J. J. Sheehan & M. Sosna (Eds.), *The boundaries of humanity: Humans, animals, machines* (pp. 36–64). Berkeley, CA: University of California Press.

Foucault, M. (1982). *Las palabras y las cosas: Una arqueología de las ciencias humanas*. México: Siglo Veintiuno Editores.

Foucault, M. (1999). *Entre filosofía y literatura: Obras esenciales*. Barcelona, Spain: Paidós.

Girard, R. (2005). *La violencia y lo sagrado*. Barcelona, Spain: Editorial Anagrama.

Gluckman, M. (1965). *Politics, law, and ritual in tribal society*. Chicago: Aldine Pub. Co.

Hagner, M. (1999). Enlightened monsters. In Hagner, M. The sciences in Enlightened Europe University of Chicago Press. pp. 175–217.

Lémery, L. (1738). Mémoire sur les monstres. M.A.R.S. *Sur les Monstres. Premier Mémoire, dans lequel on examine quelle est la cause immédiate des Monstres*. Retrieved from https://archive.org/details/mmoiresdelacad00acad

Moreno Villa, J. (1939). *Locos, enanos, negros y niños palaciegos; gente de placer que tuvieron los austrias en la corte española desde 1563 a 1700*. México: Editorial Presencia.

Paré, A. (1571/1982). *On monsters and marvels*. Chicago, IL: University of Chicago Press.

Peñalver, L. (2005). *De soslayo: Una mirada sobre los bufones de Velázquez*. Madrid, Spain: Fernando Villaverde Ediciones.

Roe, S. A. (1981). *Matter, life, and generation: 18th-century embryology and the Haller-Wolff debate*. Cambridge, UK: Cambridge University Press.

Southworth, J. (1998). Fools and Jesters at the English Court. The History Press. Gloucestershire.

Stiker, H. (1982). *Corps infirmes et sociétés*. Paris: Aubier-Montaigne.
Stiker, H. (1999). *A history of disability*. Ann Arbor: University of Michigan Press.
Turner, V. W. (1965). Betwixt and between: The liminal period in rites of passage. In W. A. Lessa & E. Z. Vogt (Eds.), *Reader in comparative religion: An anthropological approach* (pp. 234–247). New York: Harper & Row.
Turner, V. W. (1977). *The ritual process: Structure and anti-structure*. Ithaca, NY: Cornell University Press.
Welsford, E. (1961). *The fool; his social and literary history*. Garden City, NY: Doubleday.
Zijderveld, A. (1982). *Reality in a looking-glass: Rationality through an analysis of traditional folly*. London, Boston: Routledge & Kegan Paul.

Chapter 9
"Once Big Oil, Always Big Oil": Disability and Sustainability in Pixar's *Cars 2*

Shannon R. Wooden

9.1 Introduction

The Pixar universe, built on 21 feature length films across 24 years and ever-expanding, is neither acclaimed nor notorious for its representations of disability. Indeed, until 2016, none of its feature-length offerings besides *Finding Nemo* attracted much attention from disability scholars or advocates, and commentary on *Nemo*, while nearly always positive, was fairly superficial, lauding Nemo's "lucky fin" without engaging deeply with the issues central to Disability Studies.[1] With 2016's sequel *Finding Dory*, the Nemo franchise secured its status as the face of disability in Pixar, and most viewers seem comforted by its being an affirming face.[2] But Pixar's relationship to disability is far more complex, narratively and visually, than it may at first appear, and its many more problematic representations—of compulsory able-bodiedness, stigma, prosthetic appropriations of disabled bodies, and

---

[1] Ann Millett, for instance, reviewing the film for *Disability Studies Quarterly*, sees *Nemo's* "multifaceted representation of disability" as "transgressive…a flavorful ingredient in cultural diversity" even as she says the film "isn't 'about' disability at all." While I am inclined to share her pleasure in the film, I am cautioned by David Mitchell and Sharon Snyder's reminder that disability is a material and social reality that inevitably contributes to subjectivity, and our treatment of it must therefore be complex (Millett 2004, p. 58).

[2] The exceptions to this affirmation, explicitly noted by many viewers as a strange exception for such an otherwise disability-friendly film, are Gerald and Becky. Gerald, a sea lion portrayed with some sort of intellectual delay and read by many viewers as autistic, is mocked and bullied by other sea lions, presumably for comic relief; Becky, an aphasic loon, is depicted as unpredictable and unreliable (until, finally, she isn't unreliable at all). See "Finding Dory, Disability Culture, and Collective Access" at the Disability Visibility Project (2016); Picciuto (2016) at *The Daily Beast*; and Sankar-Gorton (2016) at *Huffington Post*.

S. R. Wooden (✉)
Missouri State University, Springfield, MO, USA
e-mail: srwooden@missouristate.edu

© Springer Nature Switzerland AG 2020
L. Ware (ed.), *Critical Readings in Interdisciplinary Disability Studies*, Critical Studies of Education 12, https://doi.org/10.1007/978-3-030-35309-4_9

the conflation of disability with other identities coded as inferior—are certainly worth our notice.

Even if it were true that the largely enabling space of Nemo's ocean contains all the disability of note in Pixar, there would be at least something to critique: as Halberstam (2011) enthusiastically describes the nearly limitless potential of animation to imagine and present bodies that fall outside social norms, Pixar's containing disability within just two films is a tragically missed opportunity, particularly given the pedagogical power that Giroux (1995) has ascribed to Disney by virtue of its reach, its impeccably manufactured pleasure, and its pervasive nostalgia. With merely two films, and those featuring nonhuman animals in non-anthropomorphic bodies, Disney/Pixar at best fails to capitalize on the opportunities presented by animation and a young, eagerly learning audience. Moreover, though dramatically corrected by *Finding Dory*, *Nemo's* representations of disability are not as unproblematic as they appear. The film so completely removes any obstacle caused by impairment, environment, or stigma—Nemo's "lucky fin" more cute than it is impairing, the entire plot catalyzed in fact by how well he can swim rather than by any physical challenge or limitation—that many viewers consider Dory's memory, Bruce's addiction, Flo's dissociative confusion, Jacques's obsessive tendencies (and the list goes on) as comedic, if they consider those things at all, seeing Marlin's overprotectiveness as the only truly disabling factor in the film.

Besides, it simply is not true that an exploration of disability representations in Pixar should begin and end in a coral reef. Though apparently hidden in plain sight, largely invisible to popular and critical attention, Pixar film after Pixar film uses physical impairment narratively, for plot expediency, as visual symbol, or (superficially) as a character development technique: from Buzz's broken arm in *Toy Story* to Woody's torn shoulder in *Toy Story 2* to Doc Hudson's famous accident in the *Cars* backstory to King Fergus's wooden leg in *Brave* and Carl Fredrickson's use of a walker in *Up*, Pixar characters temporarily or permanently reside outside able-bodied norms, and repair, accommodation, and stigma frequently become important plot points of conflict or resolution. More invisible but just as illuminative to the foundational theories of disability is the Pixar films' use of bodily difference to reiterate norms—and, reflexively, the use of bodily norms to quickly and efficiently tell visual stories—rather than to attempt to challenge normativity: the *Monsters, Inc.*, world of apparently infinite bodily variance, for instance, still privileges and rewards an anthropomorphic hypermasculinity, as it narratively and graphically demonstrates the inferiority of other masculine body types.[3]

Though many children's films popular in the early twenty-first century overtly construct rhetorical challenges to socially dominant standards of bodies and behaviors—indeed, this seems a minor trend over the past decade, from *Monsters University* to *Rango* to *How to Train Your Dragon*—in Pixar, at least, these rhetorical structures are nearly always disingenuous, masking visual images, thematic

---

[3] I have discussed *Monsters University* and *Monsters Inc.* elsewhere; see Wooden and Gillam (2014, pp. 62–65).

threads, and narrative conclusions that work to reinforce, rather than challenge, what Lennard Davis calls the "hegemony of normalcy" (Davis 2013, p. 10). In other words, what appear as progressive, even liberatory arguments disguise very conventional—and, in Mitchell and Snyder's (2000) construction, "prosthetic"—narrative and visual uses of difference and depend upon their audience's stigmatizing gaze to enforce sadly conventional ideas of normativity.

As McRuer (2006) argues, normative standards presume and compel not only able-bodiedness but heterosexuality, and this tendency too is invisibly present in a large variety of Pixar's offerings, despite their general resistance to romantic plots. In films like *Monsters University*, the privileged norms for (heterosexual) male and able bodies overlap so completely it is difficult to determine which bodies are "disabled" and which merely (alternatively masculine) "nerds." In terms of masculinity, such a distinction may be academic anyway,[4] particularly as long as the actual material issues of disability—access, and so on—are shunted aside to make room for an emphasis on social and self-stigmatizing. At a glance, this is also the case with *Cars 2*, wherein perpetually broken and old, unfashionable cars become the angry villains who seek revenge on superstar sports cars and the racing community at large. In *Cars 2*, though, the bully plot is intricate, underlying a spy plot bound to a criminal plot, which in its way recursively reinforces the bully plot. A deeper exploration reveals narratively foundational attitudes about bodily superiority that allow the film's protagonists (and by extension its viewers, according to the shared, if invisible, hegemonic values of both) to not only stigmatize non-normative bodies but, literally, to deny them accommodation and compassion and to punish them for venturing beyond their prescribed, stigmatized roles. Moreover, as I will discuss shortly, the convoluted narrative of *Cars 2* braids in a third and equally dangerous ideological strand to strengthen its support of normative, able-bodied masculinity. The exaltation of the "big oil" American man—built on the steel frames of Sarge and Mater but fronted by the celebrity of Lightning McQueen, whose horsepower of course exceeds even theirs—yokes the issues of disability, alternative masculinities, and global environmental consciousness, defining its superior self in unambiguous opposition to a host of progressive values simultaneously.

9.2 Cripping/Queering *Cars 2*

Cars 2 was introduced as Mater's film, an opportunity for the sidekick to get his day. The small-town, small-minded tow truck who served the first film as comic relief and foil to the superstar race car Lightning McQueen is celebrated in this sequel as having precisely the esoteric knowledge and organic genius to solve the mystery at the story's center, despite the constant, egregious, and highly public bumbling that temporarily causes his best buddy, alpha male McQueen, to be ashamed of him.

---

[4] See Klein (2012, p. 30).

Though Mater saves the day and thus resolves one of the film's major plotlines, the feel-good lesson of the film is Lightning's to learn, and it's to love and accept others warts and all. Discrimination on the basis of intellectual delay or inexperience, rural roots, bad manners, or a dented-up old body receives an overt reprimand, in the voice of Luigi's uncle, and the narrative structure shores up this moral, showing and telling viewers in no uncertain terms that individuals should be valued for their unique gifts rather than stigmatized for real or perceived limitations.

Against the hegemonic masculine ideal of his best friend—Lightning is strong, powerful, heterosexual, competitive, and professionally successful—Mater might be seen as a non-normative character by virtue of his social class, what Coston and Kimmel (2012) have described as "working class masculinity." Though at first blush this type of masculine performance may seem like almost an exaggeration of hegemonic traits, especially physical brawn, and thus strange to be understood as "alternative," but as Coston and Kimmell argue, working class males are not the main beneficiaries of white male privilege and are often stereotyped as "dumb brutes... endowed with physical virtues but problematized by intellectual shortcomings" (Coston and Kimmel 2012, p. 107). Though Mater's "intellectual shortcomings" seem not to disable him, at least in the environment of Radiator Springs, they are abundantly evident, and in the film's spy plot, it is precisely Mater's unique intellectual gifts—and the film's insistence on appreciating them—that restores his masculine status. He cannot tell when Lightning and Sally are on a date, he does not know that wasabi paste is not pistachio ice cream, and he cannot tell the difference between the names "Francesco" and "San Francisco," but he knows what type of obsolete bolts hold what kind of engine, and this esoteric, working class knowledge enables him to identify a criminal mastermind from a photograph no one else knows how to read. This small piece of knowledge earns him international renown as a literal "intelligence agent," as well as the romantic attention of the sleek, sporty, female spy, Holly Shiftwell. In other words, he ends the film with a highly public endorsement of his successful performance of hegemonic masculinity, including heterosexuality, professional achievement, and physical and intellectual authority over others.

Indeed, this conclusion of Mater's character arc might be read as "epiphanic," after McRuer's description of "heteronormative, able-bodied epiphany" (McRuer 2006), the restoration of hegemonic ideals resulting from both narrative crisis and the flexibility of a (heterosexual) character sufficient to weather it. Such epiphanies, to McRuer, create the illusion of "subjective wholeness," anchoring a character in his heteronormative status and thus anchoring the hierarchical position of that status. One might easily argue that Mater's crisis begins as a challenge to his heterosexual identity, as his desire for the attention and affection of Lightning leads him even to deliberately disrupt a romantic (heterosexual) date between Lightning and Sally. The crisis is perpetuated by Lightning's rejection of Mater in Japan and Mater's subsequent hurt feelings. Through a series of comic misunderstandings—and, arguably, resolved through the "flexibility" of Mater's identity, to the point of literal costuming and role-playing—Mater's heteromasculine success at the end of the film does seem to assert an ultimately inflexible subjectivity.

When Luigi's Italian uncle reprimands Lightning for being frustrated and embarrassed by his friend, the film unambiguously identifies Mater's constant bumbling—misnomers and misheard words and missed cultural cues—as characteristic of "who he is" and therefore, with the correct, loving interpretation, unimpeachable and unalterable. Just as Mater resents and resists the disguises that would inauthentically cover his dented body, the film narratively suggests that flexibility has its limits. Mater not only *cannot* learn to be socially adept and culturally aware, the film insists that he *should* not, new manners or intelligence being just as phony as the costumes he eschews. On the one hand, this moral message might be read as pro-disability, celebratory of difference rather than stigmatizing, shaming, or urgently insisting upon repair. Besides the fact that difference might favorably surprise us, the film says—as one's knowledge of Whitworth bolts may unmask an international criminal kingpin—we are *morally* obliged to find the unique good in people, to overlook the things about them that are different from us, even if those differences may cause social awkwardness, discomfort, or even bigger problems. On the other hand, though, with McRuer's model before us, Mater's inflexibility serves the film's reification of heteronormative, able-bodied norms.

Simultaneously, and in keeping with McRuer's own readings of popular Hollywood film, the narrative epiphany allows *Cars 2* to "disavow how much the subjective contraction and expansion of able-bodied heterosexuality… [is] actually contingent on compliant, queer, disabled bodies" (McRuer 2006, pp. 18–19). In the rhetorical construct of this ostensible moral plot of the film, in which Lightning learns to love and appreciate his friend despite Mater's deviating from a number of norms, and in the reiteration of this message by the narrative structure of the spy plot, the film all but ignores its own parallels to the nature of the crime Mater foils and the shared psychology of the perpetrators. Behind an elaborate criminal plan—which involves phases to degrade consumer confidence in biofuel and ultimately to control the global oil market but is probably most comprehensible to small children as making innocent racecars explode—is a band of small, poorly made, frequently broken, and/or notoriously unfashionable "Lemons," tired of having been abused and hell-bent on revenge.[5]

In a film whose moral message has to do with embracing difference and ending discrimination, and whose plot involves the restoration of one non-normative character to hegemonic status, we might expect characters deeply hurt by a lifetime of social ostracizing and stigmatizing to receive some sympathy or redemption, but *Cars 2* almost entirely fails to connect the crime plot with the moral one. Though Mater acknowledges their similarities, late in the film and for exactly two sentences ("I know what you're going through. I've been laughed at my whole life, too," he says), he immediately and summarily dismisses his own empathic potential by insisting that the Lemons' plan to become "powerful and rich beyond [their] wildest dreams" would not help them feel any better, an observation that at best implies no

---

[5] The criminal plot uncannily parallels many a school shooting, and the specific language used by the Lemons to justify their actions uncannily echoes the words left behind by many real-life school shooters. For a more detailed discussion, see Wooden and Gillam (2014, pp. 78–79).

solution whatsoever.[6] The inescapable fact of their inferiority, it would seem, *naturally* inspires painful social stigmatizing, so nothing can be done to relieve or prevent it. Rather than addressing the contribution of the viewer to all stigmatizing situations, as Goffman has described, Mater and the others behave as if the Lemons are "not quite human… imput[ing] a wide range of imperfections" as natural, immutable characteristics (Goffman 1963, p. 33). Even with the acknowledgment of their painful experiences with stigma, as the crime is solved, the Lemons are herded up and punished, even violently.[7]

Not only is there nothing natural or inevitable about social stigmatizing, though, as the film itself insists with regard to Mater's limitations, it is not merely negative social attitudes that the Lemons face but a medicalized naturalization of their disability. The material conditions of the film's universe purposefully and systematically disable these particular cars, creating the very disability on which the social order then insists on stigmatizing and ostracizing them. They are depicted with impairments—though some seem merely old and weird, the Lemons are lumped together as malfunctioning, in one instance commiserating over a broken clutch assembly which precludes attendance at a meeting—but in the language of the social model, disability is imposed on their bodies by physical, organizational, and attitudinal barriers. In a world of car repairs, they alone are unfixable, owing solely to the whims of the capitalist marketplace. The parts required to fix the Lemons could be easily imagined: from Lightning's first race sponsor, Rust-Eze, to the ubiquitous "pit stop" tires, to Radiator Springs' not one but two car repair businesses, a myriad other products advertised on the racing circuit, and a host of spy gadgets with which MI-6 car bodies are enhanced, the entire *Cars* world literally runs on the auto repair industry.[8] Yet the Lemons' inferiority goes without saying, understood as essential, the natural state of things. It is their rehabilitation that is depicted as unnatural. If they have the resources afforded to the highest-ranking cars in their organization, staff tow trucks will haul them around. But the path to even temporary rehabilitation is visually marked as perverse and frightening: parts are obtained in a terrifying back-alley black market, characterized by darkness, disorienting angles and speeds, and the shock of the uncanny, as when one sales car's eyes appear in her headlights rather than her windshield.

Ignoring the disabling elements of the capitalist economy and the environment to which it ideologically contributes, the film suggests that disability is a personal

---

[6] By virtue of its comic exaggeration (Mater acknowledges that the criminal plot may make the Lemons "powerful and rich beyond your wildest dreams"), his argument also seems to undercut its own veracity, suggesting that a violent ascent of the top of the pyramid is indeed the only way of attaining (masculine) dignity and respect.

[7] See also Wooden and Gillam (2014, p. 79).

[8] Indeed, for those cars initially depicted as able-bodied to become permanently disabled in this world of infinite and endless repair requires literal narrative intervention: When one captured agent, threatened with torture, scoffs that he can simply replace his engine block if need be, the evil Professor Zundapp informs him that the electromagnetic pulse that the Lemons use to destroy their enemies renders them with "nothing to replace."

problem rather than a systemic one, and chiefly an attitudinal one to boot. As a problem of one's personal attitude, disability might be simply enough overcome by changing one's mind, and/or embracing a different outlook on life. In one instance, far from back alleys and the international racecar circuit, *Cars 2* shows audiences a socially acceptable performance of disability, while retaining its status as an inherent, irreparable non-normative identity. The second scene of the film presents Otis, a friendly, docile, broken-down car whom Mater picks up on the roadside. Though it is Mater's job to retrieve him—he has a tow truck, after all, and they discuss payment—Otis shuffles around in humility and gratitude for Mater, who is "the only one who's nice to lemons like me." Otis is summarily exiled to a body shop in the second scene of the film and we never see him again, but he has served his purpose: to anchor attitudes toward disability against which the later Lemons can be measured. Animators might mark the Lemons' bodies with disability to efficiently communicate their evil to the film's young audiences,[9] but the Lemons are vilified not just by their broken bodies but by their inappropriate reactions to social stigmatization, lack of accommodation, and other forms of cruelty: rather than absorbing shame and self-stigmatizing toward an appropriate level of docility, they get angry. Then, unwilling to either restore them or redeem them after this transgression of their appropriately humble station, the film relentlessly punishes them.

It is notable that Otis is not only a self-stigmatizing disabled character but a docile consumer, his body providing the occasion for able-bodied labor to be performed. In this sense, he does more than model "good patient" behavior with which the Lemons' badness can be contrasted. As McRuer notes, the narrative site for the heteronormative, able-bodied epiphany is frequently the queer and disabled body. "Flexibility," says McRuer, works [two] ways:

> [H]eterosexual, able-bodied characters…work with queer and disabled minorities, flexibly contracting and expanding, while queer, disabled minorities flexibly comply" (18). Because all of this happens in a discursive climate of tolerance, which values and profits from 'diversity'… the heterosexual, able-bodied subject, as well as the postmodern culture that produced him or her, can easily disavow how much the subjective contraction and expansion of able-bodied heterosexuality (and… neoliberal political and economic logics more generally) are actually contingent on compliant, queer, disabled bodies (McRuer 2006, pp. 18–19).

The docile, disabled Otis provides the "diversity" on which Mater's hegemonic identity can be performed economically and in terms of performing heterosexual able-bodiedness. But the Lemons do not behave like Otis. They do not turn social stigma against themselves to become ashamed and compliant consumers, accepting of market availability and its inevitable disciplining of bodies that fall outside cultural norms. They are undisciplined, as McRuer says of Melvin in the early scenes of *As Good As It Gets*, and this behavior places them "outside the relations of docility-utility" (McRuer 2006, p. 21). Still, and even more than the passive Otis who literally requires Mater's able-bodied performance, the Lemons become the site

---

[9] See Mitchell and Snyder (2000, pp. 58–59), Shapiro (1993, pp. 30–31), and McRuer (2006, p. 23).

on which a heteronormative/able-bodied "epiphany" is staged. Mater's momentarily embracing his identification with them might be viewed as his "flexibility," his own magnanimous gesture of "tolerance," but when they yet again fail to comply with social expectations and the disciplinary structures of the market, accepting their role as consumers instead of capitalists, the narrative forces them into compliance and docility. Mater ensures their defeat and the promise (or literal actualization) of punishment,[10] and in the process cements his role as heteronormative masculine film hero, temporarily "alpha" despite his own apparent shortcomings.

9.3   Masculinity and American National Identity

In further contrast/challenge to the hegemonic masculine ideal, *Cars 2* offers a number of other examples:

- The slight-of-build, highly emotional, fashion-conscious European racecar Francesco Bernoulli, who threatens Lightning McQueen by being both a serious professional competitor and attractive to Lightning's girlfriend.
- The entire nation of Japan, which thoroughly mystifies Mater, most hyperbolically with its androgynous-looking bathroom signage, leading to a locked-stall scene in which the ostensibly gender-confused bathroom humiliates (and arguably assaults) him.[11]
- The leader of the Lemons himself, eccentric British billionaire Miles Axelrod, voiced by famous "executive transvestite" Eddie Izzard and visually introduced, in a brief expository new story, emerging from the wilderness with not only a supposed new formulation of biofuel but also flowers in his hair.

The first two of these may be seen as indirectly proving the rules of able-bodiedness as well as masculinity. Despite his horsepower, Francesco beats Lightning only by virtue of the latter's mistake (a mistake Mater causes, incidentally, catalyzing the tension between the two American friends); further, Sally's attraction has chiefly to do with the fashion of his body style, which is slighter and sleeker than Lightning's boxy bulk. His able body, in other words, is still seen as lesser than Lightning's, while his defining characteristics are his emotionality and his fashion. The overtly feminine Japanese car directing bathroom patrons through their undercarriage wash options is entirely disembodied—a transhuman construction projected on a screen. Though it is able to momentarily get the best of Mater's body, its own physical ability is beyond prosthetic-dependent, not existing at all without technological enhancement. The last of these, though, is a true Lemon,

---

[10] See also Wooden and Gillam (2014, p. 79).

[11] One can read the scene as it was apparently intended—as slapstick comedy—or as an act of deferred sexual violence, as the mechanized toilet stall, embodied by a pink, giggling, on-screen car, covers Mater's body with pink soap and forcibly shoots water into his undercarriage.

secret owner of the faculty engine held together with the elusive Whitworth bolts. Queered from the first moment by the image of flowers in his hair (even if young viewers cannot associate Izzard's voice with alternate gender performance), he is impaired by a leaky engine (visually rendered as pants-wetting) and disabled by the unavailability of parts.

The other thing these three characters share besides the markers of alternative masculinities and, if indirectly, of alternative able-bodiedness is that they are all non-American. Messner (2007), Tasker (1993), Jeffords (1993), and others have explored the relationship between American national identity and its popular cultural representations of alpha men: Jeffords explains how, through the last few decades of the twentieth century, both the celebrated personae of real-life men and cinematic depictions of fictional heroes functioned as national father figures and "emblems of national identity" (Jeffords 1993, p. 6). In the 1980s, hypermasculine, heterosexual, able-bodied, and "hard bodied" representations of *First Blood's* Rambo, *Commando's* John Matrix, *Top Gun's* Maverick Mitchell and others like them stood metonymically for American strength in the Cold War, "remasculinizing" America, argues Jeffords, and Messner echoes Jeffords in likening this particular masculine type to national identity in times of political crisis: "Conan, Commando, and the Terminator appear… when the idea of real men as decisive, strong, and courageous arose from the confusion and humiliation of the U. S. loss in the Vietnam war, and against the challenges of feminism and gay liberation" (Messner 2007, p. 464). Messner extends his analysis through the "compassionate conservatism"/"Kindergarten Cop" masculinity of the 1990s and early 2000s, as Jeffords has articulated a "New Man" model of masculinity that emerged in children's film with figures like the cursed prince in *Beauty and the Beast*. Likewise, as I have argued elsewhere, Pixar heroes narratively tend toward gentler expressions of (albeit hegemonic) masculinity. But *Cars 2* unproblematically celebrates a hypermasculine body type, a "top gun" and a Maverick, nostalgic for the "hard bodied" action figures of the 1980s. Like them, and contrasting to the slender and emotional Italian Formula One car, the pink and giggling Japanese cartoon, and the flamboyant English sport utility vehicle, Lightning's able, athletic body presents such a type as quintessentially American, a symbol of American supremacy.

Furthermore, in the convolutions of its criminal plot, the film's cheap reiteration of an adolescent bully structure of masculinity and the narrative exile of the disabled Other conflates questions of American masculinity with global environmental politics, in one of the film's most subtly damaging subtexts.

9.4 American Masculinity and Anti-Environmentalism

As the film opens, viewers learn that Axelrod has staged a world-wide auto race, the World Grand Prix, to promote his new invention, a biofuel he calls Allinol. During the race, the world's best racecars—required to run on Allinol for the duration of the event—start exploding, seemingly at random, until we find out that the Lemons, armed with an electromagnetic device the spies have observed, are triggering explosions of the new fuel. By the end of the film, Allinol is discovered not to be biofuel at all but gasoline engineered to explode when so triggered. Axelrod is then revealed to be the secret leader of the Lemons, an oil-burning, oil-leaking "lemon" himself, distracting the world from his acquisition of an enormous oil field and plans to take over the global economy. Given the fact of the film's intended audience and the power of children's film to teach, the convoluted nature of the plot may obscure the constructedness of its various associations. But biofuel is clearly marked in opposition to hegemonic American masculinity. Though adult listeners paying close attention might be able to follow the thread from Allinol-is-safe-biofuel to Allinol-is-dangerous-biofuel to Allinol-is-engineered-gasoline, and that the point of Allinol from the beginning was to drive everyone back to oil-based fuels, younger viewers (who are not likely to know the word "biofuel" any more than they know "Allinol") may interpret only the damaging associations between this concept, the Lemons (non-masculine, non-American, disabled cars), and emotional responses of anger at the "bad guys" and fear of pain or death. First, despite the weak, late corrective that Allinol is not biofuel, viewers are taught that "biofuel" makes good cars blow up. Secondly, biofuel appears as the brainchild of the *lesser man*—the stranger with the funny accent, flowers in his hair, an outsider to the beloved community of friends from Radiator Springs, and in possession of a broken-down, leaky engine. Biofuel, in other words, puts American masculinity—and, by extension, America itself—at risk.

Cars 2 does not represent a radical new association of heterosexual masculinity with able-bodiedness and anti-environmentalism, or, by converse, queerness with disability and ecology; on the contrary, such a stereotype is prevalent enough to largely avoid notice. From one of the earliest iterations of "hegemonic masculinity," R. W. Connell's "A Whole New World: Remaking Masculinity in the Context of the Environmental Movement" (Connell 1990), scholars and journalists in the popular press have begun to explore the "masculinity problem" within the environmental movement. Citing politico-historical, psychological, and symbolic roots, and linking feminism and ecology from the beginning of both the feminist and environmentalist movements, critics have offered perspectives on everything from product preference to carbon footprints to support for government spending. Richard A. Rogers (2008), for instance, links hegemonic masculinity to environmental attitudes through an analysis of advertisements for "red meat," the WWE, and gas-guzzling vehicles. Environmentalism, Rogers argues, has frequently challenged "the privilege and ideological position of the white, straight, dominating male," privilege driven to "crisis" over the latter decades of the twentieth century, in part by changing landscapes of labor and economics and the growing civil rights of women and minorities (pp. 297 and 285). Using resistance to the challenges of environmentalism to provisionally answer these contemporary anxieties about masculinity, advertisers show Hummers and hamburgers as epitomizing and "restoring" masculinity, giving men both the reassurance of masculine identity and an imperative to participate in "substantial environmental degradation" (Rogers 2008, p. 293).[12] The fragility of American masculinity, in other words, is partly supported by anti-environmentalism, rendering environment-friendly behaviors from climate change awareness to reusable tote bags not only absent from but strongly antithetical to prevailing ideas of hegemonic masculinity.

The message is driven home by positive as well as negative associations. Not surprisingly, narrative resolution assures safety and cements the bonds of friendship, and possibly it is equally to be expected that such resolution both relocates the protagonists to home turf and symbolically restores any and all compromised masculinity. But there is no obvious reason—and no structural precedent—for such a happy ending to pay explicit homage to fossil fuel. Marketed by the fictional company Dinoco (in both *Cars* and *Toy Story* franchises), gasoline is good across the *Cars* franchise. In the first *Cars*, it is directly associated with masculine "winning," as Dinoco represents Lightning's dream sponsorship; in the second, it is also credited with Lightning's success. When everyone is back in Radiator Springs, USA—heterosexual authority reestablished by Lighting's reunion with Sally and Mater's visit from Holly, who despite professional pretenses for the visit reminds him that he owes her a date—veteran Army Jeep Sarge confesses to have switched the fuels all along, ensuring that Lightning never used the Allinol. With no regret or shame at having broken the one ground rule of the World Grand Prix, Sarge proudly testifies, "Once Big Oil, always Big Oil." Biofuel is decisively dispatched as a concept that can could coexist with a quintessentially American and hegemonically masculine happy ending.

9.5 Conclusion

Pixar is widely celebrated as a pleasure-making machine, but its pedagogical function cannot be denied and must, therefore, merit critical attention as long as it retains its powerhouse position in children's entertainment. In 2016, Pixar made some progressive strides, *Finding Dory*'s unfortunate portrayals of Gerald and Becky notwithstanding. From a disability standpoint, there is something reassuring in the fact that, complicating the blandly utopian social model of *Finding Nemo* which made primarily comic use of Dory's short-term memory loss, *Dory* is upfront about Dory's unique struggle, even as it celebrates her unique gifts. From an environmental standpoint, there may be also some small comfort in the setting's dedication to the restoration and preservation of sea life. We can hope such strides signal a change in Pixar's overall direction which, as Giroux laments of most of Disney's output, trends more toward nostalgic than progress. Films like *Cars 2*, perpetuating

---

[12] See also Hultman (1993), for an analysis of Arnold Schwarzenegger's political journey into environmentalism that dovetails with Susan Jeffords's work on cultural representations of "hard bodies."

hegemonic standards of normalcy across gender, ability, and national identities, even blindly reinforcing intersectional hegemonies that unhealthily influence real-world beliefs and behaviors, continue to deserve our scrutiny.

References

Connell, R. W. (1990). A whole new world: Remaking masculinity in the context of the environmental movement. *Gender and Society, 4*(4), 452–478.

Coston, B. M., & Kimmel, M. (2012). Seeing privilege where it isn't: Marginalized masculinities and the intersectionality of privilege. *Journal of Social Issues, 68*(1), 97–111.

Davis, L. J. (2013). Introduction: Disability, normality, and power. In L. J. Davis (Ed.), *The disability studies reader* (4th ed., pp. 1–14). New York: Routledge.

Disability Visibility Project. (2016). *Finding Dory, disability culture, and collective access.* Retrieved from https://disabilityvisibilityproject.com/2016/06/27/finding-dory-disability-culture-and-collective-access/

Giroux, H. A. (1995). Memory and pedagogy in the 'Wonderful World of Disney': Beyond the politics of innocence. In E. Bell et al. (Eds.), *From mouse to mermaid* (pp. 43–61). Bloomington: Indiana University Press.

Goffman, E. (1963). *Stigma: Notes on the management of spoiled identity*. New York: Touchstone.

Halberstam, J. (2011). *The queer art of failure*. Durham, NC: Duke University Press.

Hultman, M. (1993). The making of an environmental hero: A history of ecomodern masculinity, fuel cells, and Arnold Schwarzenegger. *Environmental Humanities, 2*, 79–99.

Jeffords, S. (1993). *Hard bodies: Hollywood masculinity in the Reagan era*. New Brunswick, NJ: Rutgers University Press.

Klein, J. (2012). *The bully society: School shootings and the crisis of bullying in America's schools*. New York: New York University Press.

McRuer, R. (2006). *Crip theory: Cultural signs of queerness and disability*. New York: New York University Press.

Messner, M. (2007). The masculinity of the governator: Muscle and compassion in American politics. *Gender and Society, 21*, 461–480.

Millett, A. (2004). 'Other' fish in the sea: *Finding Nemo* as an epic representation of disability. *DSQ: Disability Studies Quarterly, 24*(1). Retrieved from dsq-sds.org/article/view/873/1048.

Mitchell, D. T., & Snyder, S. L. (2000). *Narrative prosthesis: Disability and the dependencies of discourse*. Ann Arbor: University of Michigan Press.

Picciuto, E. (2016). *Finding Dory*, disability, and me. *The Daily Beast*. Retrieved from http://www.thedailybeast.com/articles/2016/06/19/finding-dory-disability-and-me.html

Rogers, R. A. (2008). Beasts, burgers, and hummers: Meat and the crisis of masculinity in contemporary television advertisements. *Environmental Communication: A Journal of Nature and Culture, 2*(3), 281–301.

Sankar-Gorton, E. (2016). The one glaring problem with *Finding Dory. Huffington Post*. Retrieved from www.huffingtonpost.com/eliza-sankargorton/the-one-glaring-problem-with-finding-dory_b_10616630.html

Shapiro, J. P. (1993). *No pity: People with disabilities forging a new civil rights movement*. New York: Three Rivers Press.

Tasker, Y. (1993). *Spectacular bodies: Gender, genre, and the action cinema*. London and New York: Routledge.

Wooden, S. R., & Gillam, K. (2014). *Pixar's boy stories: Masculinity in a postmodern age*. Lanham, MD: Rowman & Littlefield Press.

Chapter 10
"I'd Prefer Not To": Melville's Challenge to Normative Identity in *Bartleby, the Scrivener*

Natalie M. Fleming

10.1 Introduction

Okay, I know this may sound strange, but I often catch myself wondering about Bartleby. Herman Melville's enigmatic subject from his 1853 novella, *Bartleby, the Scrivener: A Story of Wall Street*[1] and his canonical refrain, "I'd prefer not to," comes to mind at the most inconvenient of times: while I am typing my final semester papers, while staring at a sink full of dirty dishes, or admiring the hardly worn soles of my running shoes. These are things that I know should be doing in order to feel proud and productive, things that I eventually convince myself to do, but still I get a perverse pleasure in simply imagining, through Bartleby, a space for my preferences to reign over my rationality.

I am not the only person that Bartleby has managed to stick with. Although Melville's contemporary critics mostly ignored *Bartleby, the Scrivener* when it was first published, in the twentieth century it earned the status as one of the masterpieces of American short fiction.[2] For those of you who may be unfamiliar with the story, an unnamed narrator relates to his readers the tale of a scrivener, a professional copyist, named Bartleby. Although at first Bartleby is an overly productive worker for the narrator, after 3 days he shocks the narrator by telling him that he would prefer not to check over his copies for errors, a standard but tedious part of the profession. The narrator decides that this is an inconvenient quirk that he can learn to ignore, but soon afterward Bartleby announces that he prefers not to work

---

[1] Originally published anonymously in two 1853 issues of *Putnam's Magazine* and published again by Melville 3 years *later in the Piazza Tales with five other short stories.* Melville (1967).

[2] Murray is one of many scholars who notes that it was well beyond Melville's death in 1891 that *Bartleby, the Scrivener* was recognized by literature critics and academics. See Murray (2008a, p. 51).

N. M. Fleming (✉)
University at Buffalo, Buffalo, NY, USA

L. Ware (ed.), *Critical Readings in Interdisciplinary Disability Studies*, Critical Studies of Education 12, https://doi.org/10.1007/978-3-030-35309-4_10

at all, but also, much to the narrator's frustration, he would rather not leave the office either. Try as he might to explain Bartleby's behavior, Bartleby confounds all of the narrator's excuses for him. Over time, the narrator grows more and more desperate to either cure Bartleby of his strange preferences or be rid of him, which ends in his forced removal to the New York City prison known as the Tombs. When Bartleby decides that he prefers not to even eat, he wastes away and dies there, leaving the narrator to guiltily wonder what could have possibly been so wrong to make Bartleby… well… Bartleby.

10.2   Explaining Away Bartleby's Behavior

The story's appeal surely stems from our own inability to understand what drives him. Like the narrator, we search for a justification for Bartleby's nonconformity, his refusal to play by the rules of his professional environment. Scholars have gladly taken up the task of explaining Bartleby with wide-ranging results: through a Marxist lens that paints Bartleby as a hero in the face of capitalist demands,[3] as an actor of early nonviolent resistance,[4] and even as a Messianic figure.[5] In addition, scholars suggest that Bartleby's refusal to comply is a message from Melville to his own contemporary audience: his resistance to compromise his writing for their approval, a refusal to become a mere copyist of his earlier successful themes.[6] Some have also searched for a medical explanation, diagnosing Bartleby's puzzling preferences as proof of mental illness. First, in the 1960s and 1970s Bartleby was seen as schizophrenic[7]; now, according to some scholars, he is autistic.[8]

---

[3] For example, David Kuebrich sees the relationship between Bartleby and the narrator as a representation of the conflict between capital and labor in the antebellum period. For Kuebrich, Bartleby's preferences are a response to the exploitative working conditions of Wall Street that Melville himself was sympathetic to. Kuebrich (1996).

[4] Desmarias describes Bartleby's passive resistance as a tool for fighting the imposing structure of his working environment. According to Desmarais, his refrain "I would prefer not to," is highly effective because, although it indicates that Bartleby will yield in his preferences to the narrator's requests, he will not. His polite and passive word choice is difficult for the narrator to challenge because it allows him a way out without ever overtly refusing. He becomes a hero to twentieth-century political movements interested in the strength of nonviolent resistance. Desmarais (2001).

[5] Deleuze defines Bartleby as the "new Christ": an "Original," that does not act in accordance to established laws and traditions, but is a unique and generative force to those around him. Deleuze (1998).

[6] Described in Chase (1949, pp. 147–148) and Arvin (1950, pp. 242–244).

[7] Beja diagnoses Bartleby as schizophrenic, suffering from a particular catatonic type of schizophrenia. He describes Bartleby's actions in the novella as symptoms of schizophrenia and mentions that Bartleby may have autism as well. Beja (1978).

[8] Murray states: "I want to claim that 'Bartleby the Scrivener' presents a radical narrative of autistic presence, and that it does so some ninety years before the condition began to be recognized within the terms of clinical medicine." Murray details the ways in which Bartleby's behavior connects this character to today's medical explanation of autism and believes that the interpretation of Bartleby as autistic is not simply one possible explanation for the story, but the story's foundational meaning. Murray (2008b, pp. 27–64).

Bartleby's historical diagnoses reflect changing attitudes within the medical field at large. Our understanding of autism emerged out of the study of schizophrenia, as the medical term was used first by Swiss psychiatrist Eugene Bleuler in 1911 as a symptom: "schizophrenics who have no more contact with the outside world live in a world of their own… This detachment from reality with the relative and absolute predominance of the inner life, we term autism."[9] In 1943, child psychiatrist Leo Kanner borrowed this term to define a separate condition he claimed was present in the 11 children he studied.[10] These early explanations linking autism to detachment are reflected in the current American Psychiatric Association's (APA) definition of autism spectrum disorder as a "complex developmental disorder that can cause problems with thinking, feeling, language, and the ability to relate to others."[11] According to the APA, currently the largest professional organization for psychiatrists in the world, there are three main characteristics of autism: first, difficulty communicating with others, including using and understanding language; second, difficulty interacting and relating to people, which often presents as an inability to make eye contact or read facial expressions; and finally, repetitive body movements and behaviors, including repetitive speech patterns.[12]

One of the difficulties of assigning the diagnosis of autism to Bartleby is that Melville wrote his novella almost 100 years before the medical term and its meaning even existed. How can Bartleby have autism, if autism did not exist? However, scholars have written convincingly about the ways in which Bartleby almost perfectly fits the model used by our contemporary medical community. There is a lot at stake for disability studies in claiming Bartleby as autistic, and therefore, disabled. It establishes autism as an authentic part of society, not an epidemic rampant only in our current period, as it has been claimed in certain incendiary political debates.[13] Also, Melville's story itself becomes a narrative about disability, its autistic figure not only central to this particular tale but to the larger canon of American literature. A Bartleby with autism stakes a strong claim for disability's crucial role in Western cultural production; disability cannot be concealed.

---

[9] Bleuler (1911). Translated in Parnas et al. (2002).

[10] Kanner (1973).

[11] American Psychiatric Association (2016a).

[12] American Psychiatric Association (2016b). APA's classification of autism is outlined in its Diagnostic and Statistical Manual of Mental Disorders, a publication trusted and utilized by its international psychiatric community.

[13] This is a common claim in contemporary popular culture, particularly in the discourse concerning the disputed connection between required vaccinations for children and the development of autism. What is much less rarely debated is how a person with autism can positively impact society and live a meaningful life. It is often taken for granted that a life with autism is not a "full" or "social" one. I most recently came across this debate while reading a *New York Times* article about whether or not the Tribeca Film Festival should allow for the screening of a film that links vaccines to the development of autism in children. The film, *Vaxxed: From Cover-Up to Catastrophe*, claims that the Centers for Disease Control and Prevention is covering up the knowledge that the measles, mumps, and rubella vaccine causes autism. Its claims are divisive, angering doctors, disability experts, and a large part of the filmmaking community, who call for its censorship. Belluck and Ryzik (2016).

However, even with the seeming appropriateness of the diagnosis for explaining Bartleby's actions, and while keeping in mind this reading's potential benefits for disability studies, I am wary about using any medical lens to explain Bartleby. I am worried about the ways in which a diagnosis of autism solidifies a particular understanding of Bartleby that allows us to end our search for answers. This interpretation brings both a kind of sympathy and self-satisfaction to Melville's story that was not previously available: Bartleby's death could have been prevented *if only* his nineteenth-century narrator possessed the knowledge granted by the gods of science to all of us now. The narrator and his readers are let off the hook; we could not understand Bartleby because of his *own* inability to relate. His repetition of "I'd prefer not to" takes on no deeper meaning than as a symptom of his condition.

10.3   The Limits of "Normal"

As scholar Michael Rembis warns in his book *Defining Deviance: Sex, Science and Delinquent Girls*, the so-called factual and unbiased medical knowledge often conforms to and supports hegemonic normativity. He argues that mental impairment "is not an immutable essence embodied in the disabled subject"[14] but instead a product of culture and its medical discourses, created and negotiated in an uneven relationship between professionals, patients, and others.[15] Although the scientific and social associations linked to autism are culturally constructed, its diagnosis for many individuals closes off any other lens for interpreting their behaviors. In an interview,

---

[14] In *Defining Deviance: Sex, Science and Delinquent Girls, 1890–1960*, Michael Rembis places Illinois's 1915 Involuntary Commitment Law within a larger national eugenics movement. The law allowed for the legal segregation of first-generation, white, working-class, American women who had been labeled deviant and defective through medical discourse, in order to "protect" both society and the women themselves from their own hypersexuality and potential offspring. Rembis reads against the grain of both medical and governmental archives, pointing out the socially constructed nature of seemingly fixed scientific categories such as impairment and intelligence. Scientific discourse gave authority to middle-class men and women to pathologize female sexuality. Rembis crucially elucidates the ways in which conceptions of impairment were modified to fit evolving scientific knowledge, all while continuing to connect the female body with an inherent and dangerous mental deficiency. Rembis (2011, p. 7).

[15] Rembis points out how necessary it was for scientists to prove that the defects within female patients were observable and quantifiable. If mental deviance was written on the body, then the American public wanted to know how in order to better protect themselves from exposure to the so-called defective. However, Rembis is quick to show us that institutionalized women were not simply passive victims in the creation of scientific discourse. Women were able to negotiate and push back against their prognosis, challenging scientific authority by running away, forming sexual relationships within the institution, continuing their educations, appealing to family members for release, or in their responses to scientists during the ritual of the exam. By describing them as neither complete victims nor guilty instigators, Rembis' narratives display the nuanced and complex lives of institutionalized women. Rembis (2011, p. 117).

blogger Amanda Baggs describes the cultural weight of the autistic label for her own everyday life:

> My strategy is to find what I need to do, then find a way to do it. If what I do seems to fit an autism stereotype, then so be it. If what I want to do seems to fit a stereotype of not being autistic, so be it too. I have had it with being controlled mindlessly by a set of requirements. I view "autistic" as a word for a certain part of how my brain works, not for a narrow set of behaviors, and certainly not for a set of boundaries of stereotype that I have to stay inside.[16]

Even a cursory study of autism reveals that science knows far less about the disorder's specificities than popular stereotypes suggest. In our collective minds, we conjure up an image based largely on the original scientific models linking autism to detachment: a male figure, isolated in his own body from the joys of social interaction.[17] However, autism in many ways serves as a catchall for a variety of communicative behavior labeled non-normative, with most scientists in agreement that there is no one cause and no singular manifestation of autism.[18] The problem then with labeling Bartleby as autistic is that it reveals more about our desire to control and reduce that which we do not fully understand than it does about the nature of the individual diagnosed as autistic.

Even without the label of autism, however, Bartleby remains a significant figure for disability studies because he defies and destabilizes the seeming logic of normativity. His presence calls into question our almost universal acceptance of what terms like "normal," "strong," "successful," and "productive" look like.[19] Although Bartleby seems to refuse to produce within his working environment, his "I'd prefer not to" is indeed productive, but not through a narrow capitalist lens. And certainly not in the narratives that we often encounter in popular disability depictions—the model of the so-called super crip—individuals whose disabilities are overcome through their unique effort, talent, and perspective and in spite of their bodily differences.[20] We see this model being used as a redemptive tool for people with

---

[16] Baggs (2007).

[17] Draaisma argues that Kanner and Hans Asperger both offered influential models for autism, which have led to the development of the disorder's powerful contemporary stereotypes; for example, its depiction as a condition solely effecting men. Draaisma (2009).

[18] The Autism Spectrum Disorder fact sheet published by the American Psychiatric Association notes that autism acts as a "catch-all diagnosis of pervasive developmental disorder not otherwise specified." American Psychiatric Association DSM-V (2013).

[19] Scholar Julian Carter has proven in his book, *The Heart of Whiteness: Normal Sexuality and Race in America 1880–1940*, that, at the turn of the twentieth century, the concept of "normal" was actually a racially and sexually marked ideal formed as a goal for all Americans. Although usually defined as standard or customary, Carter argues that the discourse of normalcy allowed Americans "the ability to construct and teach white racial meanings *without appearing to do so*." Therefore, the danger in normalcy is that the concept appears innocuous while it establishes a hierarchy that privileges hegemonic identity categories such as whiteness, heterosexuality, and ability. However, normalcy is only one of a slew of seemingly innocent terms hiding biased ideals that came to dominate the twentieth century. Carter (2007).

[20] Clare discusses his own battle to overcome the super crip narrative in the introduction of his book while detailing his attempt to climb Mount Adams with cerebral palsy. He contemplates the reasons why he feels compelled to perform certain acts to prove to himself and others that he has conquered his disability. Clare (2015, pp. 8–9).

autism, perhaps most famously in the case of the livestock scientist Temple Grandin. She not only pioneered cattle-handling facilities throughout the United States but also wrote in *The Way I See It: A Personal Look at Autism and Asperger's* that without autism, "You would have a bunch of people standing around in a cave, chatting and socializing and not getting anything done."[21] Researchers and activists claim that respected figures such as Albert Einstein, Sir Isaac Newton, and Charles Darwin would not have been able to advance civilization without their autistic characteristics.[22] Scholars have even asserted that Bartleby fits such a model, identifying Bartleby's skill as his "exceptional knack for copying"[23] in his first 3 days of service. In other words, Bartleby is extraordinary because of his ability to assist his boss in an office environment before his pesky preferences begin. But Bartleby's narrative also creates a space to question why people, regardless of their differences, should have to execute some standardized level of industry in order to be tolerated in society. Who defines what makes a life successful?[24] Who exactly are we performing for?

Bartleby is extraordinarily productive: of such questions, of instability and uncertainty. Although the narrator prides himself on his constancy, Bartleby disrupts that self-image. When Bartleby utters, "I would prefer not to," the narrator moves through various extreme reactions: confusion, excitement, repulsion, fear, melancholy, and attraction. The narrator insists: "Indeed, it was his wonderful mildness chiefly, which not only disarmed me, but unmanned me."[25] Contrary to the ways in which we usually frame discourses of production, it is Bartleby's inaction that commands such disruptive change in the narrator's sense of being.

As Bartleby remains unmoved in his preference to opt out, the narrator notes that his influence permeates the office, infecting those around him. He worries:

> Somehow, of late, I had got into the way of involuntarily using this word 'prefer' upon all sorts of not exactly suitable occasions. And I trembled to think that my contact with the scrivener had already and seriously affected me in a mental way. And what further and deeper aberration might it not yet produce?[26]

---

[21] Grandin (2011).

[22] Herman Melville has also been retrospectively diagnosed as autistic in the book *The Genesis of Artistic Creativity: Asperger's Syndrome and the Arts*. Fitzgerald uses biographical details from the book *Melville: A Biography*, by Laurie Robertson-Laurant, to make his case that Melville's writing was influenced by his undiagnosed Asperger's syndrome. Fitzgerald (2005). See also Muir (2003) and Lyons and Fitzgerald (2005).

[23] Pinchevski (2011, p. 42).

[24] Garland-Thomson sees Melville's narrative as one that reveals the workings of our institutional and ideological systems that judge whether a life with disability is worth living, what she refers to as the "cultural logic of euthanasia." For Garland-Thomson, Bartleby is a figure that cannot conform to cultural expectations and therefore can be eliminated, if not cured. She uses the example of Bartleby to explain how difficult the choice between living and dying can be for someone with a disability when societal standards teach us that unless one can find a cure and conquer disability, life will not be worth living. Garland-Thomson (2004).

[25] Melville (1967, p. 20).

[26] Melville (1967, p. 25).

The narrator understands Bartleby's behavior as dangerously contagious for those around him. His medical language helps him rationalize the necessity of amputating Bartleby for the sake of his corporate body. Although he cannot convince Bartleby to implicate himself in an excuse for his removal, the narrator realizes that a justified response is no longer necessary now that his office's health is at risk:

> Then something severe, something unusual must be done. What! Surely you will not have him collared by a constable, and commit his innocent pallor to the common jail? And upon what ground could you procure such a thing to be done? -a vagrant, is he? What! he a vagrant, a wanderer, who refuses to budge? It is because he will *not* be a vagrant then, that you seek to count him *as* a vagrant. That is too absurd.[27]

Irrational or not, Bartleby is charged and removed to prison under such vagrancy laws.

10.4 Conclusion

How weak is our normative system if it cannot overcome the inexplicability of one man? How strong must Bartleby have been to stand in his difference against the pressures of conformity? In one of the only occasions in which he diverts from his famous line when asked once again to explain himself, Bartleby demands: "Do you not see the reason for yourself?"[28] With that question he challenges the narrator and us all. Melville's story points to the fragility of our own self-definitions as normal as we unquestioningly perform acts to support a system that is made to seem bizarre by Bartleby's presence. The line between productive and useless, accepted and intolerable, normal and deviant is revealed to be insubstantial. Isn't it strange that the narrator, at the end of his life, feels compelled to tell us this tale about Bartleby? Why am I still thinking about him? Will you all now also find yourselves repeating the story of Bartleby, even if you would prefer not to?

References

American Psychiatric Association. (2016a). *Help with autism spectrum disorder*. Retrieved March 6, 2016, from https://www.psychiatry.org/patients-families/autism

American Psychiatric Association. (2016b). *What is autism spectrum disorder?* Retrieved March 6, 2016, from https://www.psychiatry.org/patients-families/autism/what-is-autism-spectrum-disorder

American Psychiatric Association DSM-V. (2013). *Autism spectrum disorder*. Retrieved March 6, 2016, from http://www.dsm5.org/Documents/AutismSpectrumDisorderFactSheet.pdf

Arvin, N. (1950). *Herman Melville*. New York: W. Sloane.

Baggs, A. (2007). *Putting autism on trial: An interview with Amanda Baggs*. Interview by Donna Williams. Polly's Pages. Retrieved March 7, 2016, from http://blog.donnawilliams.net/2007/07/03/putting-autism-on-trial-an-interview-with-amanda-baggs/

---

[27] Melville (1967, p. 35).

[28] Ibid., p. 26.

Beja, M. (1978). Bartleby and schizophrenia. *The Massachusetts Review, 19*(3), 555–568.

Belluck, P., & Ryzik, M. (2016). Robert De Niro defends screening of anti-vaccine film at Tribeca Festival. *The New York Times*. Retrieved March 27, 2016, from http://www.nytimes.com/2016/03/26/health/vaccines-autism-robert-de-niro-tribeca-film-festival-andrew-wakefield-vaxxed.html?_r=0

Bleuler, E. (1911). Dementia praecox oder gruppe der schizophrenien. In G. Aschaffenburg (Ed.), *Handbuch Der Psychiatrie*. Leipzig: Deuticke.

Carter, J. (2007). *The heart of whiteness: Normal sexuality and race in America, 1880–1940*. Durham, NC: Duke University Press.

Chase, R. V. (1949). *Herman Melville, a critical study*. New York: Macmillan.

Clare, E. (2015). *Exile and pride: Disability, queerness, and liberation*. Durham, NC: Duke University Press.

Deleuze, G. (1998). Bartleby; or, the formula. In *Essays critical and clinical* (D. W. Smith & M. A. Greco, Trans.). London and New York: Verso.

Desmarais, J. (2001). Preferring not to: The paradox of passive resistance in Herman Melville's "Bartleby". *Journal of the Short Story in English, 36*, 25–39.

Draaisma, D. (2009). Stereotypes of autism. *Philosophical Transactions of the Royal Society B: Biological Sciences, 364*(1522), 1475–1480.

Fitzgerald, M. (2005). *The genesis of artistic creativity: Asperger's syndrome and the arts*. London: Jessica Kingsley Publishers.

Garland-Thomson, R. (2004). The cultural logic of euthanasia: "Sad Fancyings" in Herman Melville's "Bartleby". *American Literature, 76*(4), 777–806.

Grandin, T. (2011). *The way I see it: A personal look at autism and Asperger's*. Arlington, TX: Future Horizons.

Kanner, L. (1973). *Childhood psychosis: Initial studies and new insights*. Washington, DC: V. H. Winston and Sons.

Kuebrich, D. (1996). Melville's doctrine of assumptions: The hidden ideology of capitalist production in "Bartleby". *The New England Quarterly, 69*(3), 381–405.

Lyons, V., & Fitzgerald, M. (2005). *Asperger syndrome: A gift or a curse?* New York: Nova Biomedical Books.

Melville, H. (1967). Bartleby, the Scrivener. In *Five tales*. New York: Dodd, Mead & Company.

Muir, H. (2003). Einstein and Newton showed signs of autism. *New Scientist, 30*, 36–39.

Murray, S. (2008a). *Representing autism: Culture, narrative, fascination*. Liverpool, England: Liverpool University Press.

Murray, S. (2008b). Presences: Autistic difference. In *Representing autism: Culture, narrative, fascination*. Liverpool, England: Liverpool University Press.

Parnas, J., Bovet, P., & Zahavi, D. (2002). Schizophrenic autism: Clinical phenomenology and pathogenetic implications. *World Psychiatry, 1*(3), 131–136.

Pinchevski, A. (2011). Bartleby's autism: Wandering along incommunicability. *Cultural Critique, 78*, 27–59.

Rembis, M. A. (2011). *Defining deviance: Sex, science, and delinquent girls, 1890–1960*. Urbana: University of Illinois Press.

Chapter 11
Co-Constructing Frames for Resistance: Reflections on Disability by a Daughter and Her Mother

Suzanne Stolz

11.1 Introduction

Following the recommendations of my dissertation committee some years back, I half-heartedly revised my plan to include interviewing parents, ultimately mothers, in addition to the disabled teens who were the focus of my study. To my surprise, in comparison to the time I spent easily relating to the experiences and feelings of the teens, the time I spent with mothers, hearing about their journeys and recent revelations, somehow intrigued and delighted me more. As I later analyzed transcripts, I felt a sense of understanding in ways I had not before and began to think more about my relationship with my own mother. I began to see our shared journey, in negotiating conceptions of disability and the consequent interactions in our lives, in building and bettering our legacy together from different vantage points.

The narrative I share here was crafted by emails, revisited journal entries, and phone conversations exchanged over a year following the invitation to contribute to this book. Through the email exchange, topics and themes emerged as my mother and I pieced together a life looked at from two distinct perspectives.

11.2 Taking the Freeway

Twenty years ago, my parents helped me pack up and move from Kansas to California, driving long distances south on I-35, west on I-40, south on I-25 from Albuquerque, and farther west on I-10 and finally ending the journey on I-8. After arriving at the coast and looking together out across the Pacific Ocean, remembering that it was named for its peacefulness, we rested at a cheap hotel.

S. Stolz (✉)
University of San Diego, San Diego, CA, USA
e-mail: sstolz@sandiego.edu

© Springer Nature Switzerland AG 2020
L. Ware (ed.), *Critical Readings in Interdisciplinary Disability Studies*, Critical Studies of Education 12, https://doi.org/10.1007/978-3-030-35309-4_11

Using apartment listings in the newspaper and a foldout map, Mom and I set out hunting for an accessible place. She navigated while I drove. Intimidated by the rush of the freeways, she found surface street routes to every address. Even in that, I felt the familiar tarnish of over-protection she named caution and her unyielding impulse to shelter me from the world I was eager to live in. After scouting out a very inaccessible treehouse and a number of units with stairs, I finally signed a lease on an apartment in a building that had an elevator. Heading back to the hotel to meet my dad and sister, I turned to my mom to declare: "I'm taking the freeway."

We celebrated New Year's Eve in my new apartment, drinking Manischewitz and hanging art we found at the swap meet. The Manischewitz was Mom's idea. She said, "Tim, remember when we used to drink this?" Their old living room furniture was now mine. The white bedroom set of my teen years fit nicely in my new room. My parents made sure everything had a place and confirmed that I could reach what they named to be my liquor cabinet.

In the morning, they kissed me goodbye and began the long drive back to Kansas. Mom later told me that she cried for some time on the road out of San Diego. Although I would miss them, I do not remember that I cried. Maybe I did.

11.3   Unspoken Rules

My mother's emotions, vivid in my memories, are often more clear than my own. The emotions I recall, those evoked through her experiences mothering me, have impacted me, marked certain events as meaningful in our shared story, and also have taught me to shield her from certain parts of my own story. Her efforts to protect me have annoyed me and yet I see that I do the same to her.

While our emotions and experiences are intertwined, our vantage points in regard to disability and other aspects of our lives can keep us circling like opposing magnets, until we finally take the extra time to communicate on a deeper level.

A couple years ago, while celebrating Christmas, we gathered for a family photo—two parents, six siblings, spouses, and 15 grandchildren. In the December cold, common to central Kansas early in the winter season, we arranged ourselves in no particular order, surrounding my parents who sat in the center. Always in the front row, I parked my wheelchair near the perimeter and held my seven-year-old niece on my lap.

If we are lucky, we all come together in the same place once or twice a year. Living in California, I am one variable that makes more frequent reunions at the Kansas homestead rare. My mom often expresses that she wants everyone to be together, to remain connected. "The whole family" I hear her repeat in my mind—an appeal, more than a restatement of the obvious.

After the photographer snapped a number of photos, the woman described another pose she wanted. "Now, we're going to spread out a bit, have mom and dad stand in the center, and then cluster each family together behind them with some space between each cluster." As the only unmarried sibling, I objected.

Initially I projected sarcasm in response—a failed effort to disguise my disapproval. The photographer instructed me to join my parents, and rather than explain my objection, I quietly complied. All was made better by simply setting aside my reaction to that particular moment in an otherwise richly layered day. Weeks later, when the photographer sent along the proofs, I urged my mom to choose the first pose as the one she would frame and display. She agreed, but also printed the other, albeit in a smaller frame. I have secretly schemed to steal it or attach a disclaimer to it: "disability mythology." But it was because of this very photo shoot and all that it represented to me that I chose to launch this mother-daughter exchange with the hope that probing this event might give shape to our shared yet disparate experiences. In my first email, I asked Mom to look at the photo, think about her life as a mother, and tell me what came to mind. Nervously, I awaited her response, wondering if she might feel I was bringing up a point of tension by referring to the photo.

> Mom: I am proud of all six of our children. They are uniquely different, and yet have some of the same qualities ... They are all financially independent, they are emotionally stable, they are spiritually motivated to live their lives for others, and most of all love others the way God intended. That photo, I will admit, represents a sense of accomplishment, a sense that my life was indeed worthwhile.

At the end of her email, she noted that nothing in her response was about disability and she was sorry about that. I assured her that her reply was not off-target and asked her what she had done to encourage her children's independence and stability.

> *Me*: As a mother, what did you intentionally do to raise us this way?

> Mom: What did we intentionally do to raise you to be independent? I have to think it may fall under an unspoken rule. I never thought of reliance on my parents as an option, so financial independence was a given. The same held true for you and your siblings. Do you ever remember a conversation about this, or was it not one of those unspoken, but unquestionable expectations?

> You had a lot of friends, school friends, camp friends from the Muscular Dystrophy Association, cousins who contributed to your emotional health. Your parents loved you; our marriage was secure ... There is a list of things we did where you could recognize that help ing others was part of who our family was ... I think of the telethon we worked at for the MDA and the yearly swim party. I think of the taco sales for Fr. Servando to start his new order of priests in Mexico, being part of the Christian Children's Foundation, helping out at church, and housing the Totus Tuus volunteers.

Within other projects, I have reflected on my own experience and considered the role my parents have played in shaping who I have become. When I have attempted to bring light to the strength of her efforts, my mom has often passed the credit to me and even more often to God. I understand her devotion to God, but I want to learn more about her parental intentions and actions. I am not a mother myself, and yet, I have relied on the example my parents provided in counseling my then secondary school students' parents and now in my teaching of preservice teachers.

Me: Yes, I think your unconditional love and our community of family and friends helped build emotional stability for me. I've been open to sharing my home and my time with a wide range of people because it seems like a social responsibility and I saw you do it many times. The expectations of financial independence and independence in general may not have been explicitly spoken, but I can remember plenty of lessons you created for us. We all had chores and were encouraged to have jobs as teenagers. In the summer, you paid me to do household chores and then expected me to buy my school clothes with the money. I'm sure these lessons were intentional.

Mom: That was the way I grew up; you work for a living, you take care of your family first, then you help those in need.

Accomplishment—as my mother explained it—followed on her persistent effort and investment in her family and the role she embraced as "our" mother. Without actually stating it, prior to this email exchange, her sense of accomplishment was measured by my success (and that of my siblings), which is not something I always attributed to her.

We at times butt heads over otherwise "non-events" and small, inconsequential moments past that I release to wordless places. As I continued our email exchange, naming one of these places and sharing my view of it, I found surprising clarity.

Me: I didn't like the photo because of the story it told, the story about disability that I don't think is true. In a hundred years, when your great-great-great grandchildren view the photo, what will they know about our lives? What will the photo tell them? One might assume that all of your children moved out, got married, had families … and the one using the wheelchair had to stay close, didn't find love, remained dependent. I later thought it might have told my story more accurately if I had been a "group of one." But I think that would have made other people uncomfortable.

One more thing about the photo and the story … it's my story, but it's also a bigger disability story, an image that can be used to make sense of what disability is. It's the story your young self had when you thought you would always have to take care of me. A young mother in the future could see it and believe what you did. The other photo that we took tells a very different story.

Mom: Suz, I would like to tell you that your legacy of independence will be told and retold in our family, down to the great-great-grandchildren. Well, once your nieces and nephews that know you are gone, perhaps those viewing that photo will not know your story. If we could go back in time, you could have been by yourself in that photo. The only thing I can say now is, if there is a next time, we will request a different pose. Love you lots. Even now, it helps to explain things to me; it takes a lifetime to understand.

"But wait!" I want to scream—I don't really want my legacy to be a legacy of independence! I tell my students that independence is a myth that we all rely on others in some way. I have not gotten where I am on my own and they won't get far on their own either—disabled or nondisabled. Even with this realization, though, I am a product of a society that places great value on this perceived independence. My mom has watched me pull away from her many times over. "Would you just let me do it?" I say.

I remember, years ago, I took my mom to the coffee shop I frequented while writing my dissertation. Following me up the long ramp, she started pushing me and sighed, "I don't know how you do this."

I held tight to my wheels and grumbled, "Would you just let me do it? I come here all the time! Why are you always imagining that things are too hard for me to do?"

My niece, who was with us, took a call from my sister and relayed the message that Grandma was "hovering" and Aunt Suz was "crabby." We all laughed then.

Mom explained, "It's just that I see you struggling and want to make it easier."

"I'm not struggling, Mom. That's how I move," I said.

I went on to tell my mom a story about one of my students, a preservice teacher, who saw a young man at the airport using a wheelchair. Upon seeing a woman pushing him, she acknowledged her feelings of discomfort. "She told me, 'Professor, he was about 20 and really good looking but I felt sorry for him. I thought, 'Oh my god, he's *always* gonna have his mother right there'."

Mom nodded, "I get it."

In the past few years, I have noticed a change in my physical strength in that I *do* need a push up that ramp. Likely, as I age, I will learn to embrace more wholly what I teach my students about the myth of independence. While I certainly acknowledge the fictitiousness now, I have yet to let go of the notion that I *must* be as independent as I can be. Independence still feels non-negotiable.

Can I please claim a legacy of better understanding instead? While a family photo may communicate or miscommunicate the nature of our relationships, it does not capture the complexities with which we live. We can all fall victim to the various social mythologies that swirl through families and communities. The mythology of independence has likely contributed to where I am in this world; certainly not a bad place, but quite far from the natural supports of the family I was blessed with. I wonder, *Has my drive for independence led me away from the family togetherness my siblings more frequently enjoy?* More and more, I consider the ways I can contribute to interdependence, giving what I can and gracefully accepting what I need from others. *Would I have better contributed to my family had I stayed living close?*

11.4   Imagining a Life—Separate

Mom: When I learned of your disability, my main concern was to do everything possible for you to have a good life. The concerns I had were for my future as well as yours. I wondered how disabled you would be, and how that would affect me. One of the things I thought, that I am not proud of, was that you would always need care. You have to understand that I was in my late 20s, and quite selfish yet. So for a little while that struck me: "Here is someone I will have to take care of forever." Boy, was I wrong about that. It's almost laughable … if I wasn't so ashamed of those thoughts. I wanted you to be able to walk, to dance, to do everything Donnie and Sandi could.

I cannot deny the power of her influence. Recognizing her love and patience in raising six children, my siblings and I often say we "won the lottery" in getting the mother we have. I see my relationship with her as something different than what my siblings have, as the presence of disability shapes interactions in expected and unexpected ways. As I write this chapter I struggle to avoid judgment. I want instead to focus on what we have made in the four decades of our knowing and loving one another. I wonder, though: "What's our story, Mom? What's different about our relationship, different than your relationships with my sisters and brothers?" I asked her on the phone. She does not hesitate to respond, and of course, begins with the obvious.

"What's different? You live in San Diego. You don't need us!"

She did not mean this in the way some accuse others of not caring. It was a straightforward declaration! "We do so much for everyone here and we don't do anything for you." Yes, my mom exaggerates on this point—that is my first thought. But instead I probe, "Does that have anything to do with disability?"

"No! Of course not" she quickly replied.

In an article I use in my teaching, "Diego's Life Without Her," Ware (2006) describes an interaction she and her disabled adult son have with another family to illustrate how mothers of disabled children can have difficulty imagining their child's life without their immediate presence and support. With this, she offers a piece of her own story and shares that she decided at some point to afford her son the space to have a life without her (to the greatest extent possible), and, yet, she does not divulge the struggle she likely had in coming to this decision and to living with this decision over time. I imagine she and Justin know it best. I imagine their story against my own and wonder.

When I decided to move to California, I did not describe moving away as a means to having a life separate from my mom. Both of my parents tried to convince me not to move and, I think, struggled to imagine how I could live without them. In the way that my mom represents to me a presence and the support of someone who *has to be there*, I thought about the separation from them to be a way to test my own strength and to establish a life that I chose.

When I imagine how my life might be different had I stayed in Kansas, I see that family photo that was staged to place me—the disabled daughter—beside my parents and I imagine the way people would view me, represented as the adult tethered still to her parents. Even if my family gave me the same support they give each other now, I would still be seen as the child my mom would *have to take care of forever. Could I have learned to willingly submit to a life of long term "care" and the erasure of my desires, wants and needs as I have pursued them? Could that have been my life?*

11.5 Resisting Confinement

Mom: The doctors we saw at the MDA clinic were not really much help. In fact, sometimes they did more harm than help. One said, "You can send her to school, but not sure what good it will do." Not his exact words, but you get the picture. That still irritates me. It made me not trust everything doctors say, to this day. Really, for the first three days after finding out, I couldn't think or smile. Then at the dinner table, Donnie or Sandi said something funny and I laughed. From that moment, I made a conscious decision to let laughter in again and look for hope in this situation.

When my parents learned of my diagnosis, my mom drove straight to her parents' house to cry about it. Her dad told her, "Betty, if God wants to take her, you have to let her go." But she did not want to let go. Instead, she picked me up and carried me with her outside and away from such notions. Unvoiced fury formed the very resolve she would eventually summon when she tackled the medical professionals' prognosis.

Doctors were the first to put limits on what she wanted for me. At one point, a doctor told her that she might expect me to live to be about 40.

Me: I remember you told me about Dr. G. saying I would probably live to be 40 and about not being sure what good it would do to send me to school. The school comment didn't bother me much because I always knew I could prove him wrong. For a long time though, I wondered if he might be right about my longevity. I'd like to say this didn't cause me fear, but I remember feeling relief when another doctor told me she didn't think my life expectancy was any different than the average person. I was in my 20s then.

At the time of my diagnosis, my mom had seen few disabled people living outside the confines of the family home, living fully active lives in community with friends. Still, she wanted me to have the kind of life she imagined my siblings could have. Sometimes my siblings pushed for Mom to see my capabilities as greater than my dependencies. When she asked Jay to do something for me that I could do, he would reply, "She has legs, Mom." Neither of us, we came to realize, had useful models to follow.

Building on hope, she dismissed the low expectations of my doctors when she enrolled me in public school. She soon learned that she would have to sometimes fight for my rights to be included in the same school my siblings attended without question.

Mom: When you were to go from kindergarten to first grade, the teacher was unsure of your abilities and most likely unsure of her ability to have you as a student. I remember having to assure her that all you needed was someone else's arm to hold onto when you walked. The physical education teacher was also difficult. We wanted you to be a part of the activities he had planned for the class. His idea of including you was sitting by the wall and watching.

I remember sitting on the sidelines in PE class. As a child, I did not like this, but used it as an extra study hall. Mom recalled encouragement from a school-based physical therapist, parental involvement with others through MDA, and gathering with charismatic prayer groups. With this support, she kept me involved in exercise, social activities, and school.

Me: I try to remember any foresight I had as a child about my adult life, and really, nothing comes to mind. Yes, I said I wanted to be a teacher, but I had no idea what that would look like. Usually, I attribute this to not knowing or seeing disabled adults who had lives that appealed to me. Perhaps I could blame the fear that I might not live long. Or maybe I did have ideas and just don't remember well.

The conscious decision my mom made to "let laughter in and look for hope" allowed me to be optimistic about the future. I learned from her to brush off the negativity that some imagined for me. Her advocacy called into question others' assumptions that my participation was burdensome, and over time, I adopted the ability to critique that mindset.

11.6   Too Few, Too Uninspired

As a young girl, I looked for disabled adults in the community and yet I can recall looking away from the lives of those I did not want to follow. I remember only a few who I could not keep my eyes off of, soaking up the evidence that something good was possible. During doctors' appointments, Mom sometimes asked about what was possible. While she always showed some degree of skepticism with what doctors said, I have often questioned how much she was impacted by the medical model, how much of my existence seemed to be a problem to be solved or a loss to be endured. In our email exchange, I told her about one disabled adult who gave me hope.

> Me: You say you always wanted to be a mother. As a child, I remember seeing a mother at church once. She walked in with a limp and sat a few pews away with her husband and children. That was meaningful to me. I still remember it vividly.

This memory has stuck with me even though I never mentioned it to anyone when it happened. In my community, most women were mothers and I wondered if I might one day be a mother too. I had seen a TV movie once in which disabled women were forcibly sterilized. As a girl, I wondered if there was a secret plot among doctors to assault me this way.

When my sister, nine years younger, was small, I rocked her, fed her, and comforted her when she cried. Mom always called me Mary's second mother. This is the way I learned to mother other people's children, loving my sister and being validated by my mom. I never had the strong desire for motherhood that my mom describes. Was I socialized away from it?

> Mom: My desire for motherhood culminated in having six of the most admired human beings ever. You, of course, are at the top of the list. Who you are and what you have accomplished is mind-boggling. Living with a disability, as you do every day, you inspire others, me included.
>
> The most important thing I learned from you, when you were still a small child, is real love. Suddenly material things were less important to me. My motherly concern for my child took precedence over everything else. Your health and well-being was my concern.
>
> That is unconditional love and I recognized that in me. That is how I grew through adversity.
>
> To answer the original question, doctors did have an effect on me; it was usually a negative one, but my hope in prayer and healing had a much greater effect.

11.7   Measured Steps to Imperfect Truths

After several months of email exchanges in preparation for a draft for my mother to consider, I struggled to see the sense we were making—again, disparate and imperfect. I excerpted the longer text to build this dialogue. Of course, in the process I edited the text into my narrative. Mom would certainly have created another story—her story. And here I find myself interrupting her in a sense, something I admit I have always done when it is not the story I want to be told.

> Me: What you've written here makes me think you still do not believe disabled people have the potential that others have. Why is it mind-boggling and why is it inspiring? You gave me stability and unconditional love. How could I live any other way? You sometimes talk about me as some super human and when in reality, I'm just a woman who was privileged to have loving parents and who has had to fight to get what I want.

> Mom: You find it hard to believe that your incredible ability to accomplish what you have is mind-boggling? I only heard of well-known people with physical disabilities who did extraordinary things. Helen Keller for instance. I did not know too many people with disabilities.

> Me: You didn't when I was a child. You do now!

Helen Keller! Yes, the woman born in 1880 who lived her entire life before mine even began is who she could point to! The scarcity of disabled models during my childhood diminished some when I met older girls at camp, and finally was rectified when, as an adult in another state and a bigger city, I finally found a community of disabled adults. Through this community, I took on a coordinator position with a mentoring program for disabled youth, creating a curriculum and facilitating mentee/mentor events. In this role, I recruited disabled mentors and once again found myself in search of those who could represent the limitless possibilities of living a life, disabled and whole. I told my mom about the wide range of people I met and befriended. I presume her focus had already shifted to a more current interest, the grandchildren she had.

11.8   A Pilgrimage of Loss and Acceptance

When doctors painted a grim future and the local community offered no models, a friend invited my mom to a prayer meeting. That was the beginning of her hope for healing. Understanding that she could not control the outcome of my life, she turned to God, became involved in the charismatic renewal, and began praying for my "complete healing." I became the center of prayer meetings and the reason for traveling to healing services and religious pilgrimages. Believing that I would be healed, my mother taught me to do the things my siblings did, including household chores, family activities, and enrolling in my neighborhood school. It was as if to qualify me for an imagined future and the mandate for full participation.

I started walking when I was four. Although I have no memory of that, I do remember my parents carrying me around a lot. Having given much time to prayer, my parents saw my walking as an answer to their pleas and something to celebrate. Mom kept a journal and gave it to me after I had moved away. I dug it out while working on this project and reading it in my present was provocative on many levels. Although there are sections written about each of my siblings, the majority of her entries focus on me and her relationship with God:

> This was Wednesday, January 17th, 1979, our 9th wedding anniversary ... Donnie and Sandi said, "Mom, come in here. Suzanne is really walking good." She walked so steady and well like she had never done before. Back and forth across the living room, she walked from the davan to the stairs and back again. She was delighted and so were we. We all watched and praised God as she walked ... I'm not sure why He chose or the Blessed Mother chose our anniversary, but since we were so honored, we shall certainly try to honor those days that are special to Our Lord and the Blessed Mother. (Mom's journal, January 1979)

My mom found hope in attending and hosting prayer meetings and in seeing my physical strength grow. I remember being placed in the center of the group as adults put their hands on me to pray. I did not like it, but did not complain. We traveled to neighboring states for healing services at big churches and convention centers. When I started school and got involved in going to MDA camp, there was less time and focus put on prayer meetings, but I know my mom continued to pray and to tell me her hopes that I would be "well."

In the late 1980s, my parents learned about Medjugorje, a small village in the former Yugoslavia where people reported miracles. The miracles, associated with apparitions from the Blessed Mother to six teenagers, were said to include the physical healings of travelers to the site. Even though she had just started a new job and the trip would be expensive, Mom knew she wanted to take me. Because it was so important to her, my dad agreed to make the financial sacrifice.

So we went: my mom, Aunt Mary Catherine, my sister Sandi, and me. At age 14, I recall that I was the youngest on the tour group from the local Catholic diocese. Thousands of pilgrims from around the world flocked to the village. Staying at the home of a family who provided accommodations in guestrooms at their home, we enjoyed breakfast, dinner, and Turkish coffee in the basement. Together, we walked the chalky white roads, visited the church, climbed "the hill" of the first apparitions, prayed rosaries, shopped for souvenirs, and listened to the stories of other travelers. I wondered how disappointed my mom would be if I went home with the same body I arrived with. Years later, she told me that in Medjugorje, she realized she was the one who needed healing. From her journal, I read a sort of detachment in her words:

> For about 10-plus years, I thought you would be physically healed. There were times of answered prayer. There were times I would tell you that you could be a ballerina if you wanted to. Not until Medjugorje did I accept any thoughts of you living with a physical disability.
>
> There in Medjugorje, a man walked into church, holding onto what appeared to be his son. The son looked to be in his early 20s, the man, 60 plus. The younger man did not appear to have any physical disabilities, but mental perhaps, or perhaps sight. The older man very

gently and lovingly guided the younger man. It moved me so, that with many tears, I could tell God, "If that is what you want from me, I will be a loving mother and guide for my daughter." From that day on, I no longer took you to faith healers. Once I said okay to God and stopped my non-stop begging for healing, it was a feeling of relief.

I believe you accepted your life much quicker and faster than I did. Another "ah ha" moment in my life was when I told you, "I don't know if you will ever be well." This was after Medjugorje and by "well," I meant healed. "Either way, I like myself," you told me.

That was the end of the faith healers, thank goodness. Although I have written about my experience in enduring faith-healing efforts (Stolz 2006), reading my mom's perspective stirs emotion for me. She put so much into that search for physical healing and then she let go. Seeing the man leading his disabled son into church, she may as well have been looking in a mirror, accepting her life as my mother, with tears to acknowledge the limits of our own desires and what we can control and what we cannot. Even as a child, I had a sense of the weight this carried for Mom; and, perhaps, that is what made our journey difficult for me. I knew it would take several decades to fully express that the challenge of my life was less about my disability than the systems that attempted to bind me.

Me: I think it was after I went to the National Endowment for the Humanities Summer Institute in Chicago and spent weeks immersed in disability studies that you and I began talking about these things more. Hearing about the changing conversation on disability in the works we read and discussed led me to wonder more about how I came to the critique I had. For the first time I told you how uncomfortable all the faith-healing events were to me. But at the same time I realized that as much as it made me uncomfortable, I believe the hope it gave you benefited me. You raised me as if I'd grow up to do all the things my siblings would do—whether it was in anticipation of a miracle, or not—I never questioned that I belonged.

Mom: I am grateful to the Charismatic Renewal. It gave me hope when I needed it most. It began for me a love of God that has continued to strengthen over the years.

11.9   Feeling an Absence

In the memoir he wrote about his mother, *You Don't Have to Say You Love Me* (Alexie 2017), Sherman Alexie shares tales of his mother's erratic and sometimes abusive behavior, his discoveries about the abuse she survived, and his grief about losing her. In an interview, he describes his overt affection for his own children as "me attempting to fill the absence from my own childhood." He explained that if he could, he would "defy physics, defy time and go back in time and be my mother's parent (National Public Radio 2017)."

Unlike Alexie's desire, filling the absence of my childhood is not a matter of defying physics or parenting my mother. I have never had to question my mom's love for me as he did. I did not feel a lack of affection in my childhood, and yet I have experienced the desire to fill an absence for my mom, a different absence that was not easily named. I have worked to be the teacher to my mom, to reassure her that life with disability is okay. I have become the model of living a life of choice in community, with both struggles and successes.

> Mom: I learned sensitivity about language usage from you. Adults unknowingly, or unwittingly, use words that describe disabilities in a negative way. For instance, I remember my sister, whose daughter was in a severe car accident, describing her as "brain damaged" right in front of her. For years people used words like "crippled" to describe someone who has difficulty walking or someone who uses crutches or a wheelchair. Perhaps this is all they knew to say, saying it without malice, but nonetheless affecting the person. We have a new generation, learning positive ways of describing a disability. That gives me hope for the future. I also had to learn and am still learning.

Growing up in a world where she saw disabled people as "homebound," Mom had to start imagining I could have something different. She was a young mother and could have used models to make sense of what was happening in our lives. It took years to find those who offered help, advice, and information that countered what doctors told her.

> Mom: You, from small on, maybe 8 or 10 yrs old, talked about being a teacher. We encouraged you to be whatever you wanted to be.

11.10   Redefined by Rupture

How do you understand a child whose life is markedly different than your own? Andrew Solomon (2012) names this phenomenon "horizontal identity," when a rupture emerges between the child's life and the lived experience of their parent. Often what follows is a life-long disruption to an otherwise "normal" family structure as it is redefined by rupture. Solomon's work is not necessarily a one-to-one correspondence to that which I describe here, but it comes very close. My mother wanted to understand my experience and support me at every juncture, and as a child, I could not articulate the experience of exclusion that often followed outside the confines of my home. Aside from crying "They're ugly, they're ALL ugly!" about my lack of options for shoes that would fit with metal braces and getting "sassy" about something she asked me, I was often not vocal about how I felt about my disability and the experiences I knew she could not know. In the absence of describing the feeling of an absence of her experience, I knew there were some things I could not tell her. When people said disrespectful things to me about disability or denied me opportunities because of disability, I knew that protecting her from such episodes would protect me from seeing her face crumple tragically. Those were details I saved for conversations with my disabled peers at MDA camp, where my stories evoked knowing laughter or suggestions for how to respond with pride.

On good days, I remember that my mom's experience is different than mine, but while growing up and even more recently, I have not always been patient or graceful. I unrealistically have expected her to have an understanding that is similar to mine. I say I want there to be understanding between us, but to this day, I still filter what I tell her.

After retiring from her job as a histologist at a local clinic, Mom took a job as a paraprofessional working with autistic high school boys. At the time, she knew little about autism, but she committed to learn experientially. Coincidentally, at that time, I worked for a non-profit agency that served Boys and Girls Clubs, YMCAs, and the Department of Defense programs in training youth and childcare workers about supporting disabled children. Mom often told me about the students she came to know and soon realized the value of my suggestions to support her young charges. What I also respected even more was that in witnessing others' unfair treatment of the boys, she volunteered to work with those among them who were the most mistreated by adults.

From a distance, I witnessed her experience with this group of disabled boys as quite different than her experience with a disabled daughter. She did not pray for their healing; she prayed that those around them would treat them with respect. She sat with them on difficult days, chose to be there daily, and without words conveyed her acceptance. Her support was nonetheless unconditional and it mattered.

Over the years, I think I have heard her and she has heard me. She says she always just wanted life to be easier for me. I say the biggest challenges in the lives of my people have not stemmed from impairment, but instead from the ways others have perceived them and their experience. If she had known that earlier, we would have all prayed for something quite different.

In all of this, I see how I have interrupted her story time and time again, the story of what her family would be, the story of what disability would mean, the story of keeping faith. We have both grown through these ruptures. We have gained a deeper understanding of what has been difficult for each other and what we have appreciated. Our differences can be resolved more quickly than ever. Today, we feel good about the story we share. After reading the last draft of this chapter, Mom emailed back, "It's perfect." I sat back and grinned, accustomed to her affirmation, trusting that it truly reflects her perspective.

Although I still find places to interrupt, edit, and clarify, I am relieved and humbled to know that she can call our story *perfect.*

References

Alexie, S. (2017). *You don't have to say you love me: A memoir.* Boston, MA: Little, Brown.

National Public Radio (Producer). (2017, June 20). *Sherman Alexie says he's been 'Indian Du Jour' for a 'very long day [Interview transcript].* Retrieved from https://www.npr.org/templates/transcript/transcript.php?storyId=533653471

Solomon, A. (2012). *Far from the tree: Parents, children, and the search for identity.* New York: Scribner.

Stolz, S. (2006). Physical healing. *Disability Studies Quarterly, 26*(3).

Ware, L. (2006). Diego's life without her. *Equity & Excellence in Education, 39*(2), 124–126.

Part III
Praxis and Pedagogical Intervention

Chapter 12: *Relational Pedagogies of Disability: Cognitive Accessibility in College Classrooms*—Michelle Jarman and Valerie Thompson-Ebanks, University of Wyoming. This chapter engages directly with the critique authored by Margaret Price in *Mad at School* (2011). Price challenged those in higher education to think more critically about addressing mental health accessibility issues in formal and informal academic environments. Specifically, Price suggests that college instructors be mindful of the power dynamics embedded not only in formal assignments, tests, and lectures, but of informal academic environments, in the "kairotic spaces" such as small-group, online, or class discussions; conference meetings between student and faculty; peer-review interactions; and informal gatherings. Drawing upon qualitative interviews with students with learning, cognitive, neurological, and psychiatric disabilities, this chapter engages with specific barriers to participation, as well as strategies for success and insights for greater accessibility in higher education classrooms. Using student voices as a starting point, the authors draw upon universal design principles and disability studies pedagogy to map out relational approaches to teaching and learning.

    Chapter 13: *The Totem Project: Pluralizing Access in the Academic Classroom*—Louise Hickman, Lisa Cartwright, Elizabeth Losh, Monika Sengul-Jones, and Yelena Gluzman, The University of California, San Diego. This chapter considers the initial emergence of what Louise Hickman and her interlocutors coined, "the totem project." The authors recount the evolution of the totem project during a graduate seminar at the University of California, San Diego, a pilot course in the DOCC 2013 (Distributed Online Collaborative Courses), Dialogues on Feminism and Technology, a networked learning experience initiated by the FemTechNet. Totems can be examined not only as a resource through which to understand how "access" might be pluralized across multiple bodies using mobile objects, but also as a relational process that considers both access in the classroom and how this exercise is translated through forums such as the networked course and the FemTechNet coalition.

    Chapter 14: *"I Have to Be Black Before I Am Disabled": Understanding Agency, Positionality, and Recognition in Higher Education*—Lauren Shallish, The College of New Jersey. This chapter outlines a qualitative research study on undergraduate college students who identified as disabled to demonstrate the complex ways in which racism and ableism entwined to extend or deny benefits in a postsecondary setting. At tension in the informants' experiences is both the suppression of personhood and the celebration of it. These testimonies make apparent the racial, linguistic, ethnic, and dis/abled positions that support or deny student agency on a college campus. They also signal the "interconnected and collusive" properties of racism and ableism (Annamma et al. 2013, p. 6). The chapter is not intended to set up a racialized dichotomy about disability-related experiences but rather to explicate the ways race and ability entwine to frame students' agency, positionality, and recognition in higher education settings.

Chapter 15: *Writing, Identity, and the Other: Dare We Do Disability Studies?*— Linda Ware, Independent Scholar. This chapter first appeared in the Journal of Teacher Education.

Chapter 16: *Sharing International Experiences to Develop Inclusion in a German Context: Reflections of an American Inclusive Educator*—David J. Connor, Hunter College. David J. Connor offers the metaphor of "running on the spot" in his example of education's slow embrace of disability studies. Too often, DSE scholars attempt to exert "energy toward movement (of the field), yet find oneself in the same place." The problem is one of a "constant morphing of the educational landscape as it shifts in accordance with changes in laws, governmental priorities, policies at federal/state/local levels, leadership, personnel, research, cultural values, and so on". Connor's tracings over his career as an educator, who sought to maintain a disability studies identity, reveal challenges that many of our colleagues do not encounter in the humanities. This conversation raises issues of inclusive education and its intersection with disability studies—making clear that the educational landscape is stymied by confusion by the aims of disability studies and the sub-topic of disability studies in education.

Chapter 12
Relational Pedagogies of Disability: Cognitive Accessibility in College Classrooms

Michelle Jarman and Valerie Thompson-Ebanks

12.1 Introduction

Students with disabilities are entering colleges and universities in growing numbers. Data collected by the U.S. Department of Education from 2008 to 2012 indicate that 11% of undergraduate students enrolled in two- and four-year postsecondary institutions report having a disability. From the 2008 data, 31% were identified as having learning disabilities, 18% reported diagnoses of attention deficit disorder (ADD) or attention deficit/hyperactivity disorder (ADHD), 15% reported having psychiatric diagnoses, and 2% were on the autism spectrum (Raue and Lewis 2011). This chapter focuses on the unique access needs and experiential insights from a sample of students with disabilities, such as those listed above, specifically with non-apparent conditions to frame a larger discussion about relational pedagogical approaches grounded in critical disability studies. By relational approaches, we refer to teaching strategies designed to enhance a sense of belonging among these students within their larger campus communities.

The unique struggles and barriers to success for students with disabilities in higher education are of great concern in the field of disability studies. Although greater numbers of students with disabilities are entering postsecondary institutions and disability support services offices are now well established within the structure of university life, these students continue to face greater barriers than their nondisabled peers. Research indicates that students with disabilities withdraw from postsecondary education at higher rates than their nondisabled counterparts (Kranke et al. 2013; Wessel et al. 2009); in addition, disabled students have lower graduation rates, ranging from 21 to 34% (Newman et al. 2010) compared to a 58% graduation

M. Jarman · V. Thompson-Ebanks (✉)
University of Wyoming, Laramie, WY, USA
e-mail: mjarman@uwyo.edu; vthomps4@uwyo.edu

© Springer Nature Switzerland AG 2020
L. Ware (ed.), *Critical Readings in Interdisciplinary Disability Studies*, Critical Studies of Education 12, https://doi.org/10.1007/978-3-030-35309-4_12

rate among students without disabilities (U.S. Department of Education, National Center for Education Statistics 2016).

These graduation numbers are compelling, and the situation for students with psychiatric diagnoses is even more complex. In a national study of campus disability services, Mary Collins and Carol Mowbray looked specifically at these students, reporting that "86 [percent] of individuals who have a psychiatric disorder withdraw from college prior to completion of their degree" (2005, p. 304). Further, they found that disability support staff were often uncertain of the most appropriate accommodations or which supports would be most useful to these students. In a qualitative study looking at the support needs of students with psychological disabilities, Stein (2015) found that students benefitted greatly from accommodations provided by disability support services (DSS). In fact, many students in Stein's study not only considered DSS support "necessary" to their academic success, but having support also made them feel less "alone" and more integrated into the campus community (p. 76). However, while disability supports and services on university campuses are becoming crucial to some students' success, many students are unfamiliar with the system, unable to provide necessary documentation, or the supports offered do not directly address unique student needs.

A keyword in providing support for students with disabilities is *access*, but this term is also broad and contextual, so exploring the *meaning* of access is crucial to these efforts. In practice, access usually comes in the form of extended time, quiet testing environments, materials in alternative formats, note-takers, interpreters, captioning services, and audio texts, among other supports, but all of these involve diagnosis, qualification, requests, and granting of services. Tanya Titchkosky, who has written extensively about access in university life, invites a critical engagement with this term in order to better understand how processes and structures of disability access illuminate our perceptions of and relations to each other: "Exploring the meanings of access is, fundamentally, the exploration of the meaning of our lives together—who is together with whom, how, where, when, and why?" She suggests that such questioning allows us to "regard disability as a valuable interpretive space" (Titchkosky 2011, p. 6) that we can return to and reflect upon to better understand relations between people and the spaces and systems they inhabit.

Margaret Price has also critically engaged with the meanings of access, focusing specifically on the complexities of university life for students with mental disabilities. In her groundbreaking book, *Mad at School* (2011), Price argues that the very expectations of academic life are set up to exclude or at least create barriers for many students with mental disabilities. Price uses the term mental disability to be inclusive of anyone with a diagnosis associated with cognitive processes. This umbrella term links together people with psychiatric diagnoses, autism, learning disabilities, brain injury, distress, among other issues. She connects these diverse conditions because, in many ways, they are already discursively linked by their seeming incompatibility with traditional academic ideals of the rational, intellectual, and ordered mind. As Price explains: "I perceive a theoretical and material schism between academic discourse and mental disabilities. In other words, I believe that these two domains, *as conventionally understood*, are not permitted to coexist" (2011, p. 8). Price sees addressing this schism as a necessary project if students, faculty, and staff with mental disabilities are really going to gain a sense of belonging in colleges and universities. In other words, this represents an expansive project of reimagining access—of reimagining academic spaces, expectations, and practices to not only include but to be informed by mental disability. To set the stage for this project, we engage with Price's provocative question: "What transformation would need to occur before those who pursue academic discourse can be 'heard' (which I take to mean 'respected'), not *in spite of* our mental disabilities, but *with* and *through* them?" (2011, p. 8).

Our approach brings together Titchkosky's questions about the relational nature of access with Price's appeal to inform campus culture and classroom pedagogy *through* insights from students with mental disabilities to frame the interviews in the following section. As students describe experiences with access and mental disability, they address disability services, faculty support, classroom dynamics, and personal relationships as elemental in shaping their sense of belonging and *un*belonging in campus life.

12.2 Participant Recruitment and Scope of Study

The eight interviewees discussed here were participants in a larger study designed to better understand student choices about disclosure and use of campus disability support services. Following the University's Institutional Review Board (IRB) approval, an online survey was distributed in 2014 to all undergraduates at a Western U.S. land-grant university. The survey instrument included comprised 14 open-ended short answer questions and gathered demographic data such as gender, age, ethnic/cultural background, hours employed while a student, military status, relationship status, college credits completed, academic major, stop out experience (leaving college for one or more semesters), disability identity, including disclosure to the university's disability services office, and whether or not students used any formal accommodation.

Of the 111 students who completed the online survey, 31 indicated that they have or had a disability during enrollment at the university. A total of 80 students did not report having a disability. At the end of the survey, students had the option to contact the researchers if they were interested in participating in a follow-up face-to-face interview. Ten students with disabilities completed face-to-face interviews, and notably, eight of the ten disclosed mental disabilities, including learning disabilities and psychological disabilities and one student diagnosed with Asperger's syndrome. One of the interviewees had a physical rather than a mental disability, while the other had chronic pain so they are not discussed in detail here. An analysis and discussion of interviews with the nine students who reported having non-apparent disabilities is written up separately (Thompson-Ebanks and Jarman 2018). Data pertinent to the one student with the apparent physical disability was not included to protect the identity of the individual, given that others can easily identify their distinct experiences at the university.

After completing the interviews, we were struck by the prevalence of mental disability, and the insight offered by these students. While one major interest of the interviewers was learning about student use of disability support services, a larger goal was to understand how students negotiated academic spaces and what barriers they had experienced, as well as what supports they accessed or personally put in place to be successful. As disability studies scholars, we have been particularly interested in disability studies pedagogy and universal design as these overlap with student insights. Grounded in student encounters with accessible and inaccessible spaces and contexts, this chapter engages directly with Titchkosky's relational inquiries and with Price's invitation to consider the "transformation" needed to produce a "sense of belonging" for students with mental disabilities within the academic spaces of the university. Using student voices as a starting point, the authors draw upon universal design principles and disability studies pedagogical approaches to map out relational approaches to teaching and learning.

12.3   Discussion of Interviews

12.3.1   Overview of Interviewees

This section introduces the interviewees (with pseudonyms), their self-described disabilities, their experience with stigma, access barriers, or disability support and advocacy, and how these have shaped decisions of disclosure and nondisclosure. As would be expected, disclosure of mental disability is dynamic and contextual, and these interviews capture students in a process of responding to social pressures as well as using their experiences to inform others' understandings. As stated above, all eight of the interviewees self-identify as having some form of non-apparent, mental disability. Notably, five of these identify anxiety and/or depression as the most significant condition they experience. Two female students, Sasha and Dana, describe anxiety directly associated with trauma—Dana's diagnosed PTSD is specifically attributed to military sexual trauma (MST). A male in this group, Michael, associates his anxiety with a congenital heart condition; he describes an emotional spiral as exams loomed—where nerves increased his heart rate, which increased his anxiety, and so on. Another in this group, Veronica, describes anxiety and depression compounded by an undiagnosed (and unsupported) learning disability. Ray, a male international student, struggles with depression, which has been exacerbated by intense familial shame. Of the final three interviewees, two have diagnosed learning disabilities: Joshua has dyslexia and Chris central auditory processing disorder (CAPD) with attention deficit disorder (ADD). The final interviewee, June, identifies as having Asperger's syndrome, and describes struggling at times with the complex social dynamics of academic life.

Half of these students describe seeking academic support from the university disability support services (DSS) office, but notably, four of the five students with anxiety or depression chose not to disclose to receive services. For the most part, students with psychological and emotional issues consider their diagnoses as individualized "problems" or worry that disclosure would lead to professors and peers misunderstanding their disability—or judging them as lazy. By contrast, students with learning disabilities and the student with Asperger's describe actively seeking out support services and offer specific suggestions about improving academic supports. However, even with these contrasts, all of these students are sensitive to misperceptions and stigma, and articulate a desire for family members, peers, and professors to be more knowledgeable, understanding, and accommodating of mental diversity. As discussed in more detail below, these range from wanting families to believe in the realities of a diagnosis to wanting professors to better support their learning needs, individually and in classroom contexts.

12.3.2 Social Context, Stigma, and Fluidity of Disclosure/ Non-disclosure

While none of these students has a background in disability studies, as they articulate personal academic histories, they begin to unpack access as an interpretive space—identifying social barriers as well as experiences with ableism and saneism. Sasha received diagnoses of depression and generalized anxiety her freshman year in college. She struggles with panic attacks, and recounts a history of self-harm, including a suicide attempt connected to family trauma. Sasha has tried to share some of her experience with emotional distress in classroom discussions—when relevant—but has found some peers to be judgmental or invasive. In these situations, she grapples with conflicting impulses: wanting to share but not wanting to risk follow-up social expectations to share MORE. This is especially difficult because invasive questions (even those meant to be compassionate) often trigger emotional distress: "It's just a lot easier for me to avoid triggering feelings by not bringing up the subjects at all." Sara Ahmed's (2010) concept of "inhabitance" is useful in understanding the dynamics of such social encounters. Ahmed explains that the work of inhabitance involves "extending bodies into spaces" (p. 11) in an effort to make these spaces inhabitable. However, social spaces are not neutral, and while Sasha attempts to orient her peers to her experience, their rejection closes down the potential of that exchange. Ahmed explains this in terms of "orientation" and "disorientation": "If orientation is about making the strange familiar through the extension of bodies into space, then disorientation occurs when that extension fails. Or we could say that some spaces extend certain bodies and simply do not leave room for others" (p. 11). In effect, Sasha's attempts to extend her bodymind experience and knowledge into these discussion spaces are met with failure, the result being that she silences herself and her peers lose the opportunity to gain insight—and productive disorientation—from her unfamiliar, yet rich, perspective.

The pressure to silence herself extends to interactions with professors. She fears they will not think mental health is as important as a physical disability, and that they will think of her "as less of a student or less of a hard worker." Sasha attempts to shrug these experiences off as "no big deal," but then immediately corrects herself, admitting, "In reality it is kind of a big deal; it does affect my education." Ironically, even as she knows anxiety and depression impact her ability to fulfill her academic goals, this fact also looms large as "… the biggest reason why I don't really tell instructors." Sasha knows that by not disclosing to instructors, she actively removes herself into spaces of isolation, withdrawing from discussions in which she would like to participate.

Other students describe similar self-imposed silences. Ray, an international student, and Michael, now graduated, also recount concealing their diagnoses. Ray fears peers and professors will pity him if they know about his depression. Based on his family's religion, his mother views his depression—especially his suicide attempt—as sinful, so his family offers little support for therapeutic resources. With distance from his family, Ray now sees one source of his depression as his parents' excessive fighting when he was a child: "The triggers happen sometimes when people fight … like my roommates fight. I have these memories come back to me from when I was a kid." Ray seems to allow himself to feel his emotions when they emerge, but he remains private about them, sharing only with very close friends.

Michael also keeps his mental and physical health conditions to himself. His anxiety, OCD symptoms, heart condition, and migraines were episodic and temporary when he was a student, so he never sought accommodation. Now working full-time, and reconsidering his undergraduate experience, he better understands how disability services might have benefitted him. As a student, migraines most affected his academics and work, but he was uncomfortable telling professors or co-workers about them. He suggests that unless people have had experience with migraines, anxiety, or disability, they often misunderstand the nature of persistent conditions. In his current position, when he misses hours or days at work, he worries that people assume he is "sick all the time when what's really going on is that [he is] dealing with these persistent medical conditions or these persistent sometimes debilitating … disabilities." Michael is acutely aware, from his own experience with disclosure, that everyone brings their own understanding (and lack thereof) to conversations about disability, and he sees education as key to creating more accepting, inclusive environments.

June, diagnosed with Asperger's in elementary school, came to college with years of experience navigating the schooling context and its mechanisms to support learning through Individual Education Plans (IEPs). At the university, June actively uses support services, primarily extended test time, and she usually speaks to professors early in the term to avoid misperceptions about her "quirks." She sees Asperger's is part of her individuality: "[T]here is no … cookie cutter, every person has their own quirks, they have their own eccentricities … people who have [autism] can't always be put … into one box, into one category … it's just really, really individualized."

While June has enjoyed a very supportive family, a strong network of friends, and recognizes that people are "starting to understand" autism, she also describes instances of feeling patronized by classmates, as well as being offended by ableist language, specifically the word "retarded." She explains, "Something that just really, really frustrates me is when people say something like, that's so retarded, or such a retard, and sometimes I just want to say that is such an outdated and really degrading term." Her concerns are not only personal, but are connected to other people with disabilities being misunderstood and mistreated; she wants nondisabled people to be more educated about disability as a valued dimension of human variation.

Both Dana and Veronica describe anxiety related to trauma and share feelings of isolation and stigmatization by classmates and friends. Dana is a non-traditional student in her forties, a veteran, and has PTSD from military sexual trauma (MST). Self-confident and unapologetic about her diagnosis and history, Dana actively uses disability services, discloses her diagnosis to professors to discuss accommodations, and often "comes out" in class about PTSD. Dana describes faculty and university staff as uniformly supportive, but classroom dynamics are often challenging. She thinks classmates "look at [her] weird" because they think she will "go off at any minute." Even more troubling to her is that some traditionally aged, female friends are dismissive of PTSD and MST; her non-combat trauma is brushed off by peers as not being a "big deal," and Dana struggles intensely with this erasure of her emotional pain. Much like Sasha, Dana feels disoriented when she attempts to extend her bodymind experiences into social spaces only to be rejected, misunderstood, or dismissed.

Similarly, Veronica feels judged by other students. She believes peers find her "annoying," especially because she is "hyperactive"; in response, she withdraws socially and isolates herself. She describes struggling all her life with learning— with reading, staying focused, and remembering assignments. Veronica believes she has ADHD, but after going to a psychologist and spending $400, the results were inconclusive. She wants to work with the psychology clinic on campus, but the cost, especially after essentially losing money on an unconfirmed diagnosis, has become prohibitive. Veronica suspects much of her depression and anxiety stem from an undiagnosed learning disability: "I feel like my depression isn't the base symptom I have," she explains. She elaborates to describe her experience:

> […] just not being able to, to focus in life, I mean what makes me exhausted is that I have to put in all this extra time and effort and … it doesn't always pay off and … I can't concentrate, my relationships suffer because of it.

Although Veronica describes her mind as "jumping around all the time," she has little support for her view that she has a learning disability. Not only does the psychologist resist making a diagnosis, her family members dismiss ADHD as a fake condition. Her mother refuses to accept ADHD because she does not like "labels," which causes Veronica to fear doctors may suspect her of "faking" to get medication. This situation of suffering her family's dismissal of her experience, coupled with economic and diagnostic barriers to accessing support, illustrate the exhausting loop of extra labor many students get caught in—labor that exacerbates emotional distress.

The other interviewees with learning disabilities also mention feeling discounted by friends and family members who have challenged the validity of these students' diagnoses. Joshua, an engineering student who uses disability services, admits family members have questioned his diagnosis, suggesting that he just needs to work harder; however, he is unaffected by such comments. Joshua describes having to fight for accommodations in high school, specifically for extra test time and transcription services. He also resisted biased assumptions about his abilities held by educators who did not understand dyslexia. These experiences have engendered strong self-advocacy skills, which he utilizes on campus to access disability services, seek assistance from professors, and pursue the academic goals he sets for himself.

Chris, diagnosed with ADD and CAPD, is also confident and open about his disabilities, even as peers occasionally say "mean and derogatory" things about him and his father and sister openly question the veracity of his diagnoses. Chris admits that his family has never been supportive: "That's going to sound bad, but I've never really had a support system." Chris feels that disclosing his disability is crucial to his success, not only to access key accommodations such as extra time and materials in alternative formats, but, as he explains, "Had I not told some of my professors, they would have thought I might have just been another lazy student that didn't care or didn't want to do things they say." However, while disability supports are essential, Chris echoes other interviewees by stressing that he does "twice as much work as other students." As he further explains, "… not only do I have to sit through a class and take notes, I have to decipher what that teacher says at home as well." Like many students with disabilities, he wants people to understand that while it is difficult, he has "busting butt … to get this done."

A final complication for many of these students is that although they share some experiences of disability, they still experience the complexities of impairment, of pursuing accommodations, and negotiating social and "kairotic" spaces as highly individualized. As Chris succinctly concludes, "I mean it's … my problem … I don't know what people can do." This perception of disability as an individual problem is reinforced by the structures of DSS in university life, but, as Titchkosky (2011) reminds us, these structures of access reveal our relations to disability and to each other. She points out that access is constructed as a goal, an endpoint, but it is better understood as perception—as a process in which we are always already involved:

> As perception, as talk and conduct, as a form of consciousness, access leads us to ask how access can be an interpretive move that puts people into different kinds of relations with their surroundings … Every single instance in life can be regarded as tied to access—that is, to do anything is to have some form of access (p. 13).

From a disability studies perspective, this relational register of access needs to be more visible in academic spaces in ways that support the social extensions students with disabilities make into learning spaces, where peers, faculty, and staff can share the labor of making these environments habitable.

12.3.3 Classroom Dynamics and Interactions with Professors

As these students recount, one of the complexities of achieving fully accessible environments is the wide range of perspectives about mental disability, including persistent stigma and suspicion among faculty, staff, and student peers about the legitimacy of diagnoses and corresponding accommodation requests. We asked interviewees to reflect upon difficulties they have had in classes or with instructors, to tease out specific issues exacerbated by ableist attitudes or unwelcoming classroom environments. One student recounted a professor who publicly "outed" him as having a learning disability and shamed the student for needing more time on exams; however, this incident was uncommon, and the instructor soon left the university. Many faculty members follow disability support guidelines, but nonetheless set a subtle tone of resistance to providing access. Veronica notes that many professors shut down conversation early in the semester by stressing the rigidity of the course requirements: "I mean you can tell because they're the teachers that walk in and they're … like I'm not going to help you work around your stuff, I'm not that kind of teacher, your responsibility is to get this, this is college, blah blah blah … there's no extensions, no matter what." Some instructors give students the "cold shoulder" and others, like the one described here, make it clear they are unwilling to participate in open-ended conversations about accommodations. Some students avoid classes with such professors, but this is not always possible. Other students select classes based upon physical environment, class size, or format. For example, Dana negotiates her PTSD by taking small classes, and actually adjusts her schedule to avoid large lecture halls. Small class environments allow her to better focus on the professor, the course materials, and to participate in discussions.

These examples of rigidity demonstrate the ways academic environments continue to be shaped to exclude non-normative minds. As Margaret Price suggests, "Academic discourse operates not just to omit, but to abhor mental disability—to reject it, to stifle and expel it" (2011, p. 8). Syllabi, course requirements, and classroom dynamics are all part of academic discourse, and faculty members can render these spaces and conventions more disabling by enforcing norms of able-mindedness. On the other hand, instructors who are flexible and committed to inclusive strategies often have overwhelmingly positive effects on students. In fact, in a research review on postsecondary strategies for supporting students with learning disabilities, Orr and Hammig (2009) stress the overarching importance of implementing universal design principles in course design—multiple modalities of presentation, expression, and assessment—but they also underscore that student success is strongly influenced by faculty support. In fact, "instructor behavior was seen as a powerful contributor to, perhaps even determinant of, the quality of [students with disabilities'] experiences in postsecondary education" (p. 193).

These interviewees also underscore how crucial faculty support has been to their success. Several students describe unique connections with professors based upon disability experience. Michael recounts a story of an instructor who shared his own struggles with migraines, an experience that became a meaningful bond between them. Sasha's band director revealed his history with depression, and this openness and support became deeply important to her. Other professors intuitively integrate universal design elements and flexibility into course processes and assignments. Chris describes having many supportive professors—several who have gone "above and beyond." Indeed, it was a professor early in his college career who encouraged Chris to get tested for a learning disability in order to have access to disability supports.

June and Joshua also describe supportive faculty, especially in office hours where they are able to gain additional help with class material and assignments. Sasha and Dana have both asked for flexibility to leave class on occasion in order to manage their anxiety. One of the Sasha's instructors allowed her to leave the room for a while during a lab final to avoid a panic attack. Dana, who actively discloses to advocate for herself, describes her professors as "the best" because they have been very accommodating of her need to move within the classroom in order to navigate the effects of PTSD.

These anecdotes of flexibility, compassion, accommodation, disclosure, and vulnerability often take place in what Margaret Price calls "kairotic space" of the university: "These are the less formal, often unnoticed, areas of academe where knowledge is produced and power is exchanged. A classroom discussion is a kairotic space, as is an individual conference with one's professor" (2011, p. 60). Informal conversations where professors upend power dynamics by disclosing disability to a student, through purposeful rewriting of rigid expectations of bodymind comportment in classroom spaces, and by allowing students to leave or be absent as strategies to support mental health are examples of expanding accessibility in kairotic space. Price encourages college instructors to be mindful of the potential access barriers built into formal assignments, tests, and lectures—where universal design strategies such as note taking, outlines, study aids, and captioning can easily be built in—and can benefit all students. Faculty need to be especially aware of the stressful power dynamics present in everyday, casual academic environments, in the kairotic spaces of small-group conversations, online or class discussions, office hours, peer-review interactions, and even informal academic social gatherings.

From our interviews, classroom discussions emerged as kairotic spaces of particular potential and vulnerability for students with mental disabilities. As discussed above, most students describe instances where they have felt silenced or openly judged, or where they have silenced themselves rather than risk being pitied or misunderstood. Because many instructors—even those who willingly accommodate individual needs—do not publicly call attention to classroom dynamics or the complexity of facilitating accessibility for mental disability, students often do not know what to request or how to ask for accommodations. Several students describe difficulty sitting still or focusing in class due to medications, learning disability, migraines, or emotional distress. In Dana's case, for example, instructors have allowed her to get up and move or excuse herself, but if this level of flexibility were built into the classroom expectations, all students would understand this as part of the collective accessibility, not as something one student has "special" permission to do.

When instructors gloss over accessibility and students feel compelled to be silent about both their needs and their experiential insights related to non-apparent disability, everyone in the class loses the opportunity to learn from each other and to collaboratively create more accessible spaces. Sasha speaks powerfully to this internalized tension, acknowledging that she is often silent about what she calls her "problem."

> I feel like I have missed out on discussions that are … that could be beneficial to not only myself but other people in my class, by avoiding subjects and by keeping quiet … and kind of hidden away, I feel like I might be missing out on a chance to participate at my fullest potential, which is the reason I take classes like those … to get a different perspective and it's hard to get the different perspective when other people don't really know …

Sasha provides a compelling example of the productive disruption mental disability may bring to classrooms; further, if faculty are prepared to facilitate the inclusion of such students' insights, not only do they reinforce a sense of belonging to students with disabilities, but also other students benefit from important perspectives that are too often silenced or ignored. As Price suggests, "Students with mental disabilities may disrupt conventional agendas of participation not out of laziness or malice, nor even rebelliousness, but through sincere efforts to participate in ways that reflect their own abilities and needs" (2011, p. 76). Faculty committed to ongoing engagement in relations and processes of access would be wise to remember, "An accessible classroom neither forecloses emotion nor is overrun by it, but makes constructive and creative space for it" (Price 2011, p. 80).

12.4   Conclusion: Pedagogies of Relation and Care

As students reflect upon what they would ultimately like to see in classrooms from faculty members or in the form of accommodations, a common theme emerges: while individualized supports are crucial and appreciated, students want an overarching shift in environments and attitudes—where diverse learning styles are valued and supported, where mental disabilities are acknowledged and better understood, and where anxiety and emotional distress are validated. While not using the language of universal design, trigger warnings, or kairotic space, these students intuitively understand that these pedagogical approaches would benefit their learning, participation, and sense of belonging.

Universal design models provide dynamic strategies to support more students within classroom contexts, but instructors committed to access *as perception and relation* must also think across diversity categories in the pursuit of inclusive pedagogy, remaining open to the ongoing learning process inherent in making academic spaces accessible to all learners. Kristina Knoll draws from feminist disability studies pedagogy to encourage instructors to take privilege and oppression of all kinds seriously as we work toward enabling pedagogies. While she values universal design principles, Knoll also warns instructors not to use these strategies to construct universalizing ideas of disability. She explains, "The concept of universal design must always be tempered by a commitment to recognize and address unforeseen barriers and needs of individual students" (2009, p. 127). The unique and varied concerns of students with mental disabilities underscore the need for instructors to be flexible and responsive to student accommodations and insights—and to acknowledge and encourage expressions of multiple dimensions of disability experience.

Supporting students with mental disabilities in classroom contexts and welcoming discussions of disability experience along with other expressions of diverse identity may present complications for instructors in terms of facilitating discussion, such as when to encourage more participation and when to interrupt discussion to provide context about power dynamics; however, planning with mental disability in the foreground also invites—even demands—collaborative, participatory engagement with access as a process. Jay Dolmage and Alison Hobgood invite instructors to adopt an orientation of care in pedagogical approaches to disability, not caring *about* or caring *for* disability, but caring *through:* "To care through is not to contain, define, or discipline disability but to provide space for what disability is and, more so, might become" (2015, p. 565). Caring through disability, especially mental disability, also promises the unexpected, the surprising, and new insight from students whose perspectives have too often been marginalized or misunderstood. Relational pedagogies of care invite those perspectives into the formal and informal spaces of the academy, and also engage in the labor of making those spaces habitable.

References

Ahmed, S. (2010). *Queer phenomenology*. New York: Routledge.

Collins, M. E., & Mowbray, C. T. (2005). Higher education and psychiatric disabilities: National survey of campus disability services. *American Journal of Orthopsychiatry, 75*(2), 304–315.

Dolmage, J., & Hobgood, A. (2015). An afterword: Thinking through care. *Pedagogy, 15*(3), 559–567.

Knoll, K. R. (2009). Feminist disability studies pedagogy. *Feminist Teacher, 19*(2), 122–133.

Kranke, D., Jackson, S., Taylor, D., Anderson-Fye, E., & Floersch, J. (2013). College student disclosure of non-apparent disabilities to receive classroom accommodations. *Journal of Postsecondary Education and Disability, 26*(1), 35–51.

Newman, L., Wagner, M., Cameto, R., Knokey, A. M., & Shaver, D. (2010). *Comparisons across time of the outcomes of youth with disabilities up to 4 years after high school: A report of findings from the National Longitudinal Transition Study-2 (NLTS2)*. Menlo Park, CA: SRI International. Retrieved from www.nlts2.org/reports/2010_09/nlts2_report_2010_09_complete.pdf.

Orr, A. C., & Hammig, S. B. (2009). Inclusive postsecondary strategies for teaching students with learning disabilities: A review of the literature. *Learning Disability Quarterly, 32*(3), 181–196.

Price, M. (2011). *Mad at school: Rhetorics of disability and academic life*. Ann Arbor, MI: University of Michigan Press.

Raue, K., & Lewis, L. (2011). *Students with disabilities at degree-granting postsecondary institutions*. Washington, DC: US Department of Education, National Center for Education Statistics. http://nces.ed.gov/pubs2011/2011018.pdf.

Stein, K. F. (2015). DSS and accommodations in higher education: Perceptions of students with psychological disabilities. *Journal of Postsecondary Education and Disability, 27*(2), 60–82.

Thompson-Ebanks, V., & Jarman, M. (2018). Undergraduate students with nonapparent disabilities identify factors that contribute to disclosure decisions. *International Journal of Disability, Development and Education, 65*(3), 286–303.

Titchkosky, T. (2011). *The question of access: Disability, space, meaning.* Toronto, Canada: University of Toronto Press.

U.S. Department of Education, National Center for Education Statistics. (2016). *Digest of education statistics, 2014.* Retrieved from http://nces.ed.gov/pubs2015/2015167.pdf

Wessel, R. D., Jones, J. A., Markle, L., & Westfall, K. (2009). Retention and graduation of students with disabilities: Facilitating student success. *Journal of Postsecondary Education and Disability, 21*(3), 116–125.

Chapter 13
The Totem Project: Pluralizing Access in the Academic Classroom

Louise Hickman, Lisa Cartwright, Elizabeth Losh, Monika Sengul-Jones, and Yelena Gluzman

13.1 Totems

1. Sweet charm packet, printed foil wrapping
2. Post-it Note, pink paper
3. Penknife, metal; Reading: *Meeting the Universe Halfway: Quantum Physics and the Entanglement of Matter and Meaning (Cutting),* Karen Barad (2007)
4. Data Traveler Zip Drive, metal and plastic device; Reading: *Database Aesthetics: Art in the Age of Information Overflow (Electronic Mediations)*, Victoria Vesna (2007)
5. Travel water bottle, glass, plastic, and green rubber
6. Photographic memory card, plastic and metal
7. Nesting bird sugar bowl, ceramic
8. Juggling ball, foam and laminated fabric; Reading: *Critical Play: Radical Game Design*, Mary Flanagan (2013)

L. Hickman (✉) · M. Sengul-Jones
Department of Communication, University of California San Diego, La Jolla, CA, USA
e-mail: lizlosh@wm.edu; mmjones@uw.edu

L. Cartwright (✉)
Visual Arts, Communication and Science Student, University of California, San Diego,
La Jolla, CA, USA
e-mail: lisac@ucsd.edu

E. Losh
William & Mary, Williamsburg, VA, USA
e-mail: emlosh@wm.edu

Y. Gluzman (✉)
Department of Communication UCSD Vesna, La Jolla, CA, USA
e-mail: egluzman@ucsd.edu

© Springer Nature Switzerland AG 2020
L. Ware (ed.), *Critical Readings in Interdisciplinary Disability Studies*, Critical
Studies of Education 12, https://doi.org/10.1007/978-3-030-35309-4_13

13.2   Introduction

Objects as communicative devices have been compulsory among many individuals who are deafblind. Within such communities, deafblind individuals utilize a "talking stick" to orientate corporeal relations that are defined through spatial organization. The talking stick guides individuals toward mutual proximity—one individual orients to the other by occupying each end of the talking stick. This chapter introduces an object called the totem that functions, like the talking stick, to mediate conversation. Whereas the talking stick mediates conversation among two people, the totem is designed to facilitate group conversation.

The *Totem*, then, is the name given by Louise Hickman to any tactile object at hand—a ball, a penknife, or a soft toy, as demonstrated in the list above—that has been introduced into a graduate seminar to resist normative time and re-situate the process of turn-taking in an academic space, where access-oriented services such as in-class captioning do not correlate with real-time conversation. As a material response to a temporal problem, the totem is designed to slow down time. Requiring participants to exchange a totem before they speak inserts moments of pause between conversational turn-taking and, therefore, expands the temporal window of access by enabling the CART (Communication Access Real-time Translation) operator to complete the previous speaker's statement. This type of accommodation is specific to the USA, and is designed partly in response to the Americans with Disabilities Act (ADA).

This chapter considers the initial emergence of what Louise Hickman and her interlocutors coined as "the Totem Project" during a graduate seminar at the University of California, San Diego, which was among a few pilot courses in the USA for DOCC 2013 (Distributed Online Collaborative Courses), Dialogues on Feminism and Technology, a networked learning experience initiated by the FemTechNet. Totems can be examined not only as a resource through which to understand how "access" might be pluralized across multiple bodies using mobile objects, but also as a relational process that considers both access in the classroom and how this exercise is translated through forums such as the networked course and the FemTechNet.

13.3   The Beginnings

In Spring 2012 a group of about a dozen feminist media and technology scholars, activists, and artists met at USC to discuss feminism and technology practice, scholarship, and teaching. The meeting was convened by Anne Balsamo (then of USC) and Alexandra Juhasz (then of Pitzer College). Balsamo, a renowned scholar of feminist communication and technology theory and digital designer, had launched a dialog project with Juhasz, a renowned scholar of video and social media activism and a media producer, around feminist media practice and theory. Each brought to the table for dialog and planning people from their respective networks of feminist technology scholarship and activism.

This was the year that many universities and mainstream media were discussing and promoting the MOOC (Massive Open Online Course), which many feminist scholars considered to be a patriarchal reaction to new practices in the academy. There was lightning energy, and the idea was launched to expand the network around the shared objective of teaching a distributed online course that would foreground feminist method and feminist content around technology, media and digital production, and theory. Balsamo introduced the concept of the DOCC (its principles are described below) as an alternative to the MOOC (of which a critique is offered below). Balsamo and Juhasz headed up the FemTechNet initiative for the ensuing year. Lisa Cartwright and Elizabeth Losh, both at UC San Diego, collaborated as instructors offering one of the three pilot courses in Spring 2013. Their UC San Diego course was offered at the graduate level through the Department of Communication and drew together 15 graduate students from programs including science studies, studio art, and literature. The decision was made prior to the first class meeting to forego the standard approach of teaching through standard methods and offering accommodation for individual students as needed. The instructors chose instead to adopt a seminar format that would take what might be called "accommodation" and make it the general method of instruction and communication for the entire seminar. The infrastructures of the classroom became a matter for explicit discussion in what Star and Bowker have called "infrastructural inversion" (Bower and Leigh Star 1999, p. 34).

Cartwright and Losh consulted with Louise Hickman, a scholar of communication and disability and a future member of the class in planning, to consider best practices. It was decided that the course would operate using two methods around which Hickman had done initial classroom testing and design work. The first was to use the totem, introduced above, and described at length below. The second was to decelerate the pace of engagement with texts, so that the class could delve more deeply and systematically into readings and discussion.

13.4 Authors' Discussion

13.4.1 Louise

The Totem Project developed as a direct response to my own personal experience as a deaf person with visual impairments in a PhD program in Southern California, and someone who is a non-ASL (American Sign Language) user. In order to facilitate academic access, I was provided with real-time captioning CART (Communication Access Real-time Translation) to transcribe classroom speech into text on a screen. The transfer of speech to text has certain limitations that are important to note. The CART operator types using a stenotype keyboard that operates at a different speed than that of the words spoken in the room. The time between the speaker and the typed speech differs, often significantly. The seamless interactions between speakers around the seminar table presume the ability to hear the subtle, culturally embedded pauses in the space between a speaker's comments, and such practices assume that tacit knowledge is similarly transferred through real-time captioning. Further, in this form of tacit knowledge, the textures of language and personas of individual speakers are reduced to their categorical role in the classroom. Emotions that are present in everyday speech are dropped from real-time captions. Moreover, the highly technical, specialized, and often-abstracted language used in different academic disciplines can vary sharply from one to another. The stenograph operator is often unfamiliar with the esoteric language produced in the classroom. High abstraction translates to phonetic mishaps, and therefore knowledge production and exchange within the classroom frequently begins to unravel. Sometimes, these moments are translated as "[inaudible] [inaudible] [inaudible]," or replaced with long dashes, "——." These abstractions are coupled with the production of speaker anonymity, since the yellow text on the royal blue background identifies the PROFESSOR, while multiple speaking STUDENT(s) share a singular identity. In this way, the names of speakers are omitted and replaced by standardized classroom roles. Here, the Totem Project was designed to offer a material response to a temporal problem that exists in the graduate seminar: namely, that the in-class captioning service does not correlate with real-time speech.

To negotiate some of these conditions, I proposed to introduce to the classroom the totem, an object that could disambiguate the subtle textures of classroom speech, in coordination with CART captioning and my directed attention. Whereas the talking stick has ends or sides and is meant to be touched by two people, the totem is meant to be held by the one speaker, then handed off or tossed to the next speaker. Large enough to be tracked by someone with low vision, the totem is small enough to be handled and used gesturally. The totem may be any item ready at hand that can be drafted into the exchange. In this regard it is somewhat more flexible, mobile, and malleable than the talking stick.

Ironically, when the idea of the talking stick was first introduced to me, and even now, I hear both "totem" and "token"; the phonetic sounds each of these words make, when spoken, are not easily distinguishable from each other. Due to these slippages in sound, practices of naming this device move interchangeably between the two terms, and the conditions that necessitate the device also mark its surface. This effect does not exist for me alone. Since token and totem are exposed to situational appropriation, both the discussion content and peer members shape the naming of the device which is passed among seminar participants. The two terms operate at opposite ends of the spectrum: the device is both situated as a capitalist token, a tangible object with value to be exchanged for goods. Alternatively, the totem gestures towards a spiritual object that is connected to ideas of kinship. In fact, the seeming opposition between these terms evaporates, as the token/totem finds value in its ability to coordinate, and in doing so, creates temporal kinship.

As a pedagogical intervention, the totem seeks to redefine educational access through a dynamic model that accounts for a specific type of sociality, one that binds learning with a unique form of physical interaction with the totem. The materiality of the totems has been central to how subjects relate to one another; experimentation with different sized and textured objects has oriented a range of different interactions and encounters within the space of the seminar.

13.4.2   Lisa

By introducing Louise's practice of using a totem, we could be said to have introduced an accommodation to the classroom. But it was an accommodation for all of us, and not just for Louise. This is a key idea that inverts the common belief that it is just for the "one" disabled person who has so inconvenienced us with their presence. The totem facilitated something that classrooms often need, which is a mechanism to distribute turn-taking and slow down the rush of exchange. In this sense, it could also be said that we introduced universal design. But the group expressly did not embrace the concept of universal design for learning (UDL), or imagine ourselves to be making an "accommodation." We were cognizant that universal design (a term introduced to US practice in Mace 1985) had undergone important critiques, notably for its focus on individual "consumers" or "clients." Our aims were aligned with the ideas of Aimi Haimraie, who has proposed that we "conceive UD as a project of collective access and social sustainability, rather than as a strategy targeted toward individual consumers and marketability" (Hamraie 2013, np). But what was the "collective" and what is it that we were making more accessible? The totems we used worked for our group, and they changed the ways we each accessed one another's words, but I would not presume that the ways in which we used the totem are necessarily generalizable (universal) or that communication became more "accessible" to all. In some ways the totem introduced useful impediments to communication. It was at times, and in interesting and productive ways, frustrating. The totem had a personality of its own at times, intruding on the speaker's point or interfering in the "smooth flow" of conversation, sometimes in hilarious ways. On more than occasion, a speaker would stop mid-sentence, an idea half-formed, look askance at the token as if to say "what do I really mean?" smile, and then either reformulate the idea, or pass the token along to let somebody else finish the thought. If this was "accommodation," what did it accommodate? I think the token at time facilitated breakdown and interruption, which was incredibly useful and productive, given that one of our goals was to practice a distributed development of ideas, and not to facilitate something like "improved" binary teaching and learning.

In class, we handled the totem with trepidation and affection, not as a transparent medium or user-friendly interface that made everything oh so accessible, but as a useful and always unruly agent. Through our totem, we were all in dialog not only with one another, but also with the totem itself, the agency of which was neither smooth and facilitative nor malleable in our hands. As we handed off the right to speak, or held it in our hands just a bit more, the totem itself became a charged subject. The totem was changeable and always interesting. But here we should say more about what it was and how we handled it.

13.4.3 Monika

Yes, each class, someone would volunteer a totem. Memorable totems include a Swiss Army knife, a ball, a Girl Scout badge, and a pendant. Totem volunteers would tell the story of their object. The pendant, for instance, was a gift from the course participant's former lover. And each totem introduced different dynamics of integration within the seminar space. A ball is quite playful, and lent itself to being caressed and tossed gleefully, while the pocketknife elicited commentary about cutting: When you are facilitating classroom conversation, do not hurt yourself. The material and cultural constraints that informed how each object was experienced meant that each experience speaking using a totem was always different. At times, depending on the topic and the totem, no one would forget to use the totem. But there were instances when, in the heat of discussing the rich menu of feminist texts and topics during a seminar, someone would forget to use the totem and interrupt, interject, or just not pass it along. Why did totem use in these moments become difficult? We did not always know at the time. Other participants in the course would correct each other when lapses happened—passing the totem after the fact, or waiting to speak once again. And once reminded, the participants who had momentarily failed at the project—such as I did a number of times—may have blushed. While it may have felt awkward to break from the logic of typically flowing seminar conversation and use a totem, it was more awkward, and slightly embarrassing for both the speaker and the audience, when you failed to do so.

But the awkwardness of the project, and the embarrassment of failing, perfectly encapsulates how the project pushes back against the tenets of universal design. Totems do not perfectly resolve tensions that arise when an in-class captioning service does not correlate with real-time speech. Moreover, each encounter between the members of this class, a material object, and a set of texts and ideas introduces different anxieties and excitements. Awkwardness is a given. And more crucially, awkwardness illustrates beautifully the intersections between the embodied experience of slowing time with the theories of feminism we were reading and discussing in the seminar. Imagine summarizing and analyzing the political hopefulness of un-doing the liberal subject that undergirds many a feminist theory, as we did while reading Jack Halberstam's (2011) work on "shadow feminism," while un-doing the liberal subject assumed to be the classroom student through using totems. What does feminism look like when remaining silent, unraveling, and refusing are the basis of the subject?—the non-liberal subject is the starting point for action. "Can we find feminist frameworks capable of recognizing the political project articulated in the form of refusal?" (Halberstam 2011, p. 126). Translate this question to the classroom: What does pedagogy look like when refusal is the starting point for action?

The course materials enriched how we, as students in the thick of intellectual dialogs on feminism and technology, might connect feminism to disability studies. But such connections were made by experiencing the discomfort of questioning at the level of the body. The Totem Project was a refusal, and a deep disruption of time, that organically lent itself to critique of the MOOC (that our DOCC itself was a response to) and for connecting the theory of access to feminist theories. Sarah Pink's (2009) work on sensory ethnography (which was among the rich reading list of recommended readings) also served as instructional texts for how we might make sense of our seminar experience. Every discussion was punctuated by little reveals of the normativity of seminar conversational pacing; the pauses, the exchanged glances, the tones.

13.4.4 Liz

As an instructional technology, the totem exerted its agency upon the facilitators of the class as well, who similarly fumbled with its use, particularly in the context of attempting to demonstrate team-teaching ideals and the supposed interoperability of our pedagogy. The urge to finish a partner's sentence, improvise with the board to develop an emergent idea, or move dramatically around the classroom to demonstrate a concept might have been techniques in an instructional repertoire of bodily engagement, but these tacit practices now needed to be consciously synched with other people. As instructors, we became woefully aware that too often even our own classroom technologies might be merely treated as neutral forms of amplification for a message or as a means to boost a signal rather than actants in their own right.

In the rhetorical tradition in which I was trained, such totems were often presented as magnifying the speaker's verbal appeals to an audience with a visual signifier. Conventional emblems were to be brandished in a relatively noiseless channel of unidirectional one-to-many communication, as in the case of a classical orator holding up the shield of a fallen comrade in a speech or George W. Bush grasping the badge of an emergency first responder in a presidential address after the September 11th attacks. In contrast to these signifiers of emphasis that seem to punctuate syntax in an orderly and predictable way, totems often had other possible purposes: to bounce, to cut, to store memory.

13.4.5 Yelena

The generative awkwardness of handling and handing over totems was inflected by the awkwardness of CART captions. Picture it: We were in a university classroom, set up seminar-style with students and faculty oriented towards each other around a table. One of the members of the class, who was neither student nor faculty, was the CART provider, or "captioner," officially tasked with producing a real-time transcript to facilitate the participation of a deaf student. She was and was not at the table, since her stenograph machine was mounted on a stand and placed just in front of, and tucked under, the seminar table. The few inches that displaced her from the table marked her particular relation to the proceedings of the class: on the one hand, she labored to maintain an exquisite proximity to the ongoing classroom interactions, and at the same time, her gaze, her spatial relationship to the table, and her silence stressed her non-involvement in these interactions.

In class, we were talking about the histories of invisible labor and women's work, especially women working as "computers," secretaries, and (*yipes*) stenographers. Awkward, since we engaged in this talking while collectively doing what we could to background the presence of the captioner. I do not mean to imply that the captioner in this room is a modern-day version of the de-skilled, de-valued secretarial work that characterized women's stenographic work until the 1970s; indeed, CART providers are highly skilled and take great pride in their ability to do this difficult work. Further, their non-participation and relative invisibility allows them the space and focus to do that work, and to keep up with the emerging bursts of talk and interactions.

Still, awkward. Precisely because CART, as a service that is meant to "create access" to a compulsory normative participation, foregrounds the individual "needing accommodations" and presumes that the event in which accommodations are given is, and should remain, unchanged. This insistence on the failure of individual capacities, I think, is what made looking at the captioner so awkward, impolite, and unwarranted.

The totems had some very straightforward effects on captioning, as Louise explained early on: passing totems created pauses and allowed the captioner to catch up; it created markers to visually identify a speaker. But most interesting, it seemed to me, was the way in which the task of coupling your speech to the grasp of an object respecified the work of the captioner. Without calling her out, or dragging her in, the movement of totems extended and distributed the ongoing work of the captioner, as well as destabilizing the idea of who needed these accommodations, and why. In passing and fumbling totems, we ourselves performed a visual-haptic transcript that supported (and maybe also challenged?) the work of the captioner. At the same time, allowing these objects, so loaded with meaning, to affect our feeling-thinking-speaking on the fly suggested the possibility that the event—the classroom discussion—was itself being constituted by multiple sorts of engagements and participations. Ironically, the totems became less about creating access to a singular, meaningful event, and more about exploring the ways in which meanings could layer to circumscribe and de-center the event.

13.4.6   *Louise*

Situating classroom discussion as a meaningful event through the inclusion of totems, in the way that Yelena previously described as "destabilizing," can de-center how sociality is organized in educational spaces. The informal structure of this approach poses an interesting dilemma for the practice of self-disclosure, or understanding the ways in which privacy is perceived and enacted in these spaces. Even as these terms (disclosure and privacy) are deployed in this space, I will treat them as synonymous to further complicate the process of how peers and professors facilitate accommodation, and how the CART operator might gain access to this discussion. Earlier I have disclosed my deafness to situate how the Totem Project came about, but I have not previously referred to the relationship this hearing impairment has to my (visible) disability. The hesitation of disclosure in this forum has been largely shaped by how disability and deafness are translated into their own scholarly disciplines. For Deaf scholars and activists, self-disclosure is part of organizing an orientation towards a D/deaf culture that is structured around language. This accounts for a social network of encounters that require self-disclosure to foreground "deaf selves," thus allowing for a type of "deaf sociality" (Friedner 2015). For Disability Studies scholars and activists, the conversation around self-disclosure is different, and one that is often fraught and contested (Kerschbaum 2014; O'Toole 2013). In academic spaces, for example, nondisclosure of disability is preferred, but activists like Corbett O'Toole often stress the importance of positioning oneself in relation to the lived experience of disability (2013). Disclosure is therefore situated by one location in relation to an individual's own activism and scholarly commitment, but the repeated performance of disclosure in the classroom offers us another location from which to think this through. As Stephanie Kerschbaum expands further: "Many of these disclosures reveal their authors' consciousness of audience expectations as well as anticipated reactions to utterances, claims, and gestures. These texts also emphasize the decision-making behind self-representation in these encounters, most often telling stories in which the writer has a preferred means of managing a situation or context" (2014, p. 58). How the totems become entangled in these utterances, claims, and gestures have been marked by the awkwardness mentioned by both Monika and Yelena, and indeed the totems themselves are also bound by the risk of disclosure. As these totems expand the ways that access is distributed across multiple bodies as a form of technology, the risk of disclosure cannot be conflated with the embodiment of these objects; rather, this exchange sets up an interplay between the individual who is speaking, whoever is handling the object, and how these objects are cared for, while it simultaneously suspends the question of disclosure.

13.4.7   Lisa

As for the risk of disclosure, for me the further question is, disclose what? The captioner "discloses" who is being facilitated in the room in the narrow sense of accommodation. There is the tacit "I'm with her" that comes from the seating arrangement and the close work that happens there. The totem moves around—the iconic thing that marks the fact an accommodation is happening. Someone entering the room mid-class and following the totem probably would not be able to tell who was being accommodated. The totem discloses accommodation as always distributed. When there is just a captioner, the speaker can be lazy and does not have to think too much, because the whole idea is for the captioner and the person for whom the captioner is working to do the work to keep up. With the totem, what gets disclosed is the negotiation everybody in the room has to make to take turns, listen, speak, and be heard. The totem distributes the site and human subjects of accommodation, and it also flags accommodation as a performance that involves work and reflexive thoughtfulness and one's activity as a speaker. Using the totem, I became hyper-aware of how much of speech is in fact visual and spatial, involving gesture and gaze direction. Watching the totem move around the room and seeing people, including myself, struggle with it made visible something that is always true about accommodation—it is always a distributed process, even if we mask the contributions of "nondisabled" individuals when we adopt practices that put the onus on the "disabled" person to manage the process.

13.4.8 Louise

The distribution of accommodation as brought up by this project involves the potential undoing of an autonomous understanding of access, but I do not want to simply translate this as a move towards a crippling of interdependence. Rather, I want to draw on this project's experimentation with a crip form of sociality, which entangles orientation within self-disclosure or nondisclosure through multiple modes of access. The voluntary contribution of the totem, as Mia Mingus might claim, is an example of the "collective access" that blurs the boundaries to formal curation of access in the classroom, and also considers, as Mingus writes: "[how] we would also think about social time and what social spaces were accessible and how we would make sure no one was isolated or left out" (Mingus 2010, np). The curation of these objects is a project that supports a distributed effort and an ethics of care; these totems are garnered from homes, rooted out from personal belongings, or appropriated from nearby offices, illustrating a phenomenological approach to the collective effort of distributed care. In the way that these objects have come together to collectively curate access, they also act within a form of perceived access that is often shaped and translated by peers, and are thus shaped by their own expectations within the university. If these objects are to mediate sociality, it is also useful to consider the totems' place within a contact zone of subjectivity, to reveal the inherent awkwardness demonstrating that these totems are not part of everyday vernacular, and lack tacit fluency in the seminar space. Again, the entanglement of utterances, gestures, and awkward exchanges actually begins to transform how these contact zones might disrupt the neat configuration of assimilation; the totem's transitions are not smooth, at times risky, and largely not welcomed. How totems experimentally move through pedagogical spaces indexes problems around the temporal structure of the university system at large. Can the Totem Project question the boundaries of assimilation predicated on normative contributions of listening and speaking (as seen through compulsory able-bodiedness) and the boundaries of how we think about disability (compulsory able-mindedness) (McRuer 2006; Kafer 2013)? Regarding Monika's call to situate refusal as "the starting point for action," I want to expand on this not simply as equating refusal with a way to deconstruct compulsory participation in the classroom, but rather by imagining how *touch* as a contact zone of refusal is reshaped by individual subjectivities, or how the participants directly care for these objects to enact their perception of access. The expression of awkwardness is an awakening to an alternative way of knowing, constantly redirected to (real-time) embodiment, while bringing attention to the problematic limits of accommodations as prescribed by the ADA. The totems find themselves oscillating between mediating refusal, and producing new ways of knowing that undermine sensory exclusion in the classroom. A situated orientation towards crip/queer ways of knowing, or in this case the touch of failure, as noted by David Mitchell, Sharon Snyder, and Linda Ware, highlights a need for a curricular of cripistemologies, which as they write: "undertake[s] pedagogical practices suppressed (or, at least, devalued) by normative neoliberal educational contexts" (Mitchell et al. 2014, p. 307). The notion of a crip/queer art of failure (also explored by an assigned text during the graduate meetings) provides the class with the theoretical grounding required to engage with the totem, while simultaneously following the cues from Mitchell, Snyder, and Ware when they write: "an alternative ethical mapping of non-normative living coordinates privilege interdependency over liberal concepts of the autonomous subject" (Mitchell et al. 2014, p. 301). If we recognize these totems as opening up a dialog between the rejection of inclusion (under the neoliberal umbrella of equality and diversity) and embracing failure as the potential redressing of pedagogical space, the totem becomes an artifact of crip culture, and one that celebrates the failure to become normate (Mitchell et al. 2014).

13.4.9 Yelena

One of the great successes of the totem-mediated seminar in which I took part was the fact that, under the guidance and example of the instructors, the totem very quickly became unmoored from a strict role of providing access. These objects were present to touch, throw, slide across the long table, to place into an outstretched hand that waited impatiently for the opportunity to speak. We took our cues from the objects, both temporally and also emotionally and semiotically, since these were not neutral objects but real things that carried meaning, and thus could assist or resist the unfolding articulation of a comment or question in the seminar space. The totems did not point to Louise, but to the dynamic material and semiotic spaces between all of us. I think this has to do with the shift towards explicit intersubjectivity Louise wrote about earlier. The totems cut through the room like vectors. They were expressive media. They allowed for a range of movement, gesture, and coordination that is typically impossible in a seminar classroom. I remember throwing a rubber ball in the air to punctuate something I said. I remember hugging a plush Totoro doll while trying to find the right words. I remember putting a flash drive on a keychain into the hand of the student next to me, and the instant of intense care we took in not dropping it. Something about all this created opportunities for thinking together that felt very different from a standard seminar.

13.4.10 Louise

Thus far I have reflected on the totems as a constructive surface from which to mediate subjectivity through touch; now I will bracket this discussion to consider how the totems give visibility to language in the "hearing" classroom and how access enacted through these complex orientations shared between speakers, the totems, and the operator of the CART machine is also enabled by embodied forms of discourse. In Leanna Hunter's *Embodied Classroom: Deaf Gain in Multimodal Composition and Digital Studies*, which draws on the d/Deaf cultural narrative of "visual metaphors" and "embodied discourse" as ways to inform new practices of learning in a hearing classroom (Hunter 2015, np), the embodied classroom provides an opportunity to extend the reading of cripistemological curricular to include aspects of Deaf Studies, particularly the ways in which this discipline can build on new epistemologies through "hearing ways of knowing" (as quoted in Hunter 2015, np, from Bauman and Murray 2013). The curation of affective encounters encouraged by the Totem Project shares a likeness with Hunter's tracking of different ways of knowing, to reveal how embodied actions are equally important as the uses of speech in the classroom. The adopted totem of the penknife, for instance, induced affective encounters for those who chose to speak while handling this sharp object. In this instance the totem invited speakers to handle the object with care, engaging participants to negotiate with their neighbors, or even to cross the room to ensure safe passage of the fragile object, while conversely ball-shaped totems were often flipped from hand to hand, slid across the table, or thrown across the room. To situate these objects as props that might belong to Hunter's theater of learning allows us to transform the classroom into a space of embodied interface that includes prioritizing the use of nonverbal communication (facial expression, body language) alongside analogue technology (totems) and linguistic technologies (social media and online learning). Even as these totems were found to guide discussion in productive ways, I argue that the use of everyday objects also functions to structure embodied discourse; as Deaf Studies scholars have shown, this places value on a "highly visual, spatial, and kinetic structure of thought and language" (Hunter 2015, np). In social settings, the conceptual design of the Totem Project can also be reassembled for use at the dinner table by conceptualizing the forks that direct food to one's mouth as totems that serve to either punctuate speech or discipline conversational turn-taking around the table. Such embodied practices might be particularly noted by the lip reader at the table; here, consuming food as an event is marked with the notations of sociality and loss. In the classroom, however, Hunter's advocacy of student-centered pedagogy builds on the concept of multimodal composition to include human technologies, thus reconfiguring the roles and privileges of compulsory participation through speaking and listening. Nonverbal communication, as shaped by deaf culture, gives insight into a classroom shaped by "indefinite articulation" (Hunter 2015, np). The question might be asked whether or not it is still possible to integrate these embodied articulations into the future of educational space as it diversifies and diffuses. With the emergence of MOOC (Massive Open Online Courses), we encounter a learning environment that is predominantly determined not by nonverbal cues but by verbal language only, limiting and de-emphasizing the expressiveness of embodied discourse. In part, then, the Totem Project in its current incarnation gestures towards the importance of using our own bodies as the most rudimentary forms of technology (through face-to-face pedagogy) to co-produce knowledge in the classroom. The collective practice at the core of this project not only attempts to situate bodies and objects as forms of potential technology, but draws attention to the grammar of access as it is understood and pluralized across different experiences of subjectivity.

13.5 Conclusion

As a way to understand how access might be a collective and collaborative effort, the Totem Project reveals that accommodation and access are always distributed in some way, whether that is through forms of familiar technology, human labor, or a composite of the two. The totems themselves therefore serve as representative objects of an active infrastructure that is always laboring to enable access, tactile reminders of the often invisible structures and processes through which access is distributed. The collaborative exchange at the center of the Totem Project parallels the writing process of this chapter, in which the exchange of citations, insertion of new text, and the editing process were made explicit to each contributor through tracked changes. By illuminating the process of access as a distributed process, we might reflect on the implicit labor provided by the CART operator and their technology, particularly the complex commitment to ensuring that their own system is streamlined to meet the demands of the esoteric language spoken in the classroom. Yet, how this labor is marginalized and compartmentalized in the mainstream classroom points to the problems of ADA mandates to support "disabled or d/Deaf client" needs without considering how access might move beyond simple participation. The design of the Totem Project is not only a resource to understand how "access" is pluralized across multiple bodies using mobile technologies, but also as a relational project to extend our conception of access beyond the boundaries of ADA determination in the classroom.

References

Barad, K. (2007). *Meeting the universe halfway: Quantum physics and the entanglement of matter and meaning*. Durham, NC: Duke University Press.
Bauman, H.-D. L., & Murray, J. J. (2013). Deaf studies in the 21st century: "Deaf-Gain" and the future of human diversity. *The Disability Studies Reader*, 246–260.
Bower, G. C., & Leigh Star, S. (1999). *Sorting things out: Classification and its consequences*. Cambridge, MA: MIT Press.
Flanagan, M. (2013). *Critical play: Radical game design*. Cambridge, MA: MIT Press.
Friedner, M. I. (2015). *Valuing deaf worlds in urban India*. New Brunswick, NJ: Rutgers University Press.

Halberstam, J. (2011). *The queer art of failure*. Durham, NC: Duke University Press.

Hamraie, A. (2013). Designing collective access: A feminist disability theory of universal design. *Disability Studies Quarterly*, 33(4). Retrieved February 26, 2016, from http://dsq-sds.org/article/view/3871/3411

Hunter, L. (2015). The embodied classroom: Deaf gain in multimodal composition and digital studies. *The Journal of Interactive Technology and Pedagogy*, 8. Retrieved February 26, 2016.

Kafer, A. (2013). *Feminist, queer, crip*. Bloomington, IN: Indiana University Press.

Kerschbaum, S. L. (2014). *Toward a new rhetoric of difference*. Urbana, IL: National Council of Teachers of English.

Mace, R. (1985). *Universal design: Barrier free environments for everyone*. Los Angeles, CA: Designerswest.

McRuer, R. (2006). *Crip theory: Cultural signs of queerness and disability*. New York: NYU Press.

Mingus, M. (2010). *Reflections from Detroit: Reflections on an opening: Disability justice and creating collective access in Detroit*. INCITE Blog. Retrieved May 6, 2016 from https://incite-national.org/category/reflections-from-detroit-reflections-on-an-opening-disability/

Mitchell, D., Snyder, S., & Ware, L. (2014). "[Every] Child Left Behind": Curricular cripistemologies and the crip/queer art of failure. *Journal of Literary & Cultural Disability Studies, 8*(3), 295–314.

O'Toole, C. (2013). Disclosing our relationships to disabilities: An invitation for disability studies scholars. *Disability Studies Quarterly, 33*(2). https://doi.org/10.18061/dsq.v33i2.3708/3226.

Pink, S. (2009). *Doing sensory ethnography*. London, Thousand Oaks, CA: Sage.

Vesna, V. (2007). *Database aesthetics: Art in the age of information overflow (Electronic Mediations)*. Minneapolis, MN: University of Minnesota Press.

Chapter 14
"I Have to Be Black Before I Am Disabled": Understanding Agency, Positionality, and Recognition in Higher Education

Lauren Shallish

14.1 Introduction

In a 2015 qualitative research study on undergraduate college students who identified as disabled, interview data demonstrated the complex ways in which racism and ableism entwined to extend or deny benefits in a postsecondary setting. At tension in the informants' experiences was both the suppression of personhood and the celebration of it. The following examples represent two students in particular: A disabled, female-identified, queer, international student from Botswana and a disabled, female-identified, heterosexual, US citizen from New Hampshire, respectively:

> "When I go to the international student center, I have to be black before I am disabled. There is nothing for my disability identity there."

> "Yeah, I have LD. My friends think it's cool—they actually wish they had extended time too!"

Taken from the larger context of their 90-minute interview, these testimonies make apparent the racial, linguistic, ethnic, and dis/abled positions that support or deny student agency on a college campus. They also signal the "interconnected and collusive" properties of racism and ableism (Annamma et al. 2013, p. 6). This sampling is not intended to set up a racialized dichotomy about disability-related experiences but rather explicate the ways race and ability entwine to frame students' agency, positionality, and recognition in higher education settings. In line with DisCrit theorists who assert that "ability is distributed and withheld based on race through policies and practices" (Annamma and Morrison 2018, p. 72), this chapter will lay out the bodies of knowledge and research in disability law and higher education (specifically the

L. Shallish (✉)
The College of New Jersey, Ewing Township, NJ, USA
e-mail: ShallisL@tcnj.edu

© Springer Nature Switzerland AG 2020
L. Ware (ed.), *Critical Readings in Interdisciplinary Disability Studies*, Critical Studies of Education 12, https://doi.org/10.1007/978-3-030-35309-4_14

fields of enrollment management, student affairs, and academic affairs) that have siloed inquiry on race and dis/ability, respectively, rather than contribute to knowledge about interlocking systems of racism and ableism. I will examine the literature on disproportionality in K–12 special education and offer implications for postsecondary education in an attempt to expose the larger structures that situate (or omit) dis/ability in the context of diversity work in higher education.

14.2   Disproportionality in K–12 Schools and Implications for Higher Education

Disproportionality is defined as the overrepresentation and underrepresentation of a particular population or demographic group in special or gifted education programs relative to the presence of this group in the overall student population (National Association for Bilingual Education 2002). This injustice is the product of a number of social, political, economic, educational, and historical forces—many of which are ever-present (or especially heightened) on college campuses. No one factor alone explains disproportionality. Although numerous court cases and bodies of research have documented these patterns—and federal special education law requires states to monitor and address overrepresentation (IDEA, 1997, IDEA 2004)—the problem has persisted (Voulgarides 2018). These trends can be traced throughout the history of race relations in the USA (Smedley 2007) and are symptomatic of structural forces that include the "changing demographics of public schools, the context of service outcome disparities, and the influence of color-blind ideologies" (Artiles et al. 2010, p. 282). Not only does disproportionality exist in special education identification but also in placement decisions, disciplinary consequences, academic performance, and exiting from special education services (Blanchett 2006; Skiba et al. 2008; Sullivan 2011). "Testing biases, poverty, inequities in general education, behavior management, and cultural mismatch" continue to perpetuate the marginalization of students of color (Skiba et al. 2008, p. 264). These patterns are symptoms of disparities on a global scale as Tomlinson (2004) notes: "In all countries that have developed special education sub-systems to their mainstream education and also have racial, ethnic or immigrant minorities, these minorities have always been represented in the special sector" (p. 76). Research on the topic is also somewhat unbalanced as it is primarily concerned with patterns for students who identify as African American and less frequently for Latino, Asian, and Native American (Sullivan 2011). Altogether these inconsistencies expose the cultural and ideological constructions of dis/ability and the struggles within the foundations of special education practice(s) (Bratlinger 2004; Danforth 2008).

Literature on disproportionality is concerned with special education referrals and placement decisions in K–12 education but its impact can notably be found in higher education, specifically in the fields of enrollment management, academic affairs, and student retention. While college matriculation rates "when combining all types of postsecondary education, of students with disabilities are similar across race and ethnicity, these aspects of identity are linked with significant differences in diagnostic experiences and institution level matriculation" (Evans et al. 2017, p. 160). Said another way, rates of diagnosis varied significantly by race, "with certain forms of impairment more or less often diagnosed in different populations" (Evans et al. 2017, p. 160). To frame implications for postsecondary education it is necessary to provide a cross-section of research findings that speak to the continuing effects of racial, linguistic, and class-based inequities in K–12 schooling.

14.3 Experiences of Race, Dis/Ability, and Higher Education

Research demonstrates that students with disabilities in secondary education do not experience a difference in college attendance based on race or ethnicity; 62% of Hispanic, 60% of African American, and 61% of White young adults with disabilities had enrolled in a postsecondary program within 6 years of completing secondary education. However, "racialized discrepancies in diagnosis and receipt of support services in secondary education for students with disabilities adversely affect their postsecondary experience" (Evans et al. 2017, p. 160). Just as discrimination based on racial identity often hides under the "guise of discrimination based on income, ableism may be used to justify differential treatment and rationalize schools' failure to help students of color achieve" (Ostiguy et al. 2016, p. 318). Vernon and Swain (2002) found that "black disabled people consistently speak to experiences of segregation and marginalization within services" (p. 79) that reduce their future trust in and use of resources. The consequences of being labeled as disabled, even if one does not claim that identity, can result in rejection from cultural, racial, ethnic, and gender groups (Goodwin and Morgan 2012). Research continues to demonstrate that minoritized students avoid disability resources and distance themselves from their disability, while, for example, White students with economic means *and* the label of learning disability are more likely to gain access to and recognition within higher education (Reid and McKnight 2006).

Even as students with disabilities attend college in greater numbers, and the National Center for Education Statistics found that 11% of undergraduates report having a disability (Sanford et al. 2011), this group often remains segregated in academic and co-curricular settings (Tregoning 2009). There is a wide variation in numbers of students with disabilities in higher education, as only students who identified themselves to their institutions are counted. Data disaggregated by disability category further indicates disparities in representation among campus sectors. Overall, barriers for students with disabilities include minimal financial support (Holloway 2001), difficulty in seeking accommodations (Barnar-Brak et al. 2010), and more subtle obstacles to full participation, including lack of peer awareness (Komesaroff 2005) and diminished representation in academic fields (Taylor 2011). The most common institutional barriers include a lack of understanding of disability-related experiences (Rao 2004) or the perception that services provide a "special benefit" which disability studies scholars argue is the reflection of ableist assumption that accommodations provide an unfair advantage (Williams and Ceci 1999).

Newman et al. (2010) report that 63% of postsecondary students who were identified in secondary school as having a disability no longer report they consider themselves to have a disability. Another 8.5% who do still consider themselves to have a disability choose not to identify themselves as such to their postsecondary institutions (Newman et al. 2010). Disability status works somewhat differently in higher education. There is an increase in students with learning disabilities entering college; the majority of students are white and from families whose annual income exceeded $100,000 (Reid and McKnight 2006). The experiences of students of color are qualitatively different (Blackorby and Wagner 1996). Current scholarship on disability in higher education predominately addresses the classroom context and is focused on learning disabilities. Learning disabilities predominate representations on campus while students with mental health labels, for example, experience less access to supportive accommodations. Furthermore, students labeled as having an intellectual disability are hardly represented in postsecondary spaces. Two items are at tension here. While the field of higher education began to evolve and address retention within the context of higher education, disability still maintained an issue of compliance. Course content, fields of study, and standardized benchmarks for admission and graduation remained largely untouched. Inquiry largely blamed underserved groups for their own failures in postsecondary life and did little to address ecological perspectives on persistence and retention (Winkle-Wagner and Locks 2014).

Not until the 1990s did higher education research address how the environment of colleges and universities contributed to attrition. Pascarella and Terenzini (1997) identified theoretical models of student retention that found that persistence to be largely related to a student's fit within the institutional environment and factors that affect this retention include an ethic of care, participation in college-support activities, an emphasis on support services, and a peer culture where close friendships are developed in academic, social, and psychological spheres. These examples asserted that student learning and success were connected to larger environments where students interact and were instrumental in the proceedings of the Michigan affirmative action cases and *Fisher v. University of Texas Austin* in efforts to address broader approaches to understanding diversity and student success. Material conditions like economic inequality and segregation ultimately had the greatest influence on student performance in higher education, yet a persistent focus on merit maintains color-blind racism and other oppressive structures (Bonilla-Silva 1997).

14.4   Disability Law and Compliance

Disability, by contrast, has largely stayed within the realm of legal compliance. Though Sect. 504 and Title II of the ADA apply to both K–12 school districts and colleges, the responsibilities of postsecondary schools differ significantly from those of school districts. Disability-related issues in higher education include broader questions about the roles and function of postsecondary institutions and their responsibilities for educational equity. As Matus-Grossman and Gooden (2001) write: "Before adoption of America's antidiscrimination statutes related to disability, most institutions of higher education were conforming participants in a society that, by indifference, prejudice, or structure, excluded individuals from nearly every aspect of human endeavor" (p. 1). Today several federal laws protect students with disabilities from discrimination by institutions of postsecondary education, namely Section 504 of the Rehabilitation Act of 1973, which applies to all colleges that receive federal financial assistance; and the Americans With Disabilities Act (ADA) of 1990, which applies to three primary groups: employers; government entities, such as state universities; and private entities that serve the public. This legislation requires accessibility of resources and avenues of communication and equal participation in educational communities. Notions of least restrictive environment, free and appropriate public education, or continuum of services that are foundations of K–12 special education law do not apply. The clause "essential" in higher education disability rights legislation serves to ensure that colleges and universities need never "fundamentally alter" their programs of instruction to accommodate students with disabilities. By instructing colleges to distinguish carefully between what is essential and what is tangential, "the courts have used Section 504 and the ADA to create equal educational opportunity for the disability community—without lowering academic standards" (Matus-Grossman and Gooden 2001, p. 2). Conversely, misunderstanding what the duty to provide reasonable accommodations means is a source of suspicion and fear.

Today, institutions are legally required to meet the requirements for access and participation as outlined in Section 504 of the Rehabilitation Act of 1973 and the Americans With Disabilities Act (1990, 2008), yet studies and case law indicate colleges and universities are still establishing compliance practices (Burgstahler and Cory 2008). Compared to thousands of pages of regulations for the IDEIA, there are virtually no regulations to guide the implementation of the ADA or Section 504 on college and university campuses (Harbour 2013). For persons with disabilities to access the rights afforded by Section 504 and the ADA, they must first meet the legal definition of disability as defined in the statutes. This reliance on individualized inquiry and medical documentation continue to construct categories of disability — and related research—apart from other categories employed in diversity work and affirmative action policies that are known to have larger benefits to learning and engagement (Pascarella et al. 2012). While civil rights laws have been used as one piece among efforts to restructure inequitable practices in higher education, disability is frequently understood as admissible within the strict interpretation of legal regulations, which require documentation of medical impairment. A singular focus on case-by-case compliance has provided little sense that disability has any larger benefits to the campus community or that accommodations benefit anyone other than the person who requests them (Emens 2013). Like whiteness is a "social construct of the phenomenon of differential racialization, which both expand and contract racial categories to include and exclude different people in order to limit and extend benefits of being labeled as such, ability and disability changes throughout history in similar ways and are deeply impacted by perceptions of race" (Annamma et al. 2013, p. 10). Even as numbers of persons with disabilities attending, teaching, and working in higher education have tripled over the past 25 years, the majority of research on disability and higher education consists of longitudinal surveys, quantitative studies, and case law that maintains a singular focus on compliance with legal regulations. This persists even as qualitative studies and autobiographical literature signal larger, systemic barriers that are symptomatic of ableist preferences and an overall lack of awareness about disability culture and political identities that extend beyond classroom-based supports (Holloway 2001).

There is an ever-growing body of research on cultural centers, affirmative action, scholarships, and campus climate but hardly any that address disability in these conversations. Davis (2015) asserts that it is within the repression and exclusion of disability that neoliberal notions of individuality and diversity are able to persist:

> The idea presented by diversity is that any identity is one we could all imagine having, and all identities are worthy of choosing. But the one identity one cannot (and, given the ethos of diversity, should not) choose is to be disabled. So how could disability legitimately be part of the diversity paradigm since it speaks so bluntly against the idea of consumer lifestyle choice and seems so obviously to be about helplessness and powerlessness before the exigencies of fate? … What diversity is really saying, if we read between the lines, is that "we are different and yet all the same precisely because there is a deeper difference that we, the diverse, are not." (p. 63)

Diversity work is maintained so long as there is a non-apparent other, disability. Increasing scholarship addresses the need for intersectional perspectives on identity and college-going experiences, yet this is nearly impossible when disability is not considered part of the constellations on a college campus.

14.5   Next Steps for Disability Studies

Diverse educational environments impact student learning, critical thinking, civil engagement, and attitudes toward inequality (Goodman and Bowman 2014: Pascarella et al. 2012). Sociological perspectives dismantled radicalized or gendered assumptions about intelligence and instead took into account how environments constructed students as lacking or underprepared in higher education. Hurtado et al. (2001) argued that exposure to student diversity in college was part of the education process, not only in subject material but also exposure to a wider array of perspectives. Studies have also demonstrated that diversity in the curriculum and diverse interpersonal interactions had a positive effect on learning and development (Seifert et al. 2010). Goodman and Bowman's (2014) summary of research on diversity and student learning found that diversity interactions and diversity coursework predicted many desired outcomes associated with college, including positive attitudes toward literacy, critical thinking, socially responsible leadership, intercultural effectiveness, and psychological well-being. These effects were maximized by positive campus climate features: the inclusion of diverse students, faculty and administrators; a curriculum reflecting historical and contemporary experiences of underrepresented groups; programs that support the recruitment and retention and graduation of diverse students; and a mission that reinforces the institutions commitment to diversity (Guinier et al. 1997). The application of these findings also manifested into the establishment of cultural or identity centers, learning communities, and academic fields of study. Cultural and identity centers provided a counter-space to build relationships and establish social supports that counteracted alienation based on language and cultural adjustment, heterosexism, religion, and gender (Renn 2000). Learning communities structured around academic interests also provided opportunities to interact with various backgrounds and social identities (Jehangir 2003).

14.6   Conclusion

The inclusion of critical disability studies can work to transcend a singular focus on postsecondary service delivery, legal compliance, and medical documentation in higher education and expand the discourse of disability as a valued social, cultural, and political group. As other identities—around race and gender, for example—have employed compliance with civil rights statutes as one means to address equity in higher education, so too can disability studies provide a forum to think about preferences for normativity. An institutional orientation toward the social model of disability can move the category from a biomedical deficit managed by one campus office and resist entrenched practices that view legal interpretation as the only means by which to address disability in sectors of postsecondary life including enrollment management, curriculum development, and alumni (Taylor 2011).

References

Annamma, S. A., Connor, D., & Ferri, B. (2013). Dis/ability critical race studies (DisCrit): Theorizing at the intersections of race and dis/ability. *Race Ethnicity and Education, 16*(1), 1–31.

Annamma, S. A., & Morrison, D. (2018). DisCrit classroom ecology: Using praxis to dismantle dysfunctional education ecologies. *Teaching and Teacher Education, 73*, 70–80.

Artiles, A., Kozleski, E., Trent, S., Osher, D., & Oritz, A. (2010). Justifying and explaining disproportionality, 1968–2008: A critique of underlying views of culture. *Exceptional Children, 76*(3), 279–299.

Barnar-Brak, L., Lectenberger, D., & Lan, W. Y. (2010). Accommodation strategies of college students with disabilities. *The Qualitative Report, 15*(2), 411–429.

Blackorby, J., & Wagner, M. (1996). Longitudinal postschool outcomes of youth with disabilities: Findings from the national longitudinal study. *Exceptional Children, 62*(5), 350–399.

Blanchett, W. (2006). Disproportionate representation of African American students in special education: Acknowledging the role of white privilege and racism. *Educational Researcher, 35*(6), 24–28.

Bonilla-Silva, E. (1997). Rethinking racism: Toward a structural interpretation. *American Sociological Review, 62*(3), 465–480.

Bratlinger, E. (2004). Ideologies discerned, values determined: Getting past the hierarchies of special education. In L. Ware (Ed.), *Ideology and the politics of (In)Exclusion* (pp. 11–31). New York: Peter Lang.

Burgstahler, S., & Cory, R. (2008). From accommodation to universal design. In S. Gabel & S. Danforth (Eds.), *Disability and the politics of education: An international reader* (pp. 561–577). New York: Peter Lang.

Danforth, S. (2008). Using metaphors to research the cultural and ideological construction of disability. In S. Gabel & S. Danforth (Eds.), *Disability & the politics of education* (pp. 385–400). New York, NY: Peter Lang.

Davis, L. J. (2015). Diversity. In R. Adams, B. Reiss, & D. Serlin (Eds.), *Keywords for disability studies* (pp. 61–74). New York: New York University Press.

Emens, E. (2013). Disabling attitudes: U.S. Disability Law and the ADA Amendments Act. In L. Davis (Ed.), *The disability studies reader*. New York: Routledge.

Evans, N., Broido, E., Brown, K., & Wilke, A. (2017). *Disability in higher education: A social justice approach*. San Francisco, CA: Jossey-Bass.

Goodman, K. M., & Bowman, N. A. (2014). Making diversity work to improve college student learning. *New Directions for Student Services, 2014*(147), 37–48.

Goodwin, S. A., & Morgan, S. (2012). Chronic illness and the academic career: A hidden epidemic in higher education. *Academe*. Retrieved from http://www.aaup.org/article/chronic-illness-and-academic-career.

Guinier, L., Fine, M., & Balin, J. (1997). *Becoming gentlemen: Women, law school, and institutional change*. Boston, MA: Beacon Press.

Harbour, W. (2013). Inclusion in K-12 and higher education. In A. Kanter & B. Ferri (Eds.), *Righting educational wrongs: Disability studies in law and education* (pp. 294–306). Syracuse, NY: Syracuse University Press.

Holloway, S. (2001). The experience of higher education from the perspective of disabled students. *Disability & Society, 16*(4), 597–615.

Hurtado, S., Laird, T. N., Landreman, L., Engberg, M., & Fernandez, E. (2001). *College students' classroom preparation for a diverse democracy*. Washington, DC: American Educational Research Association.

Individuals with Disabilities Education Improvement Act, P.L. 108-446 20 U.S.C. §1400 (2004).

Jehangir, R. R. (2003). Charting a new course: Learning communities and universal design. In J. L. Higbee (Ed.), *Curriculum transformation and disability: Implementing universal design in higher education* (pp. 79–92). Minneapolis, MN: Center for Research on Developmental Education and Urban Literacy, College of Education and Human Development, University of Minnesota.

Komesaroff, L. (2005). Category politics: Deaf students' inclusion in the "Hearing University". *International Journal of Inclusive Education, 9*(4), 389–403.

Matus-Grossman, L., & Gooden, S. T. (2001). Opening doors to earning credentials: Impressions of community college access and retention from low-wage workers. In: Paper presented at the Annual Research Conference of the Association for Public Policy Analysis and Management.

National Association for Bilingual Education (NABE). (2002). *Determining appropriate referrals of English language learners to special education: A self-assessment guide for principals*. Arlington, VA: Council for Exceptional Children.

Newman, L., Wagner, M., Cameto, R., Knokey, A. M., & Shaver, D. (2010). Comparisons across time of the outcomes of youth with disabilities up to 4 years after high school. A report of findings from the National longitudinal Transition Study (NLTS) and the National Longitudinal Transition Study-2 (NLTS-2). Prepared for the U.S. Department of Education (NCSER2010–3008). Retrieved from http://www.nlts2.org/reports/2010_09/nlts2_report_2010_09_complete.pdf

Ostiguy, B. J., Peters, M. L., & Shlasko, D. (2016). Ableism. In M. Adams & L. A. Bell (Eds.), *Teaching for diversity and social justice* (3rd ed., pp. 299–337). New York: Routledge.

Pascarella, E. T., Salisbury, M. H., Martin, G. L., & Blaich, C. (2012). Some complexities in the effects of diversity experiences on orientation toward social/political activism and political views in the first year of college. *The Journal of Higher Education, 83*(4), 467–496.

Pascarella, E. T., & Terenzini, P. T. (1997). Studying college students in the 21st century: Meeting new challenges. *The Review of Higher Education, 21*(2), 151–165.

Rao, S. (2004). Faculty attitudes and students with disabilities in higher education: A literature review. *College Student Journal, 38*(2), 191–198.

Reid, D., & McKnight, M. (2006). Disability justifies exclusion of minority students: A critical history grounded in disability studies. *Educational Researcher, 35*(6), 18–23.

Renn, K. (2000). Patterns of situational identity among biracial and multiracial college students. *The Review of Higher Education, 23*(4), 399–420.

Sanford, C., Newman, L., Wagner, M., Cameto, R., Knokey, A., & Shaver, D. (2011). *The post-high school outcomes of young adults with disabilities up to six years after high school. Key findings from the National Longitudinal Transition Study-2 (NLTS2)*. Menlo Park, CA: SRI International.

Seifert, T. A., Goodman, K., King, P. M., & Baxter Magolda, M. B. (2010). Using mixed methods to study first-year college impact on liberal arts learning outcomes. *Journal of Mixed Methods Research, 4*(3), 248–267.

Skiba, R., Simmons, A., Ritter, S., Gibb, A., Rausch, M., Cuadrado, J., & Chung, C. (2008). Achieving equity in special education: History, status, and current challenges. *Exceptional Children, 74*(3), 264–288.

Smedley, A. (2007). *Race in North America: Origin and evolution of a worldview* (3rd ed.). Boulder, CO: Westview Press.

Sullivan, A. (2011). Disproportionality in special education identification and placement of English language learners. *Exceptional Children, 77*(3), 317–334.

Taylor, S. (2011). Disability studies in higher education. *New Directions for Higher Education, 2011*(154), 93–98.

Tomlinson, S. (2004). Race and special education. In L. Ware (Ed.), *Ideology and the politics of (in)exclusion* (pp. 76–88). New York: Peter Lang Publishing.

Tregoning, M. E. (2009). *"Getting it" as an ally: Interpersonal relationships between colleagues with and without disabilities. Making good on the promise: Student affairs professionals with disabilities*. Washington, DC: ACPA-College Student Educators International and University Press of America.

Vernon, A., & Swain, J. (2002). Theorizing divisions and hierarchies: Towards a commonality or diversity? In C. Barnes, M. Oliver, & L. Bardon (Eds.), *Disability studies today* (pp. 77–97). Bodmin, Cornwall, England: MPG Books.

Voulgarides, C. (2018). *Does compliance matter in special education?: IDEA and the hidden inequities of practice*. New York: Teachers College Press.

Williams, W. M., & Ceci, S. J. (1999, August 6). Accommodating learning disabilities can bestow unfair advantages. *The Chronicle of Higher Education*, B4–B5.

Winkle-Wagner, R., & Locks, A. (2014). *Diversity and inclusion on campus: Supporting racially and ethnically underrepresented students*. New York: Routledge.

Chapter 15
Writing, Identity, and the Other: Dare We Do Disability Studies?

Linda Ware

15.1 Introduction

Although inclusive education is often characterized as a special education initiative, both general and special educators must assume responsibility for all children's learning as mandated by 1997 amendments to the Individuals With Disabilities Education Act. The practice and implementation of inclusion policy in both K-12 public education and teacher education necessitates close examination of many issues that extend beyond compliance concerns. This article problematizes two related aspects of inclusion reform and its implementation in practice: persistence of unexamined assumptions about disability and uninspired curriculum. The author begins with an overview of humanities-based disability studies, an emerging field of scholarship that holds great promise for reimagining disability. Then the author describes a partnership between a secondary language arts teacher and herself wherein they created and cotaught Writing, Identity, and the Other, a curriculum unit informed by humanities-based disability studies. This example provides insight to the question, Dare we do disability studies?

15.2 Building a Cultural Critique

> I can't ignore my disability, why would you?
> —Karen, high school student, *Writing, Identity and the Other*

> The messages we receive are very strong and clear and we have little access to different values, which may place a more positive value on our bodies, our lives and ourselves. Our self-image is thus dominated by the non-disabled world's reaction to us. Jenny Morris (1991)

L. Ware (✉)
Independent Scholar, Corrales, NM, USA
e-mail: ware@geneseeo.edu

© Springer Nature Switzerland AG 2020   181
L. Ware (ed.), *Critical Readings in Interdisciplinary Disability Studies*, Critical Studies of Education 12, https://doi.org/10.1007/978-3-030-35309-4_15

Cultural perceptions of disability do not emerge in a vacuum; they accrue slowly and over time, informed by normalizing discourses in medicine and psychology, and reinforced by institutions and unchallenged beliefs of deficiency and need. Historically, disability has been the exclusive domain of the biological, social and cognitive sciences that shape practice in education, rehabilitative medicine, and social work. As a consequence of this limited understanding, disabled people are generally stereotyped as weak, pitiful, dependent, passive, tragic and many times, deserving of their predicament (Gilman 1985). With the medical lens fixed on the individual and their disability, the larger political, economic and material forces at play in an abelist society fall somewhere outside the frame. Despite claims to the contrary, public education, higher education, and teacher education are likewise guilty of ignoring the complexity of disability in our society. Tensions remain when attempting to consider disability as a concept or a constituency in educational settings. In higher education when disability moves beyond the diversity category to include pedagogical issues, status as an emerging field of study, and a civil rights mandate, "teachers, administrators, and students recognize the pedagogical, scholarly, and practical implications of integrating disability fully into all aspects of academe" (Longmore and Garland-Thomson 1999, p. 2). Thus, when the context responds to disability as more than a diversity category, concept and constituency merge to create important opportunities for learning. In K-12 settings *disability* has typically been defined as constituency—special education students who receive educational services in separate settings. As a consequence of the Individuals with Disabilities Act (Individuals with Disabilities Act 1997) the inclusion of students with disabilities into general education classrooms now challenges both the constituency and concept of disability. However, there remains much to learn about understanding disability as part of the larger human experience. At large, policies and practices that have a direct impact on the material reality of living with disability are rarely examined by society, as many believe that disabled people already won their rights. In much the same way that racism is believed to have been resolved by civil rights legislation, similar unexamined beliefs hold that the Americans with Disabilities Act (1990) ended injustice for the disabled. However, disabled people and those who research the lived experience of disability know that "the fundamental issue is not one of an individual's inabilities or limitations, but rather, a hostile and unadaptive society" (Barton 1999, p. xi).

15.2.1 Media Influences: In Brief

How is it that society can still be cast as "hostile and unadaptive" despite three decades of important social policy reform for people with disabilities?[1] There are several ways to respond to this question. From a historical perspective disability has

---

[1] The reforms include, principally, the Americans with Disabilities Act, (ADA, 1990), the Individuals with Disabilities Education Act (IDEA, 1990) and the reauthorization of the Individuals with Disabilities Education Act (1997).

been a specialized field limited to analysis within medicine, rehabilitation, special education, and social work. From a sociological perspective, others suggest that because many of the legal battles for disability access were won in the courts, with little involvement of non-disabled people, the assumption follows that people with disabilities have long since won their rights (Peters and Chimedza 2000). The media have played a critical role in perpetuating hostility to disability in numerous ways, including the negative portrayals of disability in television and films (Longmore 1987; Longmore and Umanksy 2001; Norden 1994; Shakespeare 1999) and in broadcast media depictions that reify unexamined assumptions about disability culture. Consider for example, the recent newspaper accounts to mark the 10-year anniversary of the Americans with Disabilities Act (ADA) of (1990). Of the many nation-wide variations on the triumph-over-disability theme of America's overcoming narrative (e.g., "Just Keep Moving" in *The Atlanta Constitution*, "Keep the 'able' in disabled," *The Kansas City Star*; "Improved Access for All, thanks to the ADA," Minneapolis *Star Tribune*), few made mention of the *Alabama v. Garrett* case recently before the Supreme Court. *Garrett* was the latest in a series of cases in which states challenged congressional power to enact legislation regulating state conduct—in this example, its authority specific to Title II of the ADA. Despite its obvious threat to dismantle the ADA, the *Garrett* case was cast as a "states rights" issue rather than a "disability rights" issue in both the courts and the media. Although this is not intended to suggest a media conspiracy, one has to wonder how naivete plays into complicity with societal hostility when the public relies on an ill-informed media.

15.2.2 Humanities and Education Influences: In Brief

Scholars in the field of humanities-based disability studies begin with the view of disability as a cultural signifier to problematize a range of unexamined attitudes, beliefs, and assumptions (Davis 1995, 1998; Garland-Thomson 1997; Linton 1998; Longmore and Umanksy 2001; Mitchell and Snyder 1997). Finally, education is just coming to name the inherent hostility to disability in education policy and practice as an evolution of its ongoing internal critique of special education (Brantlilnger 1997; Gabel 2019b; Erevelles 2000; Gallagher 1998; Heshusius 1989, 1995; Skrtic 1991, 1995; Ware 2000b, f). Critical special education theorists interrogate teacher preparation, special education, educational administration, and educational and social policy. Among the questions raised are those that implicate the organizational pathology of schools; for example Skrtic (1991) asks, if special education a rational system. Gallagher (1998) challenges the scientific knowledge base of special education by asking if weknow what we think we know. And, borrowing from Foucault (cited in Philip 1985), my research asks, "What have we done to ourselves by doing these things to them?' (Ware 2000b). This question interrogates teacher practice that ignores its own complicity in perpetuating exclusion as well as the administrative practice of "meaning-management" (Anderson 1990) which casts disability as a non-issue in general education in both secondary and post-secondary settings.

Critical special education now in it's "fourth wave" according to Heshusius (2000), provides an increasingly sophisticated range of issues beyond behaviorism. Included here are considerations of postmodern and postsrcuturalist reimaginings of disability (Erevelles 2000; Gabel 1998, 2001; Peters 1996, 2000; Smith 1999a, b, 2000; Ware 1999, 2000a) reinvigorated calls for open inquiry motivated by concerns for equity and recovery of the original moral grounding of special education's roots (Brantlilnger 1997; Danforth and Gabel 2000; Heshusius 2000; Kleiwer 2000; Ware 2000b), and research in comparative contexts that makes linkages to international critical special education theory (Gabel 2019a, b; Peters 1995, 1996, 2000; Ware 1995, 1998, 1999, 2000b).

Regardless of the origin of the critique when unexamined attitudes, beliefs, and assumptions about disability are challenged, multiple perspectives prove more useful than any one field's perspective. This is particularly important for teacher educators who seek to interrupt the contradictory subtexts in pedagogy and practice when special education's core concerns of cure, care, and remediation are contrasted with the reflection, transgression, and emancipation that lie at the center of liberatory praxis.

In the first part of this article, I consider two important critiques that have emerged to challenge status quo assumptions about disability. The first is the Disability Rights Movement (DRM), and the second is the emerging field of humanities-based disability studies. Each of these critiques is useful alone, but when taken together they provide a strong argument for educators to consider disability through a cultural lens, one that interrogates the medicalized view that has powerfully shaped both general and special education, and more important, public perceptions of disability.

15.3   The DRM

Historically, the only choice people with disabilities had in their personal struggle to survive was to individually resist isolation, even death, by relying on others. This meant, practically speaking, begging and becoming dependents of family or charities. That has begun to change. Now there is a movement of empowered people that seeks control of these necessities for themselves and their community. (Charlton 1998, p. 165)

There are 43 million of us in this country. But we're as invisible as Casper the Ghost. (Billy Golfus, cited in Golfus and Simpson 1994)

According to Longmore and Umanksy (2001), disability has been "present in penumbra if not in print, on virtually every page of American history" (p. 2), yet, history has failed to include disability other than in medical case histories. In an effort to fill in the "historical gaps" of disability in American history, Longmore and Umansky have edited a collection of essays that capture the social, cultural, and political history of disability and disability rights activism. For example, during the Great Depression, the League of the Physically Handicapped staged actions in protest of job discrimination resulting from the medical model of disability that had begun to shape policy, professional practices and social arrangements of the early twentieth century (Longmore and Goldberger 2000). Most Americans, including historians will be surprised to read the rich documentation supporting the essays in this collection, given the commonly held belief that only a "small fraction of the population appears to be disabled" (Davis 1995, p. 6).

The origin of the DRM is typically associated with the late twentieth century, from the 1960s through the present. Activism erupted in simultaneous waves in Berkley, Boston, and Houston giving rise to the DRM and paving the way for important legislation and social policy for disabled Americans. During this time, civil rights protests for accessible housing, transportation, employment, and education invited new conversations about self-determination and the real meaning of access. Through well-planned actions, disability advocates challenged public perceptions and raised consciousness about social justice and living conditions for the millions of Americans who live with disabilities (e.g., Block 1997; Brock 1998; Charlton 1998; Golfus and Simpson 1994; Shapiro 1993). A recent show at the Smithsonian National Museum of American History, titled, *The Disability Rights Movement* (June, 2000–01), captures much of the history of this era with original protest placards, footage of activism, and reform legislation documents cast among the objects on display. According to the curator, Katherine Ott (2000), the social progress of this era is most evident when contrasted to an earlier show, *Triumph Over Disability* (Davis 1973) which displayed various medical instruments, devices, and aids that signaled the rise and development of physical and rehabilitation medicine in the United States. Consistent with the new disability history outlined by Longmore and Umanksy (2001), the Smithsonian exhibit departs from the medical model of disability to instead relocate the disability experience in social rather than biological constructs.

The DRM characterizes a rich history of liberation by individuals claiming rights and staging actions that should have earned a more central place in the history of American life. Because DRM history has been elided from common understanding, its reintroduction into the collective consciousness will prove timely as it informs humanities-based disability studies and liberatory praxis in teacher education.

15.4 Humanities-Based Disability Studies

> Humanities-based disability studies is grounded in the desire to challenge our collective stories about disability, to renarrate disability, [and] to reimagine it as an integral part of all human experience and history (Longmore and Garland-Thomson 1999, p. 2).

Recent efforts to problematize disability through a cultural analysis are found in the emerging multidisciplinary scholarship and research in humanities-based disability studies.[2] History, literature, philosophy, anthropology, religion, medical history, and rhetoric rooted in the humanities rather than in the social sciences and rehabilitative medicine inform this scholarship. With an emphasis on understanding disability as discursively and materially created, the medical model is problematized such that questions of civil rights and social justice are privileged over those cast as personal problems. Among the critical issues in humanities-based disability studies are those related to: identity, education, representation, sexuality, personal meanings of disability, access, employment, religion and spirituality, and strategies for empowerment and activism. Representing an unprecedented shift from the modernist project of biological determinism and the medicalization of disability, the new disability studies defines *disability* as a way of thinking about bodies rather than as something that is wrong with bodies (Longmore and Garland-Thomson 1999; Mitchell and Snyder 1997).

In sum, disability studies "takes as its domain the intricate interaction among cultural values, social arrangements, public policy, and professional practice regarding disability" (Longmore and Umanksy 2001, pp. 15–16). This interpretation of human differences draws from postmodernist and post-structuralist analyses in which the person with disabilities becomes the "ultimate example, the universal image, the modality through whose knowing the postmodern subject can theorize and act" (Davis 1997, p. 5). Although this scholarship is infinitely broad in topic and scope, and beyond an adequate presentation in this article,[3] a key strand that cuts across this burgeoning literature is the problematizing of the ability/disability binary. That is, when disability is considered through a cultural lens, ability is interrogated in much the same way as feminist studies scholars interrogate gender, and ethnic studies scholars interrogate whiteness. The instance of the normal/abnormal binary is central to the problematization of disability, particularly as it has morphed to the ability-disability binary central to the invention of categorical systems institutionalized by society (e.g., education, medicine, law, and social policy). Given that many cultures (primarily Western) maintain disability as alterity through the ideology of assigning value to the normal, able body and its functioning parts, stigmata is often equated with impairment and the disabled body. How we "other" the disabled body, according to L. J. Davis (1995), is determined by society.

> We tend to group impairments into the categories of either 'disabling' (bad) or just 'limiting' (good) .... Wearing a hearing aid is seen as much more disabling than wearing glasses, although both serve to amplify a deficient sense .... Loss of hearing is associated with aging in a way that nearsightedness is not" (p. 130).

The subtle, yet pervasive practice of assigning value to the body is most evident in cultural representations of disability, where, according to Garland-Thomson

---

[2] See Longmore and Umanksy (2001) for a more thorough discussion of this history in the United States, Campbell and Oliver (1996) for a discussion in the context of the United Kingdom. In academia, Berube (1997) and Cassuto (1999) provide abbreviated accounts of humanities-based disability studies.

[3] Overviews can be found in Corker and French (1999), Davis (1995), Linton (1998), Longmore & Umansky (2001), Mitchell and Snyder (1997), Shapiro (1993), and Wendell, (1996.)

(1997) disability exists in opposition to the *normate*[4]. This neologism characterizes the socially constructed identity of those who by way of the "bodily configurations and [the] cultural capital they assume, can step into a position of authority and wield the power it grants them" (Thomson 1997, p. 8). In her analysis of the cultural representation of disability, Thomson reveals how disability operates in texts, to expose the tensions between people who assume the normate position and those "assigned" the disabled position. Incomplete, prototypical disabled characters are more common than are dynamic and complex individuals and for the most part, representations rely on cultural assumptions to fill in the missing details of personhood (e.g., agency, subjectivity, desire, sexuality, etc.).

With respect to cognitive disabilities, moral philosophers have begun to reimagine reason as the center of what makes us human. The moral philosopher, Eva Feder Kittay (1999a, b) draws from her experience parenting her adult daughter with significant disabilities to pose provocative questions about independence, dependence, and interdependence in pursuit of developing a radical theory of equality that extends to both political and social life. Similarily, MacIntyre (1999) in his discussion of who contributes to the common good, suggests that many children in schools experience "too constrained and impoverished [a] view of future possibilities" (p. 75), bound as educators often are, by systems that extinguish imagination. Finally, Carlson (1997, 1998) contends that given the ambiguities and intricacies of classification systems of cognitive impairment, to more fully consider the social nature of disability, questions about cognitive ability must move "beyond the boundaries of bioethics" (1997, p. 283). She urges that when feminists theorizing physical disability, many "connections can and *should* be applied to persons with cognitive disabilities" (1997, p. 280).

Intersecting issues for educators. The cultural analyses emerging from disability studies scholarship offer challenging theoretical insights for educators to examine both societal attitudes, beliefs and assumptions, and more fundamentally, the lived-experience of disability. In example, McRuer (2001) analyzes a fundamental ideological cultural demand he terms, *compulsory able-bodiedness* borrowing from Adrienne Rich, Judith Butler, and a memior by Berube (1996), who writes about life with his son Jamie, who has Down Syndrome. According to McRuer (2001):

> Berube writes of how he 'sometimes feel[s] cornered by talking about Jamie's intelligence, as if the burden of proof is on me, official spokesman on his behalf' (p. 180). The subtext of these encounters always seems to be the same: *"In the end, aren't you disappointed to have a retarded child? … Do we really have to give this person our full attention?"* (p. 180).

In his analysis, McRuer (2001) suggests two related questions drawn from Berube's experience, and bound by the same common ground of "able-bodied consciousness" to tease out important subtext at play in interactions between able-bodied and disabled people. These often-unarticulated questions are juxtaposed to make a critical point. In the end, wouldn't you rather be hearing? In the end, wouldn't you rather not be HIV positive? Although two seemingly different ques-

---

[4] The term *normate* was originally coined by Daryl Evans (see Thomson 1997).

tions, the former typifies the subtext of the "thinly veiled desire for Deafness not to exist … and the latter, "more obviously genocidal" (p. 8). By his analysis, these questions are more alike than they are different and more reflective of the able-bodied culture posing the question than about the "bodies being interrogated" (p. 8). The dialectic is one in which abelist culture uncritically assumes an "affirmative answer to the unspoken question, *yes, but in the end, wouldn't you rather be more like me?* (p. 8). The significance of these questions is that of the "compulsory able-bodied" desire for neither people who are deaf, nor those with AIDS to exist.

Although educational researchers have just begun to challenge these unarticulated questions and their relationship to the hostility and unadaptive structures in society previously cited by Barton (1999), they parallel the issues of critical race theorists and feminists who seek to move beyond the essences and the unvoiced in policies and practices. However, these conversations are not easily had in schools or in teacher development. In my own research with pre-service and practicing teachers there is sometimes a general sense of relief as we begin to unpack abel-ist assumptions in education and society, or just the opposite occurs resulting in defensiveness and denial. Initially, teachers cite the lack of resources, training, parental support, and administrative vision that reinforces the hegemony of abelist assumptions, as if to say, "That's just the way it is." Others, upon reflection, acknowledge that they have ignored disability issues, confident that systems and specialists were better able to address these issues. And a few recount personal experiences with disability which serves as the catalyst for moving beyond the normalizing discourse of disability. Regardless of the response, each is marked by emotions similar to those outlined by Tatum (1992) in her efforts to teach race and racism in college classrooms. The parallels are more obvious when considered against the larger meaning of social inclusion and the value of creating a shared responsibility for teaching all children. In the section that follows I suggest that analyses offered by humanities-based disability studies can inform educators about educational and social inclusion.

15.5   Disability Studies in Education

At stake here is the necessity for progressive educators' studies to provide some common ground in which traditional binarisms of margin/center, unity/difference, local/national, public/private can be reconstituted through more complex representations of identification, belonging, and community. (Giroux 1996, p. 53)

Critical educational discourse informed by critical theory and critical pedagogy has, for more than two decades, inspired many activist educators to form alliances in pursuit of educational and social justice. With social transformation at the center of mutual reform efforts, this legacy of morally driven activism has its roots in Freirean efforts to promote justice, equality, democracy, and freedom through liberatory praxis--*conscientization* (Freire 1970). However in a recent special issue of *Educational Theory* (1998), the success of this reform project was challenged. Given its failure to disrupt the inequities in society related to race, class, gender, and ethnicity, critical pedagogy was problematized from several perspectives. The discussion included concerns, criticism, and solutions as in the example of Peter McLaren's (1998) 10 step manifesto for critical pedagogy in the age of globalization--a revivalist revolutionary project—"performed in the streets … [and] public spaces of potential political, cultural, and economic transformation" (pp. 452–453). In this same issue, Patti Lather (1998, cited in in Ellsworth 1997, pp. xi, 9) voiced concerns that the "big tent" of critical educational discourse had come up against a "stuck place"—thus her calls for praxis informed by Derrida's question, "What must now be thought and thought otherwise?" (p. 495).

In response to this challenge, I would answer that disability must now be thought and thought otherwise. By that I mean disability is a long overdue conversation among critical theorists, pedagogues, and educationalists, who fail to recognize disability as a cultural signifier, nor do they include disability as a meaningful category of oppression (Erevelles 2000; Gabel 2001; Ware 2000f). This silence on disability issues suggests the typical societal absorption of cultural stereotypes related to disability. Of equal significance is the unexamined assumption about the taken-for-granted category of disability in educational discourse—one shaped by ideologies, history, medicine, and social and political assumptions whose central binary is ability/disability. In an argument informed by the previously cited disability studies literature, I suggest that this binary is the root of all binarisms that inform social formations such as race, class, gender, ethnicity, sexuality, and disability.

15.6 Finding Alliances

Although critical theory might seem useful in this analysis, there exists a substantial body of critical special education literature that is readily positioned to merge with humanities-based disability studies. For more than three decades, critical special education literature has challenged the traditional normative paradigm of special education. This literature is doused with references to critical theorists and pedagogues in an effort to integrate the big tent discourse into critical special education scholarship. However, critical special education research has yet to be acknowledged by critical educationalists. In practice, critical special education literature has earned little more than sideshow status in education even though this work represents an exhaustive list of interdisciplinary and international theorists and researchers. With the exception of a handful of teacher preparation programs in the United States, alternative special education theory remains on the margins in both special and general teacher education, and it is off the page among critical theorists.

In fact, it is often the case that among general education audiences, critical issues in special education from an alternative paradigm of analysis must be "contextualized" to insure general educators' understanding. In her discussion of inclusion in a mainstream education research journal, Brantlilnger (1997) felt it necessary to provide a "brief background of the trends and issues in special education in order to place the debate about inclusion in context" (p. 427). Although the boundaries between general and special education evolved as an unintended consequence of

IDEA (Giroux 1996), why is it that these exclusionary structures remain? Given the legacy of critical theory in education and contemporary practice with multicultural issues at the forefront, the preservation of a dual and separate system of teacher training with categorical divisions and a clinical orientation to disability can no longer remain unchallenged. However, critical theorists avert their gaze from both the disabled subject and the dual system of education, as if to suggest that liberatory praxis would naturally exclude the disabled. Exclusionary practices such as these suggest clear complicity when teachers and teacher educators unwittingly preserve and prop up "cycles of oppression that operate in our courses, our universities, our schools, and our society" (Lawrence and Tatum cited in Cochran-Smith 2000). In sum, general ignorance on issues of disability as a category of educational and social oppression evidenced by its absence from professional meetings, scholarly journals, and texts devoted to critical pedagogy, prompts this author to ask, "Why does the academic nod to diversity morph to cringe at disability?" (Ware 2000e).

In the absence of purposeful alliances among critical theorists and critical special education theorists, I suggest a new avenue for solidarity through humanities-based disability studies in education and the involvement of colleagues in humanities[5]. That is, if as Giroux (1996) suggests, cultural studies promises "new spaces for collaborative work" (p. 43), then disability studies in education would invite many important opportunities to provide students with the opportunity to "study larger social issues through multidisciplinary perspectives" (p. 43).

In the section that follows, I describe one aspect of such a project situated in a high school creative writing class in which the teacher and I created a curriculum informed by humanities-based disability studies. This research builds on previous research with secondary teachers in general and special education, many of whom questioned why, despite compliance to IDEA, greater numbers of students remain excluded from the educational mainstream (Ware 1995, 1998, 2000d). Although the official data reports otherwise, the fact remains that while students may be relocated into the educational mainstream in "a rush to inclusion" they often remain excluded in many complex ways that defy a simple body count for compliance purposes. The section that follows describes how one teacher realized the subtle contradictions at play in his own inclusive classroom.

15.7   Writing, Identity, and the Other[6]

As I understand the concept of the "other," it involves two essential processes: When we make people 'Other,' we group them together as the objects of our experience instead of regarding them as subjects of experience with whom we might identify, and we see them

---

[5] One such project is underway at the University of Rochester funded by the National Endowment for the Humanities. "A Collaborative Inquiry on Understanding Disability in Secondary and Post-Secondary Settings" is attempting purposeful linkages with education, humanities, and medicine.

[6] This research served as a pilot project for a

primarily as symbolic of something else—usually, but not always, something we reject and fear and project on to them. To the non-disabled, people with disabilities and people with dangerous or incurable illnesses symbolize, among other things, imperfection, failure to control the body, and everyone's vulnerability to weakness, pain, and death (Griffin, cited in Wendell 1996, p. 60).

With an emphasis on identity and "othering," a veteran language arts teacher, Tom Painting and I developed a curriculum unit we titled, "Writing, Identity and the Other" for his ninth grade creative writing class. The class consisted of typical students and those with learning, emotional, and physical disabilities (ages 13–15). The unit aimed to promote understanding of disability as part of the human experience drawing from disability studies literature and first person accounts of living with disability. Having had no prior awareness of disability studies, Tom hoped the content would cohere with his year-long theme for the class, writing for self discovery. After several meetings and the exchange of selected excerpts from the literature (e.g., Hockenberry 1995; Mairs 1986, 1996; Shapiro 1993; Shaw 1994), we discussed the value and applicability of this content for his students. Together we identified selections from the readings each of us was drawn to, including two disability studies film standards, *When Billy Broke his Head* (Golfus and Simpson 1994), and *Breathing Lessons* (Yu 1996). Tom relied upon me to propose a structure for the content and I relied upon him to develop the writing activities that would address the following goals for instruction and research.

- What can I understand about the identity of others who appear different from myself?
- What can I learn about my own identity through understanding the identities of others?
- Can disability ever represent anything other than a negative image?

Although, there were many questions we might have focused on, these three represented our initial interests in reimagining disability in the context of a high school language arts class.

15.7.1 Teaming with Tom

Tom is a veteran teacher who has taught for 17 years in the same district, a large urban, upstate New York system. Throughout our teaming, his tenacity and intuitive sense of his students amazed and intrigued me. His teaching is difficult to script as he literally seems never to miss a beat. Each morning, prior to the class, we met over coffee, and based on the previous days' instruction, set a general "target" for our teaching. Classroom interactions were something akin to "trading fours" as I played sideman to Tom and his students. I learned early to follow their lead, or when necessary, to move completely out of the way. The students (ages 13–15), having declared creative writing their major at this arts magnet high school, were in their second year with Tom. This familiarity provided an easy atmosphere in the classroom, one that did not begin with roll call nor did it end at the sound of the bell. Early in my classroom observations (prior to coteaching), a group of his students described their teacher as suffering from "HPD."

"HPD?" I asked with hesitancy, fearing I lacked the vernacular for navigating urban New York schools—or that the DSM-IV I had conjured yet another diagnostic category.

"Haiku psychosis disorder" the students laughed, given Tom's intense appreciation and collection of haiku—a simple, image driven poetry form. True to his diagnosis, on Day 2 of our teaching Tom arrived with an overstuffed folder full of haiku, beaming with the comment, "I found some really great stuff on disability that I didn't even know I had!"

Throughout our teaming, Tom remarked on his growing disability consciousness informed by both personal history and that of his professional practice. He described his awkward encounters in the gym with a disabled man and his own uncertainty about engaging in conversation—a phenomenon that was quite uncommon for Tom. He also recalled experiences from his childhood and youth growing up with a brother who was physically disabled. Tom recalled these events in a stream of consciousness fashion, as though these prior experiences had long since been reflected on until we began teaming. His growing understanding about the cultural and material conditions of disability reminded me of the historian, Douglas Baynton (2001), who asserts, "disability is everywhere in history, once you begin looking for it, but conspicuously absent in the histories we write." (p. 46).

Day 1. We began the unit[7] with a quick review of the previously explored writing genres (e.g., autobiographical writing, poetry, and science fiction). Tom revisited the general goals he had developed for the class and invited student responses as he wrote on the board:

Writing for Self-Discovery
To know about ourselves.
    The use of language—how it convinces us to see things a certain way.
    To think about where we came from, like the Day of the Dead Stuff and the deaths we've experienced.
    Culture.
    The future.
    The past.
    Paying attention to dialogue.
    Writing new plots from our lives.
    Experiences—imagined & real!

---

[7] Because Tom had extended the invitation to work with his class in mid-year, we were forced to work around the Christmas break, resulting in a noncontinuous block of twenty-two teaching days.

After summarizing what he wrote, Tom asked the students to hang on to these goals for their writing, as in our upcoming unit we would address these targets from a slightly different perspective. While still at the board, he marked nine points in a three-by-three array with directions to the students to connect the dots without touching any point more than once. This activity is often used in workshops to depict the value of thinking outside the box as a means to creativity when the only solution to seemingly complex issues is thinking outside the box. Tom engaged the students with the challenge, bribing those who knew the solution to allow their classmates to solve the puzzle on their own. Following an excited discussion of the task, Tom wrote "the Other" beside the image of the box. In the closing minutes of the class, Tom directed the students to: "write a brief definition of the Other. What do we mean by the Other? Who is the Other?" The following are examples:

> When I hear the word Other, I think of the bad. Not the norm. I don't try to think inside of the box but its easier to sometimes. The Other to me is the parts of life and society that people don't want to think about. Maybe because its harder. The other is unwantable.
> Different, not the same, something else to choose or pick. Not including one. To me the Other means all the stuff that I've never seen before or all the stuff that has a different opinion than me. The other is outside my arms length, outside my space and outside my habits.
> The other son, the other boy, the other tree outside of the "box," the other room outside of the box.

Days 2 and 3. Building off of their definitions of the Other, we led a whole class discussion of the free write responses that extended over two class periods. Among the key comments raised were those of identity that reflected cultural trends such as body piercing and tattoos, and issues related to sexuality. The exchange was difficult to predict, as topics cut across a range of issues and levels of awareness. Comments specific to homosexuality tended towards sensationalizing, until one student offered: "I have an uncle who's gay, but, in my family, he's not outside of us. I can honestly say that he's one of the best uncles I have." Another, in response to the disdain expressed by some of his peers, raised the ante when he expressed concerns for human rights and social justice, insisting, "if being gay is who you are, no one should have the right to make you feel bad about it." Another student wondered, " Is self-knowing is sometimes about not wanting to know?" Although there was no explicit reference to disability the students demonstrated the capacity to probe complex meanings ascribed to the Other.

The students' writing began with personal definitions that later shifted to society and who has the ultimate authority to define and judge normalcy. The term *normal* was their original descriptor, but given its attendant medicalized notions of the normal-abnormal binary, I introduced the term *normalcy* (Davis 1995) to underscore thinking about social justice. The students appreciated the distinction and were quick to grasp the hegemony of normalcy in a democracy. Our discussion of normalcy led easily into locating the influences on cultural awareness they had previously considered. We closed the day by summarizing where we get our ideas about normalcy. The students' list included "those closest to me—my family, my friends, church, schools, TV—and what I tell myself." Hegemony was thus easy to examine in the context of those judged to be outside normalcy, those we "other" in society.

Pedagogically, Tom's enthusiasm for the topic was significant as it complemented the disability studies material I introduced and it complicated the issues of disability and society. His willingness to include his own experiences in the conversation provided students the opportunity to consider multilayered and problematic analyses of "local histories and subjugated memories" and to express "open and honest concern for human suffering, values, and the legacy of the often unrepresented or misrepresented" (see Giroux 1996, pp. 50–52). However, it is important to stress that it was not our intention to lead students to any particular position as much as it was to consider experiences that might support ways to reimagine disability. Working from specific disability studies materials and first person accounts of disability the students approached the task as writers might—through images, language and expression. By the end of the first week, we were able to introduce the lived experience of disability through poetry as in the examples that follow.

Days 4 and 5.

My Place
    I don't want to live in bungalow land
    On the outer edges of the urban sprawl
    In the places designed for people-like-us
    Kept safely separate, away from it all.
    I want to live in the pulse-hot-thick-of it,
    Where the nights jive, where the streets hum,
    Amongst people and politics, struggles and upheaval,
    I'm a dangerous woman and my time has come.
    (Napolitano 1998)

After providing a few minutes to read the poem in silence, Tom asked the class to read in rounds with each student reading one half of a line aloud and overlapping into the voice of the next student in a round of voices that read as one. The class repeated this for several readings. Then without discussion about the poem, Tom asked the students to "attend to the language of the poem" and to write at the board, the wor or words that "really fix your attention--what captured your imagination as you listened to the poem?"

Pulse-hot-thick-of-it
    outer edges safely separate sprawl
amongst urban sprawl bungalow land
        nights jive
a dangerous woman and my time has come

Students discussed the poem in small groups as we fielded questions about the seeming "archaic" language (e.g., upheaval, amongst, bungalow land, jive). The language of the poem and its juxtaposition to more contemporary language (e.g., urban sprawl, pulse-hot-thick-of-it, nights jive, dangerous woman) led many to speculate about the time period and its setting. Guessing whether the setting was in England, Australia, or Ireland, seemed for some, to be the sole purpose of the exercise. However, others began to speculate about the speaker and their curiosity slowly replaced the animated conjecture about the setting.

"I think the woman wants to get back into a place she's been pushed out of," one student offered.

"I think she's just getting freedom—like for the first time, or something," said another.

With an air of insistence, another explained, "She could still be struggling to get free—it's not like she won't go back to the other place."

The students were perplexed by the poem unable to make much sense of the actual lived context of the speaker until Tom posed a few questions.

"Let's think about this for a minute--who lives in places for 'people-like-us?'" Pausing, he continued, "In our society, who do we keep 'safely separate?'"

"The elderly?"

"Crazy people?"

"Or maybe, developmentally disabled people--people who can't live on their own—they're kept separate."

Before, we could bring the lesson to closure, the bell signaled the end of class—but many of the students lingered over the question, Who do we keep safely separate in our society? One student paused on his way out of class to redraw the lines that Tom had enclosed in a box around their responses. "Hey, Mr. Painting," he teased, as he erased the box that encased the words, "a dangerous woman and my time has come." With a laugh he said, "Don't you think this woman is probably outside the box?" Tom paused by the board and, with a wide smile, raised both hands wide open to the air and with approval replied, "That's it isn't it, Jose?"

When Tom and I met the next morning, he explained his hunch about where we might go after these first few days of introductory material. "Let's not try to tie everything up too neatly for them. Let's give them the space to enter where they feel comfortable." According to his analysis, the students seemed anxious, perhaps, unclear about the purpose of the work, or they were anxious to begin the holiday break. Regardless, he did not want them to feel pressured. Tom then acknowledged his growing unease with the content, remarking, "I hope I know how to stay with them on this—it's hard stuff." His comments were quite unexpected. My sense was that the students were holding their own, and I thought Tom was too. I would later learn from Tom that content provoked personal issues—some he thought he had dealt with—and others he knew still needed his attention.

Later, in class, we did not return to the Napolitano poem, but instead began with a focused freewrite. Tom asked the students to define disability leading with the prompt: "Disability is ... " Everyone began writing at once, but when the designated time elapsed, several students asked for additional time. Before inviting the responses, Tom asked, "Did anyone feel frozen at first? I was surprised at how difficult it was to come up with the right words." Many students agreed and commented about having written too many words or too few words. One student explained, "It's weird because it's something you know you know, but just don't really think about it." Others offered the following definitions.

> Disability is many things. It can be when you cannot work parts of your body or it can mean you cannot read well. To me, everyone can have a disability in some way even if you don't see it.
>
> Disability is a problem that some people have that prevents them from living a life like able-bodied people. They may need a wheelchair, a walker, a cane, a seeing-eye dog, a tutor, or captioning and interpreting for all spoken words, or artificial machine-assistance to help them carry on their body's normal functions. A disability may weaken a person physically, but their thoughts and emotions are just like all peoples [sic].
>
> Something that causes a person to become unable to function the same way other people do. They may still be able to function normally, but in different way[sic] than people without a disability do.

Overall, their responses were a mix of objective and subjective descriptions that tied into the earlier conversations on normalcy and the range of visible and invisible disabilities. The exchange prompted Tom's memory of a summer job in his college days as a home health care provider for a disabled adult—something he admitted he had not thought about in years. Tom recalled his reluctance to perform the job requirements, his inability to contend with personal feelings about dependency so starkly contrasted to his own youth and athletic accomplishment that framed his identity. All of these emotions so complicated the job that he resigned from the position in less than a week. The intersections of these very critical issues proved to be of great interest to the students as the tables were turned, and they probed their teacher's emotions and attitudes.

As a researcher, I observed Tom's easy exchange with the students despite his prior concerns about the emotional demands of the content. It is interesting that when when Tom and I initially planned the unit, he made no mention of his personal experiences with disability. However, since we both participated in the writing assignments along with the students, recounting our personal experiences was a given. On the one hand, it was valuable that Tom located himself in this inquiry with the same desire to understand disability differently, as did his students. Conversely, in his role as the teacher his vulnerability led to concerns about where our teaching would ultimately lead us. The challenge of teaching in the zone of the unknown was clearly becoming burdensome as we neared the Christmas break.

Earlier that day we had wondered how much could be accomplished given that we were at the end of the last full week of instruction prior to the holiday break. Knowing the following week would be marred by interruptions with holiday programs, early dismissals, and the general frenzy in high schools prior to a holiday, Tom made a quick decision to assign weekend homework. Despite the students' groans of protest, they were assigned an essay describing their first experience with disability. When the students returned on Monday, they had written varied accounts of family members and classmates with a range of disabilities, many provided loving descriptions of grandparents whose aging led to disability, others wrote about themselves. Karen, a student with physical disabilities titled her essay, "Telling about disability, telling about me." Her essay began with the following:

> My first encounter with disability was when I was born with spina bifida that affected my spinal chord. I wear leg braces (you probably noticed this). When I was little I didn't walk till I was 3 years old. My parents are very protective of me.

15.8 Reflecting with Tom

Although I felt that the first two weeks of instruction were a great success, the experience left Tom with new doubts about his teaching. He wondered why, prior to this unit, Karen and some of the other students had never written about disability. He was unable to recall a single student in all his years teaching who had ever written about disability. He wondered if he had somehow failed to create a place in which it was safe to examine this issue. As a consequence, he expressed doubts about whether the class, now halfway through their second year together, was really a community of writers. More important, Tom wondered if he had unconsciously avoided the topic of disability. His concerns surprised me, but they also provided the opportunity to discuss how schools silence particular discourses. Specifically, race, class, and sexuality are often cited in the educational literature as silenced discourses, but rarely is disability considered among the inequities resulting from the normalizing discourses of schooling. I explained that in the example of disability only certain professionals are sanctioned to broach the topic. That is, although conversations about disability occur in schools everyday, for the most part, they are restricted to procedural issues of identification, referral, and placement in special education, or they focus on related problems of staffing, curriculum and inappropriate student and parent behavior. This discourse of containment and control has failed to consider disability through a cultural lens or what it might mean to live with a disability over a lifetime.

As our teaching progressed, Tom recognized his reticence growing from a number of sources. He acknowledged his lack of familiarity with the materials I provided on disability and was surprised to find so many sources available to support disability studies. In addition, he was discomforted by the fact that he had not previously considered disability as an identity category. Relatedly, his lack of vocabulary to discuss disability with his students was discomforting. More important, he was slowly coming to realize that students with disabilities would not be likely to find themselves anywhere in the curriculum.

15.8.1 The Final Two Weeks

When we reconvened after the break, we began with Tom's package of haiku. In small group discussion, the students were asked to speculate beyond the moment depicted in the haiku and to flesh out a character with details of physicality and history by locating him or her in a scene. "Envision human attributes—a voice, a look, a story to tell." Tom urged.

> a girl is wheeled in--
>   chatter ceases
>   in the ladies' room
>   Jocelyne Villenueve

> MEN ONLY
>   door too narrow
>   for his wheelchair
>   Rebecca M. Osborn

Among their examples are the following:

The girl is about 23, but why is she called "girl?" She has just been in a car accident and is paralyzed. She is hooked up to all sorts of devices attached to the back of the wheelchair.

I see a little girl in a wheelchair that cannot go to the bathroom by herself. I think she is small and has brown eyes and is embarrassed a little too. I know how she feels too in some ways because I have a disability and sometimes I get a reaction similar to that.

This man has been handicapped for a while now. He's depressed but still tries to get out of the house. He's alone and has a hard time. Even though he's a man he can't get in the men's room so it's like since he's handicapped he's not a human being. I picture he's overweight, 40 years old, tight blue shirt, messy hair, jeans.

Reviewing their writing, I noted patterns that might be characterized by themes of empathy/compassion, pity/knowing, self-knowing, and rescue/saving. I prepared a handout with excerpts from their writing along with the list of themes and asked the students to confirm these themes or to identify other emotions I may have missed. The students added "anger" and "resentment" and then realized the list comprised only negative emotions. In discussion of why this occurred some students seemed at a loss to explain. Others, like Jose, seized the opportunity to remind everyone about his earlier analysis of the cultural messages we receive about disability when the class discussed the Napolitano poem. This time, he expounded on the negative portrayals of disabled people in films:

> I still dislike they way they're portryed as angry, vengeful people like in films--Davros—in Dr. Who, or the Phantom in the Phantom of the Opera, but this story I like because it showed at the end that the Phantom had human emotions.

In response, another student insisted she had really heard many adults describe other adults with disabilities as girls or boys instead of women or men—as she had written in her characterization. She challenged Jose's analysis explaining that she had borrowed language from how people really talk about the disabled, and not how they talk in the movies. Students contributed to both sides of the debate raising issues about how we infantalize disabled people, how fear frames difference, and how, without thinking, we perpetuate negative media stereotypes. It was remarkable how much the students raised in their criticism generated by two haikus. From this point, it was easy to revisit an earlier conversation on the social construction of disability and the acknowledgement that they lacked sufficient experience with disability to aptly portray characters with disabilities. One student explained, "Its funny, that we don't really talk about disability in school. If it is just another way to live, then why don't we know more about that way?"

In our final activity we viewed the documentary, *When Billy Broke his Head ... and Other Tales of Wonder* (1994). This award winning film introduces more than 20 activists who live with disability and view the experience as central to their identity. The narrator, Billy Golfus, a former radio journalist who was brain damaged after a motor scooter accident introduces the film saying, "This ain't exactly your inspirational cripple story." The students' final writing assignment was to develop characters informed by the individuals in the film. In contrast to their earlier writing, their characters—informed by the lives of the individuals they came to know in the documentary—were markedly more witty, complex, and humane.

15.9 Implications for Teachers

This research was designed to explore K-12 curriculum approaches informed by humanities-based disability studies as described in part one of this paper. Although I reported only a fraction of this classroom research, in this final section I will focus on the implications for teachers when attempting similar content to promote new understanding of disability. In many ways, one of the greatest challenges to teaching this content will be for teachers as they contend with personal issues that surface as they confront unexamined attitudes, assumptions, and beliefs about disability. Consider for example, Tom's realization of the absence of disability issues in his general teaching for over seventeen years. Obviously, this was a surprise and a disappointment given his espoused ideology and daily practice. That is, Tom attended individualized education plan meetings and worked individually with counselors, social workers, special education teachers and other team members on behalf of his students with disabilities. Among his colleagues, he was known to be an inclusive practioner, and yet disability-related topics were nowhere to be found in his curriculum. He explained this in an interview after we completed the unit: "I felt that I lacked the authority to talk about disability; that was someone else's job." In fact, because the discourse on disability in public education and society is so entrenched in the medical model, by most standards, Tom did lack the credential to address disability in his teaching. Professionals from medicine, rehabilitation, psychology, psychiatry, social work, and special education inform the discursive community on disability, which results in a normalizing discourse that informs the collective view of the disabled as diseased, weak, tragic, and too often deserving of their fate.

However by introducing disability as a cultural construct with the purposeful goal of reimagining disability, Tom was more than qualified to introduce these issues. By examining disability through a cultural lens he tapped into prior experiences to inform his insights and practice in a reflective teaching approach. Curiously, this aspect of our teaching was not addressed when we planned the unit. I shared my background as a parent of an adult son with physical disabilities and as a former special education teacher and administrator. However at the time, Tom did not realize the importance of his personal experiences to his teaching of this content, and I did not assume it was necessary to inquire about his lived experience. In retrospect, this proved to be somewhat ironic in that my work with pre-service and practicing teachers is focused on acknowledging prior experience in the formulation of our constructs about ability and disability. As our teaching evolved, the importance of personal reflection when teaching this content became readily apparent. Now that I have expanded this project to include five new teachers along with Tom, the project teachers began with a journal assignment similar to that which I use in my teaching and workshops, titled, My First Memory of Disability."

15.10   Conclusion

If teacher educators accept the challenge of reimagining disability we must begin by problematizing disability through a cultural lens. This approach will necessitate new alliances with colleagues in the humanities and new conversations informed by humanities-based disability studies. Teacher education must recognize that purposeful links between general and special education have failed to occur in most teacher education programs. Although some universities have taken the lead in this enterprise, notably, Syracuse University (Blanton et al. 1997) and the University of South Florida (Paul et al. 1993), many teacher preparation programs are institutionally sanctioned to perpetuate educational apartheid. Turf wars and age-old disputes about professional credentials for educating students with special needs remain unresolved and serve to silence more important conversations about disability as a political and discursive entity. Among these issues are those which Tom and I addressed in his class including identity, education, representation, access, employment and strategies for empowerment and activism, and most significantly, personal meanings of disability. By no means is this list exhaustive, as important related concerns include issues of sexuality, spirituality, religion, and the genocidal aspects of the human genome project. In sum, consideration of these topics would dislodge the silence buried deep inside the uninspired curriculum that restricts teacher and student imagination about disability in both secondary and post-secondary education.

Acknowledgement   I would like to acknowledge the participants of the First Summer Institute on Disability Studies (July, 2000), sponsored by the National Endowment for the Humanities and codirected by Paul K. Longmore (San Francisco State University) and Rosemarie Garland-Thomson (Howard University).

References

Americans with Disabilities Act, 42 U.S.C. §§ 12101-12213 (1990).

Anderson, G. L. (1990). Toward a critical constructivist approach to school administration: invisibility, legitimization, and the study of non-events. *Educational Administration Quarterly, 26*(1), 38–59.

Barton, L. (1999). Series editor's preface. In M. Corker & S. French (Eds.), *Disability and discourse* (p. xi). Buckingham, UK: Open University Press.

Baynton, D. (2001). Disability and the justification of inequality in American history. In P. Longmore & L. Umansky (Eds.), *The new disability history: American perspectives* (pp. 33–57). New York: New York University Press. forthcoming.

Berube, M. (1996). *Life as we know it: A father, a family, and an exceptional child.* New York: Vintage-Random House.

Berube, M. (1997, May). On cultural representation of disability. *Chronicle of Higher Education, 43*(38), B4–B5.

Blanton, L. P., Griffin, C. C., Winn, J. A., & Pugach, M. C. (1997). *Teacher education in transition: Collaborative programs to prepare general and special education educators.* Denver, CO: Love.

Block, L. (1997). *Beyond affliction: The disability history project.* Washington, DC: Corporation for Public Broadcasting. (Audiotape series).

Brantlilnger, E. (1997). Using ideology: Cases of nonrecognition of the politics of research and practice in special education. *Review of Educational Research, 67*(4), 425–459.

Brock, W. (1998). If I can't do it. [Videotape]. Available from Fanlight Productions www.fanlight.com.

Campbell, J., & Oliver, M. (1996). *Disability politics: Understanding our past, changing our future.* London: Routledge.

Carlson, A. L. (1997). Beyond bioethics: Philosophy and disability studies. *Disability Studies Quarterly, 17*(4), 277–283.

Carlson, A. L. (1998). Mindful subjects: Classification and cognitive disability. Unpublished Ph.D. dissertation, University of Toronto, Toronto, Canada.

Cassuto, L. (1999, 19 March). Whose field is it anyway? Disability studies in the academy. Chronicle of Higher Education, 45(28), A60.

Charlton, J. I. (1998). *Nothing about us without us: Disability oppression and empowerment.* Berkley, CA: University of California Press.

Cochran-Smith, M. (2000). Blind vision: Unlearning racism in teacher education. *Harvard Education Review, 70*(2), 157–190.

Corker, M., & French, S. (Eds.). (1999). *Disability and discourse.* Buckingham, UK: Open University Press.

Danforth, S., & Gabel, S. (2000, April). *Disability studies in education.* New Orleans, LA: American Educational Research Association.

Davis, A. B. (1973). *Triumph over disability: The development of rehabilitation medicine in the USA.* Washington, DC: Smithsonian Institution, National Museum of History and Technology.

Davis, L. J. (1995). *Enforcing normalcy: Disability, deafness and the body.* London: Verso.

Davis, L. J. (1997). *The disability studies reader.* New York: Routledge.

Davis, L. J. (1998, Summer). Who put *the* the *in* the novel? Identity politics and disability in novel studies. *Novel, 31*(3), 317–334.

Ellsworth, E. (1997). *Teaching positions: Difference, pedagogy and the power of address.* New York: Teachers College Press.

Erevelles, N. (2000). Educating unruly bodies: Critical pedagogy, disability studies, and the politics of schooling. *Educational Theory, 50*(1), 25–47.

Freire, P. (1970). *Pedagogy of the process.* New York: Continuum.

Gabel, S. (1998). Depressed and disabled: Some discursive problems with mental illness. In M. Corcker & S. French (Eds.), *Disability discourse* (pp. 38–46). Buckingham and Philadelphia: Open University Press.

Gabel, S. (2001). "I wash my face with dirty water." Narratives of disability and pedagogy. *Journal of Teacher Education, 52,* 31–47.

Gabel, S. (2019a). Problems of conceptual translation in cross-cultural disability studies: A south Asian immigrant example. In B. Altman & S. Barthart (Eds.), *Research in social science and disability Vol. II.* Thousand Oaks: Sage.

Gabel, S. (2019b). Some conceptual problems with critical pedagogy. *Journal of Curriculum Inquiry.*

Gallagher, D. (1998). The scientific knowledge base of special education: Do we know what we think we know? *Exceptional Children, 64*(4), 493–502.

Garland-Thomson, R. (1997). *Extraordinary bodies. Figuring physical disability in American culture and literature.* New York: Columbia University Press.

Gilman, S. (1985). *Difference and pathology: Stereotypes of sexuality, race, and madness.* Ithaca: Cornell University Press.

Giroux, H. (1996). Is there a place for cultural studies in colleges of education? In H. A. Giroux, C. Lankshear, P. McLaren, & M. Peters (Eds.), *Counternarratives: Cultural studies amd critical pedagogies in postmodern spaces* (pp. 41–58). London: Routledge.

Golfus, B. and Simpson, D.E. (1994). When Billy broke his head … and other tales of wonder [Film]. Available from Fanlight Productions, www.fanlight.com

Heshusius, L. (1989). The Newtonian mechanistic paradigm, special education, and contours of alternatives: An overview. *Journal of Learning Disabilities, 22,* 403–415.

Heshusius, L. (1995). Holism and special education: There is no substitute for real life purposes and processes. In T. M. Skritc (Ed.), *Disability and democracy: Reconstructing (special) education* (pp. 166–189). New York: Teachers College Press.

Heshusius, L. (2000, April). Breaking the silence: Disability, education, and critical methods. In: Paper Presented at the Annual Meeting of American Education Association. New Orleans, LA.

Hockenberry, J. (1995). *Moving violations*. New York: Hyperion.

Individuals with Disabilities Act, 20 U.S.C. §§ 1400 et seq. (1997).

Kittay, E. F. (1999a). *Love's labor: Essays on women, equality, and dependency*. London: Routledge.

Kittay, E. F. (1999b). "Not *my* way, Sesha, *your* way, slowly": "Maternal thinking" in the raising of a child with profound intellectual disabilities. In J. E. Hanigsberg & S. Ruddick (Eds.), *Mother troubles: Rethinking contemporary maternal dilemmas* (pp. 3–25). Boston, MA: Beacon Press.

Kleiwer, C. (2000). The collected papers of Burton Blatt: In search of the promised land [Book review]. *Journal of the Association for Severe Handicaps, 25*(1), 59–63.

Lather, P. (1998). Critical pedagogy and its complicities: A praxis of stuck places. *Educational Theory, 48*, 487–497.

Linton, S. (1998). *Claiming disability: Knowledge and identity*. New York: New York University Press.

Longmore, P. (1987). Screening Stereotypes: Images of disabled people in television and motion pictures. In A. Gartner & T. Joe (Eds.), *Images of the disabled, disabling images* (pp. 65–78). New York: Praeger.

Longmore, P., & Garland-Thomson, R. (1999). *National endowment for the humanities insitute on disability studies proposal. July–August, 2000*. San Francisco, CA: San Francisco State University.

Longmore, P., & Goldberger, D. (2000). The league of the physically handicapped and the great depression: A case study in the new disability history. *Journal of American History, 87*(3), 888–922.

Longmore, P., & Umanksy, L. (2001). Disability history, from the margins to the mainstream. In P. Longmore & L. Umansky (Eds.), *The new disability history: American perspectives* (pp. 1–31). New York: New York University Press.

MacIntyre, A. (1999). *Dependent rational animals: Why human beings need virtue*. La Salle, IL: Open Court.

Mairs, N. (1986). On being a cripple. In *Plaintext: Essays* (pp. 9–20). Tucson, AZ: University of Arizona Press.

Mairs, N. (1996). *Waist-high in the world: A life among the nondisabled*. Boston, MA: Beacon Press.

McRuer, R. (2001). Compulsory able-bodiedness and queer/disabled existence. In B. Bruggerman, R. Garland-Thomson, & S. L. Snyder (Eds.), *Enabling the humanities: A sourcebook in disability studies*. New York: Modern Language Association.

Mitchell, D., & Snyder, S. (1997). *The body and physical difference: Discourse of disability*. Ann Arbor, MI: University of Michigan Press.

Morris, J. (1991). *Pride against prejudice: Transforming attitudes to disability*. London: Women's Press.

Napolitano, S. (1998). *A dangerous woman*. Manchester, England: GMCDP Publications.

Norden, M. F. (1994). *The cinema of isolation: A history of physical difference in the movies*. New Brunswick, NJ: Rutgers University Press.

Ott, K. (2000, July). History: Disability and medical history. In: Paper presented at the National Endowment for the Humanities Summer Institute on Disability Studies. San Francisco State University, San Francisco, CA.

Paul, J. L., Duchnowski, A., & Danforth, S. (1993). Changing the way we do business: One department's story of collaboration with schools. *Teacher Education and Special Education, 16*(2), 95–109.

Peters, S. (1995). Disability baggage. Changing the educational research terrain. In P. Clough & L. Barton (Eds.), *Making difficulties: Research & the construction of special educational needs* (pp. 59–74). London: Paul Chapman Publishing.

Peters, S. (1996). The politics of disability identity. In L. Barton (Ed.), *Disability and society: Emerging issues and insights* (pp. 215–234). London: Longman.

Peters, S. (2000). Is there a disability culture? A syncretisation of three possible world views. *Disability & Society, 15*(4), 583–601.

Peters, S. J., & Chimedza, R. (2000). Conscientization and the cultural politics of education: a radical minority perspective. *Comparative Education Review, 44*(3), 245–271.

Philip, M. (1985). Michel foucault. In Q. Skinner (Ed.), *The return of grand theory in the human science*. Cambridge: Cambridge University Press.

Shakespeare, T. (1999). Art and lies? Representations of disability on film. In M. Corker & S. French (Eds.), *Disability discourse*. Buckingham: Open University Press.

Shapiro, J. P. (1993). *No pity: people with disabilities forging a new civil rights*. New York: Times Books/Random House Inc..

Shaw, B. (1994). *The ragged edge*. Louisville: The Avacado Press.

Skrtic, T. (1991). *Behind special education: a critical analysis of professional culture and school organization*. Denver: Love.

Skrtic, T. (1995). *Disability and democracy: reconstructing [special] education for postmodernity*. New York: Teachers College Press.

Smith, P. (1999a). Food truck's party hat. *Qualitative Inquiry, 5*(2), 244–261.

Smith, P. (1999b). Drawing new maps: a radical cartography of developmental disabilities. *Review of Educational Research, 69*(2), 117–144.

Smith, P.. (2000). MAN.i.f.e.s.t..: A poetics of d(eviL)op[mental] {Dos}ability. In: Paper presented at desegregating disability studies: an interdisciplinary discussion. Syracuse, NY.

Tatum, B. (1992). Talking about race, learning about racism: The application of racial identity development theory in the classroom. *Harvard Educational Review, 62*(1), 1–24.

Thomson, R. G. (1997). *Extraordinary Bodies. Figuring physical disability in American culture and literature*. New York: Columbia University Press.

Ware, L. (1995). The aftermath of the articulate debate: The invention of inclusive education. In C. Clark, A. Dyson, & A. Millward (Eds.), *Towards inclusive schools?* (pp. 127–146). New York: Teachers College Press.

Ware, L. (1998). I kinda wonder if we're fooling ourselves? In T. Booth & M. Ainscow (Eds.), *From them to us: an international study of inclusion in education* (pp. 21–42). London: Routledge.

Ware, L. (1999). My kid and kids kinda like him. In K. Ballard (Ed.), *Inclusive education: international voices on disability and justice* (pp. 43–66). London: Falmer Press.

Ware, L. (2000a, April). A collaborative inquiry on understanding disability in secondary and post-secondary settings. A research proposal to the National Endowment for the Humanities (Available from Linda P. Ware, University of Rochester, PO Box 270425. Rochester, NY 14627-0425).

Ware, L. (2000b). Inclusive education. In D. A. Gabbard (Ed.), *Education in the global economy: politics and the rhetoric of school reform* (pp. 111–120). New Jersey: Lawrence Erlbaum Publishers.

Ware, L. (2000c). Products producing subjectivities: Disability studies in education. In: *An invited paper presented at the eighth annual meeting of the international research colloquium on inclusive education*. Hamar, Norway, June 27-July 1, 2000.

Ware, L. (2000d). Sunflowers, enchantment, and empires: Reflections on inclusive education in the United States. In F. Armstrong, D. Armstrong, & L. Barton (Eds.), *Inclusive education: policy, contexts and comparative perspectives* (pp. 42–59). London: David Fulton Press.

Ware, L. (2000e). There's no easy way to say/hear this, 'As a cripple, I swagger.' In: *Paper presented at the annual meeting of American Education Association*. New Orleans, LA.

Ware, L. (2000f). *What the literature tells us about inclusion: What literature? Who was listening? Presentation to the Greece Central School Board of Education special study session on inclusion*. New York: Greece.

Wendell, S. (1996). *The rejected body: Feminist philosophical reflections on Disability*. New York: Routledge.

Yu, J.. (1996). Breathing lessons: The life of Mark O'Brien. [Film]. (Available from Fanlight Productions: www.fanlight.com).

Chapter 16
Sharing International Experiences to Develop Inclusion in a German Context: Reflections of an American Inclusive Educator

David J. Connor

16.1 Introduction: Inclusive Education: Where Are We Now?

In November 2015, the Goethe Universities Institute of Special Education and the Faculty of Education, in cooperation with the German Institute for International Education Research, hosted a symposium whose theme was *Inclusion and Transformation: Possibilities of an Educational Systems Change*. As part of the International Perspectives section, I was invited to share experiences regarding the challenges of changing educational systems toward providing more inclusive schools, with a particular focus on classroom pedagogy. In some ways, this renewed focus on inclusive education at regional, national, and international levels served as a form of stocktaking. I found myself asking: *What do we know? What successes have we had? How do we know? What else can be done?* As a career-long inclusive educator who can now look back at over a quarter-century, I have experienced the constant morphing of the educational landscape as it shifts according to changes in laws, governmental priorities, policies at federal/state/local levels, leadership, personnel, research, cultural values, and so on. In sum, the "progress" of inclusive education has been subjected to a recursive trajectory of ebbs and flows, pinnacles and pitfalls, and a perpetual feeling of two-steps-forwards-and-one-step back (or two steps back, and in some cases—alas!—three).

Although a dyed-in-the-wool optimist, I must confess to sometimes feeling that we have been "running on the spot" in terms of inclusion. This phrase aptly captures the paradoxical sense of exerting energy toward movement, yet finding oneself in the same place. This feeling was triggered by a recent request from a local superintendent to provide professional development to 40 high school principals on

D. J. Connor (✉)
Hunter College, City University of New York, New York, NY, USA
e-mail: dconnor@hunter.cuny.edu

© Springer Nature Switzerland AG 2020
L. Ware (ed.), *Critical Readings in Interdisciplinary Disability Studies*, Critical Studies of Education 12, https://doi.org/10.1007/978-3-030-35309-4_16

collaborative teaching as a means to support inclusive education. In discussion with the superintendent and staff, I realized that I was being asked to do the same work I had done two decades ago, namely a presentation for a former superintendent and her school leaders. One part of me was happy that inclusive issues were being centered for principals to engage with, and another part was saddened by the realization that all of these principals should already possess this knowledge, preferably having experienced collaborative teaching in their own careers to date. Regardless, although inclusive education has not been perfected by a long shot, the school systems in which we work *are* responding to the expectations of including students identified as disabled.

Of interest is that these two invitations from Germany and a local superintendent of schools both came at a time when I was philosophically musing on the value of professional choices made throughout my career. Like many who have supported various social movements for equality—such as race, ethnicity, gender, sexual orientation, and so on—I had wished to see more progress by now. Although I have witnessed many changes for the better, deep-rooted concerns remain about the relationship between inclusion and current trends in education such as neo-liberalism and its associations with charter schools, standards, relentless data-driven assessment, and the movement to corporatize teacher education. In this current educational climate, "creative" approaches to what some educators call inclusive education are actually the opposite (Slee 2011), and I fear losing some hard-won traction gained to date.

In some ways, these concerns increase my resolve to engage with educators in university and school systems about inclusive education. As a result, I agreed to do both presentations as long as I could incorporate the topic of Disability Studies (DS) and its sub-discipline Disability Studies in Education (DSE). Both organizations were amenable. For the purpose of this chapter I will limit my primary focus to the symposium in Germany, as I have documented using a DS-approach to engaging principals about inclusive education elsewhere (Connor 2004). To be direct, I see the inclusion of DSE in presentations at home and abroad as a way to introduce its concepts to a new audience, many of who have not had the opportunity to conceptualize disability and education outside of the very narrow, largely damaging definitions within special education. The reframing of disability as a natural part of human variation helps educators better understand the purpose of inclusive education.

16.2   Disability Studies in Education and Global Interactions

Interest in DSE has grown internationally over the last 15 or so years. The desire to cultivate global dialogs became evident in *Ideology and the Politics of (In)Exclusion* (Ware 2004), the outcome of an international symposium organized by Linda Ware in 1999 and was sponsored by the Spenser Foundation. This desire to cultivate global interest continued in journal publications such as the special double edition of the *International Journal of Inclusive Education* (Connor et al. 2008) in which scholars from New Zealand, Ireland, the USA, and Ghana shared their research on the theme of Disability Studies and Inclusive Education. The DSE book series Gabel and Danforth's (2008) *Disability and the Politics of Education* contains 33 chapters by scholars from Africa (3), Asia (4), Australasia (3), Europe (12), South America (1), and the USA. (12). The introductory chapter features international agreements on the right to education, including the Salamanca Statement (UNESCO 1994) that proclaims children with disabilities "must have access to regular schools which should accommodate them within a child-centered pedagogy capable of meeting those needs," and "Regular schools with [an] inclusive orientation are the most effective means of combating discriminatory attitudes...building an inclusive society and achieving education for all..." (Sect. 16.2). Other books in the DSE series include *South Asia and Disability Studies* (Rao and Kalyanpur 2015) an Australian focused volume *(De)Constructing ADHD* (Graham 2010), and an international collection, *Practicing Disability Studies in Education, Acting Toward Social Change* (Connor et al. 2015).

An informal network of scholars has helped cultivate DSE's evolution internationally, affording opportunities for ongoing conversations about ways to (re)conceptualize disability with a view to advocating for educational change. Several editions of DS journals have been dedicated to disability and education (see, for example, *Disability Studies Quarterly* [Connor and Ferri 2010; Valle et al. 2005]), and the *International Review of Disability Studies* (Connor et al. 2012). In addition, education has been a consistent topic of interest in *Disability & Society* (Danforth 2009; Gabel and Peters 2004; Gallagher 2001; Graham and Grieshaber 2008; Lesseliers et al. 2009; Wendelborg and Tøssebro 2010). The annual DSE conference, while largely based in the USA, has been held in Belgium (2010), New Zealand (2013), and Australia (2014) and often yields a publication of selected proceedings, such as *Disability Studies: Educating for Inclusion* (Corcoran et al. 2015). All of these publications and events have contributed to a growing body of accumulated knowledge that continues to inform our collective thinking and is of great use when engaging in forums where people do not necessarily expect what [do you mean anticipate] DSE brings to the table.

16.3   Structure and Purpose of the German Symposium

The symposium in Germany was scheduled to last a full day, preceded by an evening presentation by Dr. Eckard Klieme, Director of the Department on Educational Quality and Evaluation in Goethe University, Frankfurt. The schedule was a jam-packed 9:00 a.m.–5:30 p.m. and set in a bright, spacious conference room. The tables were set in a horseshoe configuration, allowing 40 participants to face the lecture stand and the screen. After an overview of the proceedings and an introductory lecture by Allan Dyson from England, three broad areas were addressed: (1) (Inter)national findings on the development of inclusive education systems; (2) methodological and didactic conditions for inclusive education; (3) (Inter)national experience from development research. Within each of these areas were two presenters, one from Germany or Austria and one international speaker representing Scotland, Sweden, and the USA.

The purpose of the symposium was an interesting one. A benefactor of the university expressed a wish to create an endowed professorship dedicated to inclusive education within that specific region of Germany, as it was not as progressive as other comparable regions. The symposium was designed with the dual intent of (1) hearing from educational researchers within and outside of Germany about the current knowledge base and (2) developing a better sense of the disposition, knowledge, and skills needed by the person who would be in the new position—and uniquely tailored in a subsequent posting to advertise this important position.

16.4   Symposium Highlights and Tidbits

I will not endeavor to share a step-by-step detailed description of the event, as it would likely be far too pedantic. However, before I move into describing elements within my own presentation, I will share some interesting highlights and tidbits of the symposium. For example, Germany has eight "official" types of disability categories and each has been the basis for developing separate educational structures specific to that disability (Tomlinson 2012). As can be imagined, the logistics of deconstructing this system and moving toward increased integration can seem quite challenging.

In the initial section on educational systems, Michael Urban spoke of the school systems overcoming inertia and resistance toward structural changes, and the need to use flexible pedagogical skills developed by special educators within traditional general education schools. Next came Tobias Feldhoff, who strongly advocated for a mixed-methods approach in research to illustrate the complexities involved when investigating the best ways to support inclusion in schools. In his work within Hamburg schools, Feldhoff noted how educational *structures* can be changed fast, but the *culture* within schools changes far more slowly. As the culminating part of the event's introductory segment, Allan Dyson spoke of how focusing on children with disabilities was insufficient, pressing for recognition of a greater need to address children from socially and economically disadvantaged backgrounds, including those with disabilities. He advocated for conceiving of supporting children and youth beyond the school gate through the development of integrated networks that included health care and social services.

My contribution to the second section focused on instructional pedagogy, and will be described in some detail during the next section. In the third section focusing on (inter)national experience from development research, Ewald Feyerer of Austria shared 25 years of his country's journey of developing inclusive education. Beginning in 1988 and phased in over 8 years, this systematic approach "normalized" inclusive classrooms of 20–24 pupils, with a maximum of approximately 25–30% students with disabilities. Feyerer also introduced tensions revealed within his research on inclusive classrooms, including some students with disabilities who developed a greater sense of self-esteem, increased peer relationships, and trust, yet others were prone to higher rates of victimization and loneliness as compared to their non-disabled peers. Feyerer was followed by Bengt Persson of Sweden whose research revealed how teachers still have negative perceptions of students with disabilities, and his urging for inclusion being the guiding principle for teaching and learning if our collective aim is for a wider, more truly diverse society. Julie Allan rounded out the international speakers, focusing on historical and international perspectives on inclusion, particularly in Sweden and her native Scotland. She called attention to the need for changing language so inclusion is not seen as an expanded version of special education, and the tendency of educational systems to make the simple issue of inclusive classrooms unnecessarily overcomplicated.

The last section of the symposium was dedicated to a discussion of research strategies intersecting with legal, political, and cultural factors that was mindful of current school practices. Attendees noted the need to document what has worked well in terms of inclusive education, as well as learn from failed attempts. Interestingly, there was noticeable dissention among the academic attendees as several urged for a level of criticality within inclusive research, rather than unquestionably aligning themselves with institutional and state policies. It ended with an agreement that all types of research held potential value in going forward.

16.5   Using Disability Studies in My Own Presentation

Nested in the midst of all these stimulating topics, my presentation was titled *Contemplating Teachers' Disposition and Pedagogical Skills Within Inclusive Classrooms: Responsibilities of, and Implications for, Teacher Education Programs and In-Service Professional Development*. It was admittedly a bit of a mouthful because the title was designed to make all stakeholders aware of the complexities involved in educating teachers around specific issues of disability and a larger framework for inclusive education in general. It was also the opportunity to bring DSE to a larger audience and integrate it into the general conversation. In brief, I structured the presentation to address three broad, yet related, areas: first, I discussed teacher (a) dispositions (forged by beliefs and responsibilities) about human differences; (b) skills as flexible pedagogues; and, (c) ability to collaborate with others, as three crucial areas necessary to create and maintain inclusive classrooms; second, I advocated for the use of a DSE framework to inform the field's work in inclusive education; third, I posed a series of questions to serve as a springboard for further conversations about inclusive education regarding teacher educators' responsibilities to pre-service and in-service teachers. In the following sections, I will paraphrase my major points.

16.5.1   The Importance of Teachers

The teacher is the most influential person within a classroom, who should always be working to improve student engagement through their instruction while creating an environment supportive of academic, emotional, and psychological domains. In all classrooms, but inclusive classrooms in particular, teachers are expected to be knowledgeable about and comfortable with student diversity. Even though inclusive education was a term primarily associated with students identified as disabled, it has since come to symbolize all forms of diversity, including ethnicity, sexual orientation, socio-economic status, gender, culture, and so on (Baglieri et al. 2011). What is not always apparent is the need for educators to recognize the intersectional locations of all students, as there is no single marker of identity; e.g., a male who is a working class Latino immigrant of African-descent from the Dominican Republic and gay must simultaneously navigate issues of socio-economic status, gender, ethnicity, nationality, race, and sexual orientation.

In some ways, expectations of teachers represent an ideal. Where else in society is anybody expected to be open to, and respond to, seemingly infinite forms of human variation; treat everyone as equals; connect with them at their academic, social, and emotional levels; and teach them new knowledge and skills? At the same time, it is incumbent upon each teacher to see themselves, and inclusive education, as an ongoing work-in-progress. For those of us who work in researching and teaching inclusive education at the university level, such idealism gives rise to questions about "pre-service" and "in-service" teacher education. I am obliged to ask questions such as: *To what degree can and do teacher education programs effectively support and model inclusive education at the pre-service level? To what degree can authentic professional development in schools advance and support inclusive education at the "in-service" level?*

16.5.2   Consciously Cultivating Teacher Dispositions

It is important to take a moment and illustrate some considerations for university level teacher-educators in their work with the two distinct—yet related—groups of pre-service and in-service teachers. In working with individuals within these groups, each person must consider and constantly reflect upon each area of (1) disposition toward human differences, (2) abilities in pedagogy, and (3) skills in working with other educators. Without wishing to be reductive, in some respects, these crucial areas may be perceived as *abstractions* for pre-service teachers, and lived *realities* within a specific context, for in-service teachers. This distinction certainly determines how to conceptualize the teaching of certain knowledge and skills about inclusive education for pre-service teachers perhaps without a place to see them in action. Conversely, such knowledge and skills may or may not influence change in existing classrooms. I share this point because the three interrelated areas addressed in this chapter are likely to hold different implications for pre-service and in-service teachers. That said, one area in which I have experienced some success is engaging both groups about their dispositions toward human difference. To help do this, I utilize the interdisciplinary academic field of Disability Studies (DS).

16.5.3   Using the Lens of Disability Studies

It has been my experience that many teachers are wary of inclusive education, thinking along the lines of: "That child does not belong in this classroom," "There are special ed. teachers to take care of that child," or "I will not change how I teach, so if they can't keep up they must go." However, by beginning with engaging educators with questions such as What do we think about human differences and why? Where does that information come from? we can cultivate a greater awareness of: What are the sources of knowledge about disability? Who created that knowledge? Who benefits and who does not benefit from that knowledge? What if that knowledge is inaccurate and/or damaging to people with disabilities? These are crucial areas to explore because *what we think about people influences how we teach them.*

To help promote such conversations, I cull strategically from DS as an interdisciplinary field that seeks to trouble longstanding notions of disability as a deficit, disorder, or dysfunction; in brief, as something *missing* within a person. Above all, it primarily critiques the seemingly omnipresent framing of disability within a medical model, of thinking of people as ill or broken, in need of fixing, or a "cure." In contrast, because DS views disability as a natural form of human variation, it actively challenges society to examine how widespread beliefs that continue to marginalize individuals by asking what is "disability" and its relationship to "normalcy" (Linton 1998).

In these discussions, students come to see how the world has been arranged in binaric structures of normalcy/abnormalcy, able-bodied/disabled, and general/special, with clear implications for who is desirable/undesirable. It becomes apparent that characteristics of all individuals are hierarchical in value, and that the idealized American citizen is of European-descent, male, able bodied, professional, English-speaking, heterosexual, handsome, academic, and athletic (Davis 1995). However, very few citizens fit this mold within a diverse society, but those that do are favored, and those that do not are viewed as inferior. Notions of normalcy and deviance co-exist because one cannot be defined without invoking the other. By interrogating the concept of normalcy in all that it does, DS offers an alternative lens to fields of knowledge that have traditionally constituted the foundations of special education—science, medicine, and psychology. Furthermore, by using a social, cultural, and historical lens, DS reframes the issue of inclusion from one that has been viewed as primarily legal, technical, and managerial responses to one of civil rights. Instead of requesting/persuading the majority to be included, disabled individuals place the onus on: "Why do you actively seek to exclude us?"

16.6   Civil Rights

Although it will likely not be news to many readers of this volume, I believe part of our work as DS scholars is to introduce disability as a "minority model" perspective (while being mindful of intersectional nuances, complications, and even charges of outdatedness), making it be viewed as another "Other," part of the sociological frame (Kudlick 2003). Just as differences can lead to forms of discrimination such as race and racism, gender and sexism, sexual orientation and heterosexism, the corresponding "ism" is ableism—a form of structural, systematic, cultural oppression based on beliefs that people without disabilities are "complete" and therefore superior human beings (Hehir 2005). In their seminal text *The Disability Rights Movement: From Charity to Confrontation*, Fleischer and Zames (2011) connect the major topics of the civil rights movement within a powerful narrative that incorporates pitiful portrayals of "wheelchair bound" children; alternative ways of functioning such as seeing by touch and hearing by sign; deinstitutionalization and independent living; the struggle for change in the courts and in the streets; the foundational disability rights legislation, Section 504; the Americans With Disabilities Act; access to jobs and health care; activists combatting physician-assisted suicide; disability and technology; disabled veterans and their rights; the Individuals with Disabilities Education Act; and disability identity and culture.

In *No Pity: People With Disabilities Forging a New Civil Rights Movement*, Joseph Shapiro writes, "Nondisabled Americans do not understand disabled ones" (Shapiro 1993, p. 3). This sweeping statement serves as a springboard for conversation in my own graduate education classes. It tends to open up the larger topic of to what degree can a non-minority member understand a minority member's perspective of, and lived experiences within, society in general? For non-disabled people, it comes as quite a shock that the majority of information written about disabled people is not by themselves, but mainly by able-bodied people within various fields, including education. DS, in contrast, centers upon the voices of "the disabled"—including researchers, activists, children, youth, adults, and parents—who usually claim that knowledge about them written by others is overwhelmingly inaccurate, misleading, and often harmful. Implications of such an ontological dissonance are alarming, as suggested by DS scholar Len Barton's observation:

> …it gradually began to dawn on me that if disabled people left it to others to write about disability, we would inevitably end up with inaccurate and distorted accounts of our experiences and inappropriate service provision and professional practices based upon these inaccuracies and distortions (Barton 1996, p. 16).

To counter the deficit-oriented master-narrative of disability, the field of DS is replete with counter-narratives in the form of statements, testimonies, and participatory research that challenges and rectifies discourses of disability by rethinking and reframing it as natural human difference (see, for example, Brown 2003; Linton 2006; Mooney 2007; Robison 2007). It is clear that learning about disability by using disabled people as the primary source is more authentic than most educational research (Brantlinger 1997), classic and contemporary literature (Mitchell and Snyder 2000), and mainstream media (Haller 2010). These forms of knowledge about disability have the potential to make a powerful impact upon both pre-service and in-service teachers by actively helping them *unlearn* many of the inaccuracies they have come to know with a view to rethinking about human difference (Connor 2015). In sum, scholars within DS change the conversation from conceptualizing inclusive education as approximating a norm or fitting in, to one that compels us to look at the problematics of rationalizing exclusion and segregation within our democracy.

16.7 The Need to Create Change

The challenge and beauty of inclusive classrooms is that they require changing traditional notions of education as well as questioning commonplace, longstanding beliefs. In sum, they mean contemplating schools and classrooms with new eyes and imagining possibilities of what has not yet been done on a national scale. As an educator interested in pedagogy, I welcome the opportunity to help create inclusive classrooms in different ways—from co-teaching to assessing instructional effectiveness, from developing curriculum to discussing furniture arrangements, from knowing all students to informing them of their strengths and areas they need to work on. Much has been written over the last 25 years about developing inclusive education. For example, Spencer Salend's *Creating Inclusive Classrooms: Effective and Reflective Practices* (Salend 2011) was first published in 1990 and is now in its eighth edition. Given the expanse of existing literature and the limits of this chapter, I selected six points that serve as a condensed form of what I believe are important "tools" that teachers should have in their education toolbox. These tools can be utilized within daily classroom practice to help develop and expand a teacher's flexible pedagogy. In sum, the areas I discussed at greater length within the presentation were: (1) A Sense of Fairness; (2) Universal Design for Learning (UDL); (3) Multiple Intelligences; (4) Learning Styles (LS); (5) Differentiated Instruction (DI); and, (6) Habits of Thinking: Simple, Useful Ideas. These six selected suggestions help us see inclusive pedagogy from many vantage points. To state the obvious, all of these options cannot be provided simultaneously, but should be acknowledged and incorporated into a balanced pedagogy that is respectful of all learners. In addition to these suggestions, I spent time emphasizing ways in which teachers can learn to collaborate with view to maximizing the effectiveness of co-teaching (Friend and Cook 2012). Finally, I discussed how DS must be integral in the creation of more clinically rich inclusive teacher education programs and its usefulness in in-service professional development for teachers and administrators.

16.8   Discussion: DSE in the Mix

As I have previously mentioned, the core of this chapter that consists of a brief
overview and rationale of DS will be familiar to many readers. However, I felt compelled to include it as one example of how critical it is that special educators who
are DS scholars must continue to introduce DS to a more diverse audience. This can
be at a local level such as the professional development for principals that I referred
to earlier, or the international level of a symposium on inclusion, as well as within a
college-level class (Connor 2015), high school (Ware 2001), middle school (Solis
and Connor 2007), or elementary school (Connor and Bejoian 2006).

I have found incorporating DS/DSE into presentations and in classrooms has a
significant impact upon those who engage with it as it resonates with all but the
deepest cynics of diversity. DS/DSE is encompassing and malleable that, when utilized strategically, helps people see the misinformation about what we term "disabilities," subsequent inequities in society, and our complicities in exclusive
practices and systems. As mentioned previously, in agreeing to present to principals
on inclusive education in general, and team teaching specifically, I agreed to do so
if I could frame the entire conversation within disability studies. This allowed me to
call upon individuals first as private citizens, and second as public employees, asking them to reexamine their belief system about human difference, who belongs
where, and where that knowledge comes from. It also opens up space to contemplate what does it mean to be able-bodied, and to articulate the privileges that it
brings. Once the inequities and discriminatory practices within educational systems
are rendered visible (rather than being in plain sight but not originally viewed as
such), *then* the transition can be made to what the audience has identified as their
interest. In most cases, people at presentations or in classrooms want to know HOW
to do specific things. For the principals, it was how to self-assess their school organization for currently existing practices that supported inclusive education, identify
problems and gaps, and begin to think of collaborative ways to work with their staff
to strengthen and expand team-teaching classes. For the academics in Germany,
their desired focus was on skills and knowledge needed for competent inclusive
educators.

As a very practitioner-based inclusive educator, I am quite eager to get to the
HOW of what people want to learn to do, whether it be planning a lesson, developing a unit, plotting a semester-long curriculum map, working with a co-teacher,
communicating with parents, engaging students in learning, restructuring schools,
and so on. However, I have come to learn that it is *imperative* to spend time on the
WHY inclusive work is being done. DS/DSE is an indispensable tool in creating
classes and presentations that penetrates what often feels like an inflexible, calcified
educational field that is resistant to change. The strategic use of quotations, the uti-
lization of key principles, engagement through thoughtful questions and meaningful
activities, in a cohesive and balanced manner, can work to subvert the status quo in
people's thinking about disability. Of course, the balance referred to is crucial. You
give people the content they want or need, yet in return, you also provide them with

the means to take several steps back and reflect upon what they think they know. In finding out that they have been misinformed and have actually misunderstood (many) disability-related issues, participants often experience a form of destabilization. I view this destabilization as the position from which new growth is possible. Similar to how Heshusius and Ballard (1996) carefully documented the epiphanies and insights of researchers who experienced paradigm shifts, educators must grapple with letting go of life-long beliefs. Most importantly, educators should recognize that such destabilization holds great opportunities as a productive for rethinking what is important about how we understand the concept of disability—and why.

16.9 Conclusion: Final Reflections

This chapter has allowed me to share some of my current thinking about, and experiences with, DS/DSE and inclusive education. The longer I am in this profession, the more deeply convinced I am about the need to engage with educators—whether they be pre-service or in-service—about the dispositions toward the human differences that society identifies as "disabilities." It has been my experience that the theories of DS and DSE are transformable into practice, and should continue to be utilized within inclusive education, particularly with a view to confronting the current climate that conflates standards with standardization of students.

The growth of interest in DS and DSE around the world has been gratifying. Bearing this in mind, DS/DSE scholars should continue to take opportunities in their professional work to introduce examples of DS/DSE guiding frameworks of thinking with a view to problem-solving around, and further developing, inclusive classes. Whether in local, national, or international forums, DS/DSE can and should be part of our rationale for urging and developing change. In closing, I will (re)pose two questions I asked attendees at the symposium to consider:

- To what degree can and do teacher education programs effectively support and model inclusive education at the pre-service level?
- To what degree can authentic professional development in schools advance and support inclusive education at the "in-service" level?

This, to me, is where some of our work now lies. DSE seems an integral part of developing answers to these questions. What do *you* think?

References

Baglieri, S., Bejoian, L., Broderick, A., Connor, D. J., & Valle, J. (2011). [Re]claiming "inclusive education" toward cohesion in educational reform: Disability studies unravels the myth of the typical child. *Teachers College Record, 113*(10), 2122–2154.
Barton, L. (Ed.). (1996). *Disability and society: Emerging issues and insights*. London: Longman.

Brantlinger, E. (1997). Using ideology: Cases of nonrecognition of the politics of research and practice in special education. *Review of Educational Research, 67*(4), 425–459.

Brown, S. E. (2003). *Movie stars and sensuous scars.* New York: Universe.

Connor, D. J. (2004). Infusing disability studies into "mainstream" educational thought: One person's story. *Review of Disability Studies, 1*(1), 100–119.

Connor, D. J. (2015). Practicing what we teach: The benefits of using disability studies in an inclusion course. In D. J. Connor, J. Valle, & C. Hale (Eds.), *Practicing disability studies in education: Acting toward social change* (pp. 123–140). New York: Peter Lang.

Connor, D. J., & Bejoian, J. (2006). Pigs, pirates, and pills: Using film to teach the social context of disability. *Teaching Exceptional Children, 39*(2), 52–60.

Connor, D. J., Gabel, S., Gallagher, D., & Morton, M. (2008). Disability studies and inclusive education—implications for theory, research, and practice. *International Journal of Inclusive Education, 12*(5–6), 441–457.

Connor, D. J., & Ferri, B. (2010) Introduction to special DSQ issue: "Why is there learning disabilities?" revisiting Christine Sleeter's socio-political construction of disability two decades on. Disability Studies Quarterly, 30(2).

Connor, D. J., Valle, J., & Hale, C. (2012). Forum guest editors' introduction: Disability studies in education "at work". *Review of Disability Studies, 8*(3), 5–13.

Connor, D. J., Valle, J., & Hale, C. (Eds.). (2015). *Practicing disability studies in education: Acting toward social change.* New York: Peter Lang.

Corcoran, T., White, J., & Whitburn, B. (Eds.). (2015). *Disability studies: Educating for inclusion.* Boston: Sense.

Danforth, S. (2009). *The incomplete child: An intellectual history of learning disabilities.* New York: Peter Lang.

Davis, L. J. (1995). *Enforcing normalcy: Disability, deafness and the body.* New York: Verso.

Fleischer, D. Z., & Zames, F. (2011). *The disability rights movement: From charity to confrontation.* Philadelphia: Temple University Press.

Friend, M., & Cook, L. (2012). *Interactions: Collaboration skills for school professionals* (7th ed.). New York: Pearson.

Gabel, S. L., & Danforth, S. (2008). *Disability and the politics of education: An international reader.* New York: Peter Lang.

Gabel, S. L., & Peters, S. (2004). Presage of a paradigm shift? Beyond the social model of disability toward a resistance theory of disability. *Disability & Society, 19*(6), 571–596.

Gallagher, D. J. (2001). Neutrality as a moral standpoint, conceptual confusion and the full inclusions debate. *Disability & Society, 16*(5), 637–654.

Graham, L. (2010). *(De)constructing ADHD: Critical guidance for teachers and educators.* New York: Peter Lang.

Graham, L. J., & Grieshaber, S. (2008). Reading dis/ability: Interrogating paradigms in a prism of power. *Disability & Society, 23*(6), 557–570.

Haller, B. (2010). *Representing disability in an ableist world.* Louisville, KY: Advocado Press.

Hehir, T. (2005). *New directions in special education: Eliminating ableism in policy and practice.* Cambridge, MA: Harvard University Press.

Heshusius, L., & Ballard, K. (Eds.). (1996). *From positivism to interpretivism: Tales of transformation in educational and social research.* New York: Teachers College Press.

Kudlick, C. J. (2003). Disability history: Why we need another "other". *American Historical Review, 108*, 763–793.

Lesseliers, J., Van Hove, G., & Vandevelde, S. (2009). Regranting identity to the outgraced—narratives of persons with learning disabilities: Methodological considerations. *Disability & Society, 24*(4), 411–423.

Linton, S. (2006). *My body politic: A memoir.* Ann Arbor: University of Michigan Press.

Linton, S. (1998). Claiming Disability. New York: New York University Press.

Mitchell, D. T., & Snyder, S. L. (Eds.). (2000). *Narrative prosthesis: Disability and the dependencies of discourse.* Ann Arbor: University of Michigan Press.

Mooney, J. (2007). *The short bus: A journey beyond normal.* New York: Henry Holt.

Rao, S., & Kalyanpur, M. (Eds.). (2015). *South Asia and disability studies: Redefining boundaries and extending horizons*. New York: Peter Lang.

Robison, J. E. (2007). *Look me in the eye: My life with Asperger's*. New York: Random House.

Salend, S. J. (2011). *Creating inclusive classrooms: Effective and reflective practices* (8th ed.). Upper Saddle River, NJ: Prentice Hall.

Shapiro, J. (1993). *No pity: People with disabilities forging a new civil rights movement*. New York: Three Rivers Press.

Slee, R. (2011). *The irregular school*. New York: Routledge.

Solis, S., & Connor, D. J. (2007). Theory meets practice: Disability studies and personal narratives in school. In S. Danforth & S. Gabel (Eds.), *Vital questions facing disability studies in education* (pp. 103–119). New York: Peter Lang.

Tomlinson, S. (2012). *Ignorant yobs? Low attainers in a global knowledge economy*. New York: Routledge.

UNESCO and Government of Spain, Ministry of Education and Science. (1994, June). *World conference on special needs education: Final report*. Paper presented at the world conference on special needs education, Salamanca, Spain.

Valle, J. W., Connor, D. J., & Reid, D. K. (2005). IDEA at 30: Looking back, facing forward—a disability studies perspective. *Disability Studies Quarterly, 26*(2). Retrieved from http://www.dsq-sds.org/issue/view/33.

Ware, L. (2001). Writing identity and the other: Dare we do disability studies? *Journal of Teacher Education, 52*(2), 107–123.

Ware, L. (Ed.). (2004). *Ideology and the politics of (in)exclusion*. New York: Peter Lang.

Wendelborg, C., & Tøssebro, J. (2010). Marginalisation processes in inclusive education in Norway: A longitudinal study of classroom participation. *Disability & Society, 25*(6), 701–714.

Index

© Springer Nature Switzerland AG 2020
L. Ware (ed.), *Critical Readings in Interdisciplinary Disability Studies*, Critical
Studies of Education 12, https://doi.org/10.1007/978-3-030-35309-4